ALICE GOFFMAN grew up in Philadelphia and attended graduate school at Princeton University. She teaches in the sociology department at the University of Wisconsin-Madison.

Additional Praise for *On the Run*

"Alice Goffman's *On the Run* is the best treatment I know of the wretched underside of neo-liberal capitalist America. Despite the social misery and fragmented relations, she gives us a subtle analysis and poignant portrait of our fellow citizens who struggle to preserve their sanity and dignity."   —Cornel West, author of *Democracy Matters*

"Goffman is a compelling writer, and she supports her argument with one vivid antecdote after another. . . . Goffman's book requires us to confront the limitations and failures of our criminal-justice policies to date."   —James Forman Jr., *The Atlantic*

"A remarkable feat of reporting . . . Goffman's ability to understand her subjects' motivations [is] astonishing—and riveting. . . . Goffman became such a part of the fabric of the community that she was harassed by the police [and] witnessed someone getting pistol-whipped. . . . But where others might see bedlam, Goffman finds patterns, even logic. . . . You can't read this book without a growing sense of understanding as well as outrage."   —Alex Kotlowitz, *The New York Times Book Review*

"*On the Run* is an engrossing book that should also become an ethno-graphic classic."   —Christopher Jencks, *New York Review of Books*

"One of the most eagerly awaited urban ethnographies in years . . . Ms. Goffman's book both builds on [*The New Jim Crow*] and pushes past it, closely tracking a group of young men caught up in what she characterizes as a new system of surveillance and control that reaches far beyond the walls of prison."   —*The New York Times*

"This is a truly wonderful book that identifies the casualties of the war on drugs that extend beyond the prison walls. . . . The detail is incredible. The research is impeccable. Read it and weep."   —*Times Higher Education* (UK)

"As a work of ethnography it is outstanding. As a piece of social science it is refreshingly and gloriously readable—how often can one say that of sociology these days? And as an insight into the reach and effect of the contemporary penal state on the day-to-day lives of black urban America it is unparalleled." —*London School of Economics Review of Books*

"Necessary . . . Goffman's lively prose—communicated in a striking voice rare for an academic—opens a window into a life where paranoia has become routine. . . . She goes beyond her street-level focus to argue something more profound." —*Baltimore City Paper*

"This is a remarkable chronicle, informed by Goffman's scholarship, detailed from personal experience as 'participant observer,' and related with honesty and compassion." —*Publishers Weekly*

"*On the Run* is riveting—a clear-headed and sobering account of the 'way it is' for too many of the nation's young black men who live in the killing fields called American cities. It reveals how the everyday lives of these men—their loved ones—are closely monitored and mined for evidence that is then used against them, exacerbating their alienation and fueling the prison-industrial complex. This brilliant book should be required reading for everyone, including President Obama, Congress, and public officials throughout the nation."
—Elijah Anderson, author of *Code of the Street*

"*On the Run* tells, in gripping, hard-won detail, what it's like to be trapped on the wrong side of the law with no way out—the situation of so many young black Americans today. A brilliant fieldworker and a smart analyst of what she saw and heard, Goffman has made a lasting contribution to our understanding of the administration of the law, urban life, and race relations in a book you will never forget reading."
—Howard Becker, author of *Writing for Social Scientists*

"By turns *On the Run* is heartbreaking and clear-eyed, sad and entangled. With rich ethnographic detail, Alice Goffman reveals the emotional arc of deceptively complex young lives that are criminalized daily in one black neighborhood in Philadelphia. A triumphant achievement!"
—Carol Stack, author of *All Our Kin*

ON THE RUN

Fugitive Life in an American City

ALICE GOFFMAN

PICADOR

———

Farrar, Straus and Giroux
New York

ON THE RUN. Copyright © 2014 by The University of Chicago. All rights
reserved. Printed in the United States of America. For information, address
Picador, 175 Fifth Avenue, New York, N.Y. 10010.

www.picadorusa.com
www.twitter.com/picadorusa · www.facebook.com/picadorusa
picadorbookroom.tumblr.com

Picador® is a U.S. registered trademark and is used by Farrar, Straus and
Giroux under license from Pan Books Limited.

For book club information, please visit www.facebook.com/
picadorbookclub or e-mail marketing@picadorusa.com.

The Library of Congress Cataloging-in-Publication Data is available upon
request.

ISBN 978-1-250-06566-7 (paperback)
ISBN 978-1-250-06567-4 (e-book)

Picador books may be purchased for educational, business, or promotional
use. For information on bulk purchases, please contact the Macmillan
Corporate and Premium Sales Department at 1-800-221-7945, extension
5442, or write to specialmarkets@macmillan.com.

First published in the United States by The University of Chicago Press

First Picador Edition: April 2015

10 9 8 7 6 5 4 3 2

CONTENTS

PROLOGUE

Mike, Chuck, and their friend Alex were shooting dice on the wall of the elementary school. It was approaching midnight and quite cool for mid-September in Philadelphia. Between throws, Chuck cupped his hands together and blew heat into his fingers.

Mike usually won when the guys played craps, and tonight he was rubbing their noses in it, shrugging into a little victory dance when he scooped the dollar bills off the ground. After a pair of nines, Alex started in on Mike.

"You a selfish, skinny motherfucker, man."

"Niggas is always gonna hate," Mike grinned.

"You think you better than everybody, man. You ain't shit!"

Chuck laughed softly at his two best friends. Then he yawned and told Alex to shut his fat ass up before the neighbors called the law. A short time later, Chuck called it a night. Mike announced he was going to get cheesesteaks with his winnings and asked if I wanted to come with.

"Can *I* get a cheesesteak?" Alex interjected.

"Man, take your fat ass in the house," Chuck laughed.

"Oh, so I'm walking?!"

* * *

Mike and I were halfway to the store in his car when his cell phone started ringing. When he picked up I could hear screams on the other end. Mike shouted, "Where you at? Where you at?"

He screeched the old Lincoln around and headed back to 6th Street, pulling up in front of the corner store. There in the headlights we saw Alex, all 250 pounds of him, squatting by the curb, apparently looking for something. When he glanced up at us, blood streamed from his face, down his white T-shirt, and onto his pants and boots. Alex mumbled something I couldn't decipher, and then I realized he was looking for his teeth. I started searching on the ground with him.

"Alex," I said, "we have to take you to the hospital."

Alex shook his head and put up his hand, struggling to form words with his mangled lips. I kept pleading until finally Mike said, "He's not fucking going, so stop pushing."

At this point I remembered that Alex was still on parole. In fact, he was quite close to completing his two years of supervision. He feared that the cops who crowd the local emergency room and run through their database the names of Black young men walking in the door would arrest him on the spot, or at least issue him a violation for breaking the terms of his parole. If that happened, he'd be back in prison, his two years of compliance on the outside wiped away. A number of his friends had been taken into custody at the hospital when they sought care for serious injuries or attempted to attend the birth of their children.

Mike took off his shirt and gave it to Alex to soak up the blood from his face. Chuck had come back around by this point, and carefully helped him into the front seat of Mike's car. We drove to my apartment a few blocks away. We cleaned Alex up a bit, and then he began to explain what had happened. On his way home from the dice game, a man in a black hoodie stepped out from behind the corner store and walked him into the alley with a gun at his back. This man pistol-whipped him several times, took his money, and smashed his face into a concrete wall. Later, Alex found out that this man had mistaken him for his younger brother, who'd apparently robbed the man the week before.

Over the next three hours, Mike and Chuck made a series of futile calls to locate someone with basic medical knowledge. Mike's baby-mom, Marie, was in school to become a nurse's aide, but she hadn't been speaking to him lately—not since she'd caught him cheating and put a brick through his car window. Finally, at around six in the morning, Alex contacted his cousin, who came over with a plastic bag full of gauze and needles and iodine, and stitched up his chin and the skin around his eyebrow. His jaw was surely broken, she said, as well as his nose, but there was nothing she could do about it.

The next afternoon, Alex returned to the apartment he shared with his girlfriend and young son. Mike and I went to visit him that evening. I again pleaded with Alex to seek medical treatment, and he again refused.

All the bullshit I done been through [to finish his parole sentence], it's like, I'm not just going to check into emergency and there come the cops asking me all types of questions and writing my information down, and before you know it I'm back in there [in prison]. Even if they not there for me, some of them probably going to recognize me, then they going to come over, run my shit [check for his name in the police database under open arrest warrants]. I ain't supposed to be up there [his parole terms forbade him to be near 6th Street, where he was injured]; I can't be out at no two o'clock [his curfew was 10:00 p.m.]. Plus, they might still got that little jawn [warrant] on me in Bucks County [for court fees he did not pay at the end of a trial two years earlier]. I don't want them running my name, and then I got to go to court or I get locked back up.

At this point his girlfriend emerged from the bedroom, ran her hands over her jeans, and said, "He needs to go to the hospital. Better he spends six months in jail than he can't talk or chew food. That's the rest of his life."

* * *

Alex's attack occurred over ten years ago. He still finds it difficult to breathe through his nose and speaks with a muffled lisp. His eyes don't appear at quite the same level in his face. But he didn't go back to prison. Alex successfully completed his parole sentence, a feat of luck and determination that only one other guy in his group of friends ever achieved.

PREFACE

The number of people imprisoned in the United States remained fairly stable for most of the twentieth century, at about one person for every thousand in the population.[1] In the 1970s this rate began to rise, and continued a steep upward climb for the next thirty years.[2] By the 2000s, the number of people behind bars stood at a rate never before seen in US history: about 1 for every 107 people in the adult population.[3] The United States currently imprisons five to nine times more people than western European nations, and significantly more than China and Russia.[4] Roughly 3 percent of adults in the nation are now under correctional supervision: 2.2 million people in prisons and jails, and an additional 4.8 million on probation or parole.[5] In modern history, only the forced labor camps of the former USSR under Stalin approached these levels of penal confinement.[6]

The fivefold increase in the number of people sitting in US jails and prisons over the last forty years has prompted little public outcry. In fact, many people scarcely notice this shift, because the growing numbers of prisoners are drawn disproportionately from poor and segregated Black communities. Black people make up 13 percent of the US population, but account for 37 percent of the prison population.[7] Among Black young men, one in nine are in prison, compared with less than 2 percent of white young men.[8] These racial differences are reinforced by class differences. It is poor Black young men who are being sent to prison at truly astounding rates: approximately 60 percent of those who did not finish high school will go to prison by their midthirties.[9]

This book is an on-the-ground account of the US prison boom: a close-up look at young men and women living in one poor and segregated Black community transformed by unprecedented levels of imprisonment and by the more hidden systems of policing and supervision that have accompanied them. Because the fear of capture and confinement has seeped into the basic activities of daily living—work, family, romance, friendship, and even much-needed medical care—it is an account of a community *on the run*.

*   *   *

I stumbled onto this project as a student at the University of Pennsylvania. During my sophomore year I began tutoring Aisha, a high school student who lived with her mother and siblings in a lower-income Black neighborhood not far from the campus. In the evenings we would sit at the plastic and metal kitchen table in her family's bare-walled, two-bedroom apartment, the old TV blaring, and work on her English or math homework. Afterward her mom and aunts would gather on the stoop of their building and talk about their kids or watch people go by. Gradually, I got to know Aisha's relatives, friends, and neighbors. When my lease was up, Aisha and her mother suggested that I take an apartment nearby.

Aisha's fourteen-year-old cousin Ronny came home from a juvenile detention center that winter. He lived with his grandmother about ten minutes away by car. We started taking the bus to visit him there.

Soon Ronny introduced me to his cousin Mike, a thin young man with a scruffy beard and an intense gaze. At twenty-two, Mike was a year older than I was. He quickly explained that he was in a temporary financial rut, living at his uncle's house and with no car to drive. Last year he had his own car and his own apartment, and he planned to get back on his feet very soon. Mike seemed to command some respect from other young men in the neighborhood. When a neighbor asked what a white woman was doing hanging out on the back porch with him, he replied that I was Aisha's tutor who lived nearby. Other times, he explained that I was Aisha's godsister.

Over the next few weeks, Mike introduced me to his mother, his aunt, his uncle, and his close friend Alex. Many inches shorter and nearly twice Mike's weight, Alex seemed tired and defeated, as if he weren't trying to succeed in life so much as avoid major tragedy. Gradually I learned that Mike and Alex were two members of a close-knit group of friends. The third member, Chuck, was spending his senior year of high school in county jail awaiting trial on an aggravated assault charge for a school yard fight. Mike missed him keenly, explaining that Chuck was the glass-half-full member of the trio. As Chuck later told me on the phone from jail, "I ain't got shit but I'm healthy, I ain't bad looking, you feel me? I'm a happy person."

That first month with Mike and Alex was calm—boring even. We would sit on Mike's uncle's stoop and share a beer, or hang out in various houses of his friends and neighbors. Some evenings we headed over to Chuck's mother's house so Mike could catch his friend's nightly phone call from jail.

Then the cops raided Mike's uncle's house in the middle of the night. They were looking for Mike on a shooting charge, though he vehemently denied any involvement. With a warrant out for his arrest, he spent the next few weeks hiding in the houses of friends and relatives. Then he turned himself in, made bail, and began the lengthy court proceedings.

I had never known a man facing criminal charges before, and assumed this was a grave and significant event in Mike's life. I soon learned that he had gone through two other criminal cases within the past year: one for possession of drugs and the other for possession of an unlicensed gun. Chuck was in county jail awaiting trial, and Alex was completing two years of parole after serving a year upstate for drugs. Mike's cousin was out on bail. His neighbor was living under house arrest. Another friend, who was homeless and sleeping in his car, had a warrant out for unpaid court fees.

Near the end of my sophomore year, I asked Mike what he thought of my writing about his life for my senior thesis in the Sociology Department at Penn. He readily agreed, with the caveat that I leave out anything he asked me to keep secret. When Chuck came home from jail that spring, I received his permission to include him as well. Over time, I asked other young men and their families to take part.

For the next year, I spent much of every day with Mike, Chuck, and their friends and neighbors. I went along to lawyers' offices, courthouses, the probation and parole office, the visiting rooms of county jails, halfway houses, the local hospital, and neighborhood bars and parties.

Having grown up in a wealthy white neighborhood in downtown Philadelphia, I did not yet know that incarceration rates in the United States had climbed so dramatically in recent decades. I had only a vague sense of the War on Crime and the War on Drugs, and no sense at all of what these federal government initiatives meant for Black young people living in poor and segregated neighborhoods. I struggled to make sense of the police helicopters circling overhead and the young men getting searched and cuffed in the streets. I worked hard to learn basic legal terminology and process.

That spring, Mike's gun case ended and a judge sentenced him to one to three years in state prison. A short time later, I was accepted into a PhD program at Princeton. Through four years of graduate school I continued to live in Aisha's neighborhood, commuting to school and spending many of the remaining hours hanging out around 6th Street with whichever of the 6th Street Boys were home. On the weekends I visited Mike, Chuck, and other young men from the neighborhood in prisons across the state. Over time, I got to know family members and girlfriends as we cleaned up after police raids, attended court dates, and made long drives upstate for prison visiting hours.

The families described here agreed to let me take notes for the purpose of one day publishing the material, and we discussed the project at length many times. I generally did not ask formal, interview-style questions, and most of what I recount here comes from firsthand observations of people, events, and conversations. People's names and identifying characteristics have been changed, along with the name of the neighborhood. Mike initially suggested that in notes and term papers I call his neighborhood 6th Street, and I kept this pseudonym as the project grew into a book.

Though I gratefully draw on information that a number of police officers, judges, parole officers, and prison guards provided in interviews, this book takes the perspective of 6th Street residents. In doing so, it provides an account of the prison boom and its more hidden practices of policing and surveillance as young people living in one relatively poor Black neighborhood in Philadelphia experience and understand them. Perhaps these perspectives will come to matter in the debate about criminal justice policy that now seems to be brewing.

ON
THE
RUN

INTRODUCTION

In the 1960s and 1970s, Black Americans achieved the full rights of citizenship that had eluded them for centuries. As they successfully defended the right to vote, to move freely, to attend college, and to practice their chosen profession, the United States simultaneously began building up a penal system with no historic precedent or international comparison.

Beginning in the mid-1970s, federal and state governments enacted a series of laws that increased the penalties for possessing, buying, and selling drugs; instituted steeper sentences for violent crime; and ramped up the number of police on the streets and the number of arrests these officers made. Street crime had risen dramatically in urban areas in the 1960s and 1970s, and politicians on both sides of the aisle saw a heavy crackdown on drugs and violence as the political and practical solution. By the 1980s, crack cocaine led to waves of crime in poor minority communities that further fueled the punitive crime policies begun years earlier.

In the 1990s, crime and violence in the United States began a prolonged decline, yet tough criminal policies continued. In 1994 the Violent Crime Control and Law Enforcement Act poured billions of federal dollars into urban police departments across the nation and created fifty new federal offenses. Under the second Bush administration, the near unanimous endorsement of tough-on-crime policies by police and civic leaders accompanied the mushrooming of federal and state police agencies, special units, and bureaus.[1] These policies increased the sentences for violent offenses, but they also increased the sentences for prostitution, vagrancy, gambling, and drug possession.[2]

The tough-on-crime era ushered in a profound change in how the United States manages ghettoized areas of its cities. For most of the twentieth century, the police ignored poor and segregated Black neighborhoods such as 6th Street. Between the 1930s and the 1980s, an era which saw the Great Migration, restrictive racial housing covenants, the Civil Rights Movement, growing unemployment, the erosion of social services, an expanding drug trade, and the departure of much of the Black middle class from the poor and segregated areas of major cities,[3] reports from firsthand observers paint the police in segregated Black neighborhoods as uninterested, absent, and corrupt.[4]

This began to change in the 1960s, when riots in major cities and a surge in violence and drug use spurred national concern about crime, particularly in urban areas. The number of police officers per capita increased dramatically in the second half of the twentieth century in cities nationwide.[5] In Philadelphia between 1960 and 2000, the number of police officers increased by 69 percent, from 2.76 officers for every 1,000 citizens to 4.66 officers.[6] The 1980s brought stronger drug laws and steeper sentences. In the 1990s, the tough-on-crime movement continued, with urban police departments across the nation adopting what became known as zero-tolerance policing, and then CompStat to track their progress.[7]

For many decades, the Philadelphia police had turned a fairly blind eye to the prostitution, drug dealing, and gambling that went on in poor Black communities. But in the late 1980s, they and members of other urban police forces began to refuse bribes and payoffs. In fact, corruption seems to have been largely eliminated as a general practice, at least in the sense of people working at the lower levels of the drug trade paying the police to leave them in peace. Also during this period, large numbers of people were arrested for using or possessing drugs, and sent to jails and prisons.

The crackdown on the drug economy in poor Black neighborhoods came at the same time that welfare reform cut the assistance that poor families received and the length of time they could receive it. As welfare support evaporated, the War on Drugs arrested those seeking work in the drug trade on a grand scale.

By 2000, the US prison population swelled to five times what it had been in the early 1970s. An overwhelming majority of men going to prison are poor, and a disproportionate number are Black. Today, 30 percent of Black men without college educations have been to prison by their midthirties. One in four Black children born in 1990 had an imprisoned father by the time he or she turned fourteen.[8]

Sociologist David Garland has termed this phenomenon *mass imprisonment*: a level of incarceration markedly above the historical and comparative norm, and concentrated among certain segments of the population such that it "ceases to be the incarceration of individual offenders and becomes the systematic imprisonment of whole groups."[9] Sociologist Loïc Wacquant and legal scholar Michelle Alexander have argued that current levels of targeted imprisonment represent a new chapter in American racial oppression.[10]

Since the 1980s, the War on Crime and the War on Drugs have taken millions of Black young men out of school, work, and family life, sent them to jails and prisons, and returned them to society with felony convictions. Spending time in jail and prison means lower wages and gaps in employment. This time away comes during the critical years in which other young people are completing degrees and getting married. Laws in many states deny those with felony convictions the right to vote and the right to run for office, as well as access to many government jobs, public housing, and other benefits. Black people with criminal records are so discriminated against in the labor market that the jobs for which they are legally permitted to apply are quite difficult to obtain.[11] These restrictions and disadvantages affect not only the men moving through the prison system but their families and communities. So many Black men have been imprisoned and returned home with felony convictions that the prison now plays a central role in the production of unequal groups in US society, setting back the gains in citizenship and socioeconomic position that Black people made during the Civil Rights Movement.[12]

*   *   *

6th Street is a wide commercial avenue, and the five residential blocks that connect to it from the south form an eponymous little neighborhood. In the 1950s and 1960s, the 6th Street neighborhood had been a middle-class Jewish area; by the early 1970s it was just opening up to Black residents.

When I first came to the neighborhood in 2002, 93 percent of its residents were Black. Men and boys stood at its busiest intersection, offering bootleg CDs and DVDs, stolen goods, and food to drivers and passersby. The main commercial street included a bulletproofed Chinese takeout store that sold fried chicken wings, single cigarettes called loosies, condoms, baby food, and glassines for smoking crack. The street also included a check-cashing store, a hair salon, a payday loan store, a Crown Fried Chicken restaurant, and a pawnshop. On the next block, a Puerto Rican family ran a corner grocery. Roughly one-fourth of the neighborhood's households received housing vouchers, and in all but two households, families received some type of government assistance.[13]

6th Street is not the poorest or the most dangerous neighborhood in the large Black section of Philadelphia of which it is a part—far from it. In interviews with police officers, I discovered that it was hardly a top priority of theirs, nor did they consider the neighborhood particularly dangerous or crime ridden. Residents in adjacent neighborhoods spoke about 6th Street as quiet and peaceful—a neighborhood they would gladly move to if they ever had enough money.

Still, 6th Street has not escaped three decades of punitive drug and crime policy. By 2002, police curfews had been established around the area for those under age eighteen, and police video cameras had been placed on major streets. In the first eighteen months that I spent in the neighborhood, at least once a day I watched the police stop pedestrians or people in cars, search them, run their names for warrants, ask them to come in for questioning, or make an arrest.[14] In that same eighteen-month period, I watched the police break down doors, search houses, and question, arrest, or chase people through houses fifty-two times. Nine times, police helicopters circled overhead and beamed searchlights onto local streets. I noted blocks taped off and traffic redirected as police searched for evidence—or, in police language, secured a crime scene—seventeen times. Fourteen times during my first eighteen months of near daily observation, I watched the police punch, choke, kick, stomp on, or beat young men with their nightsticks.

The problems of drugs and gun violence are real ones in the 6th

Street community, and the police who come into the neighborhood are trying to solve them with the few powers that have been granted to them: the powers of intimidation and arrest. Their efforts do not seem to be stopping young men like Mike and Chuck from attempting to earn money selling drugs or from getting into violent conflicts; whether they are helping to reduce overall crime rates is beyond the scope of this study.

Whatever their effect on crime, the sheer scope of policing and imprisonment in poor Black neighborhoods is transforming community life in ways that are deep and enduring, not only for the young men who are their targets but for their family members, partners, and neighbors.

CLEAN AND DIRTY PEOPLE

With decent, well-paying jobs in perennial short supply, Black communities have long been divided between those able to obtain respectable employment and those making their money doing dangerous, profaned work. In the 1890s, W. E. B. Du Bois dubbed this latter group the submerged tenth.[15] In the 1940s, Chicago sociologists St. Clair Drake and Horace Cayton referred to these groups as the respectables and the shadies. Drawing on terms used frequently in the Black community, sociologist Elijah Anderson famously dubbed this distinction the divide between *decent* and *street*.[16] Though the line between decent and street has been recognized and elaborated by academics, those divides first emerged as folk categories that residents of segregated Black neighborhoods used to draw distinctions among themselves.

In the current era, where police circle overhead and the threat of prison weighs heavily on neighborhood residents, the long-standing social divides within the Black community have been exacerbated by the issue of legal standing.

A central social fact about any person living in the community of 6th Street is his or her legal status; more specifically, whether the person is likely to attract police attention in the future: whether he can get through a police stop, or make it home from a court hearing, or pass a "piss test" during a probation meeting. Those who have no pending legal entanglements or who can successfully get through a police stop, a court hearing, or a probation meeting are known as *clean*. Those likely to be arrested should the authorities stop them, run their names, or search them are known as *dirty*.

These designations are occasioned ones, brought to the fore when an encounter with the authorities is imminent or has just occurred. When friends and neighbors hear that a young man has been stopped, their first question is often "Is he dirty?" This question means: Does he have an open warrant? Any probation or parole sentence he'd be violating by running into the police? Is he carrying any drugs? In short: if he meets with the police, will he come home to his bed tonight, or will he be seized?

Yet the designations of clean and dirty aren't just in-the-moment estimations occasioned by contact with the criminal justice system. They also become more general labels that attach to individuals or locations over time. While some people are widely known to be in good standing with the law, others are generally assumed to be liable for arrest should the authorities stop them. These designations become significant even when a police stop isn't imminent, because they're linked to distinct kinds of behavior, attitudes, and capabilities. For instance, a clean person can rent a car or a hotel room, or show the ID required for entry into many buildings. A dirty person may be taken advantage of in various ways, as it's assumed he won't be able to notify the authorities.

As men are largely the ones caught up in the criminal justice system, there exists in part a gendered divide—in many couples, the woman is clean, the man dirty. And the woman is not only free from legal entanglements—she likely works in the formal economy or receives government assistance, whereas the man makes his sporadic income in the streets, doing things for which he could be arrested. There is also an age divide—overwhelmingly, it is young people who are mired in legal entanglements, not older people. And third, there is a class divide, for it is most typically unemployed young men without high school diplomas who are dipping and dodging the police, who have probation sentences to complete and court cases to attend.

Dirty people are likely more aware of their status than clean people are of theirs, much in the same way that Black people may think about race more often than white people do, or gay people may think about sexual orientation more often than straight people do. But clean people living in the 6th Street neighborhood and surrounding areas so often have relatives, friends, and neighbors who are looking over their shoulder that these categories remain somewhat salient no matter which side a person is on.[17]

Residents of the neighborhood draw further distinctions between those likely to be taken into custody if the authorities do a general sweep, and those for whom the authorities are aggressively searching. The people the police are particularly interested in are said to be "hot." Places can also be hot, as in a block with a lot of recent police activity or the funeral of a young man who was gunned down, where police are likely to be looking for people related to the case or with other open warrants. In these instances, it may be said that one should not enter the area or event, or associate with the individual, until it or he cools down.

While the categories of clean/dirty and hot/cool focus on a person's risk of arrest or a place's likelihood to draw police attention, residents also draw distinctions among themselves according to how a person treats the legal entanglements of others. Those who continue to have dealings with a young man once he becomes wanted, who protect and aid him in his hiding and running, or who support him while locked up are known as *riders*—a term signaling courage and commitment. Those who turn on a man once the warrant has come in, or who fail to support a partner or family member once that person is sent to jail or prison, are said to be "not riding right." Those who go a step further and provide the police with information about the whereabouts or actions of a legally precarious person are known as "snitches" or "rats." Designations such as the clean person, the dirty person, the hot person, the snitch, and the rider have become basic social categories for young men and women in heavily policed Black neighborhoods.

The first chapters of the book concern the dirty world: the young men spending their teens and early twenties running from the police, going in and out of jail, and attempting to complete probation and parole sentences. These chapters reflect my attempt to understand this world through the eyes of Mike and Chuck and their friends—young men living with the daily fear of capture and confinement. Because the reach of the penal system goes beyond the young men who are its main targets, later chapters take up the perspective of girlfriends and mothers caught between the police and the men in their lives; of young people who have found innovative ways to profit from the legal misfortunes of their neighbors; and finally of neighborhood residents who have managed to steer clear of the penal system and those enmeshed therein. The appendix recounts the research on which this work is based, along with some personal reflection about the practical and ethical dilemmas of a middle-class white young woman reporting on the experiences of poor Black young men and women.

Together, the chapters make the case that historically high imprisonment rates and the intensive policing and surveillance that have accompanied them are transforming poor Black neighborhoods into communities of suspects and fugitives. A climate of fear and suspicion pervades everyday life, and many residents live with the daily concern that the authorities will seize them and take them away. A new social fabric is emerging under the threat of confinement: one woven in suspicion, distrust, and the paranoiac practices of secrecy, evasion, and unpredictability.

Still, neighborhood residents are carving out a meaningful life for themselves betwixt and between the police stops and probation meetings. The scope of punishment and surveillance does not prevent them from constructing a moral world in which they can find dignity and honor; and the struggles of young men and women to negotiate work, family, romance, and friendship in this hyper-policed zone, under threat of confinement, constitute as much of the story as the late-night raids or full-body searches.

ONE

The 6th Street Boys and
Their Legal Entanglements

CHUCK AND TIM

On quiet afternoons, Chuck would sometimes pass the time by teaching his twelve-year-old brother, Tim, how to run from the police. They'd sit side by side on the iron back-porch steps of their two-story home, facing the shared concrete alley that connects the small fenced-in backyards of their block to those of the houses on the next.

"What you going to do when you hear the sirens?" Chuck asked.

"I'm out," his little brother replied.

"Where you running to?"

"Here."

"You can't run here—they know you live here."

"I'ma hide in the back room in the basement."

"You think they ain't tearing down that little door?"

Tim shrugged.

"You know Miss Toya?"

"Yeah."

"You can go over there."

"But I don't even know her like that."

"Exactly."

"Why I can't go to Uncle Jean's?"

"'Cause they know that's your uncle. You can't go to nobody that's connected to you."

Tim nodded his head, seeming happy to get his brother's attention no matter what he was saying.

Chuck was the eldest of three brothers. He shared a small, second-floor bedroom with Tim, seven years his junior, and Reggie, born right between them. Reggie had left for juvenile detention centers by the time he turned eleven, so Tim didn't know his middle brother very well. He looked up to Chuck almost like a father.

When Tim was a baby, his dad had moved down to South Carolina and married a woman there; he did not keep in touch. Reggie's father was worse: an in-the-way (no-account) man of no consequence or merit, in prison on long bids and then out for stints of drunken robberies. Reggie said he wouldn't recognize him in the street. By contrast, Chuck's father came around a lot during his early years, a fact that Chuck sometimes mentioned when trying to explain why he knew right from wrong and his younger brothers did not.

The boys' mother, Miss Linda, had been five years into a heavy crack habit when she became pregnant with Chuck, and continued using as the boys grew up. With welfare cuts the family had very little government assistance, and Miss Linda never could hold a job for more than a few months at a time. Her father's post office pension paid the household bills, but he didn't pay for food or clothes or school supplies. He said it was beyond what he could do, and not his responsibility anyway.

At thirteen Chuck began working for a local dealer, which meant that he could buy food for himself and Tim instead of asking his mother for money she didn't have. His access to crack also meant that he could better regulate his mother's addiction. Now she came to him to get drugs, and mostly stopped prostituting herself and selling off their household possessions when she needed a hit. In high school Chuck got arrested a number of times, but the cases didn't stick and he continued working for the dealer.

By his sophomore year, Chuck's legs were sticking out past the edge of the bunk bed he shared with Tim. He cleared out the unfinished basement and moved his mattress and clothing down there. The basement flooded and smelled like mildew and sometimes the rats bit him, but at least he had his own space.

Tim was eight when Chuck moved out of their room, and he tried to put a brave face on it. When he couldn't sleep, he padded down to the basement and crawled into bed with his brother.

In his senior year, when we met, Chuck stood six feet tall and had a build shaped by basketball and boxing—his two favorite sports. That winter, he got into a fight in the school yard with a kid who had called his mom a crack whore. According to the police report, Chuck didn't hurt the other guy much, only pushed his face into the snow, but the school cops charged him with aggravated assault. It didn't matter, Chuck said, that he was on the basketball team, and making Cs and Bs. Since he'd just turned eighteen, the aggravated assault case landed him in the Curran-Fromhold Correctional Facility, a large pink and gray county jail on State Road in Northeast Philadelphia, known locally as CFCF or simply the F.

About a month after Chuck went to jail, Tim stopped speaking. He would nod his head yes or no, but didn't say any words. When Chuck called home from jail he asked his mother to put Tim on the phone, and he would talk to his little brother about what he imagined was happening back at home.

"Mike prolly don't be coming around no more, now that his baby-mom about to pop. She probably big as shit right now. If it's a boy he going to be skinny like his pops, but if it's a girl she'll be a fat-ass like her mom."

Tim never answered, but sometimes he smiled. Chuck kept talking until his minutes ran out.

In his letters and phone calls home, Chuck tried to persuade his mother to take his little brother to the jail for visiting hours. "He just need to see me, like, he ain't got nobody out there."

Miss Linda didn't have the state ID required to visit inmates in county jail, only a social security card and an old voter registration card, and anyway she hated seeing her sons locked up. Chuck's friends Mike and Alex offered to take Tim along with them, but since Tim was a minor, his parent or guardian had to go, too.

Eight months after Chuck was taken into custody, the judge threw out most of the charges and Chuck came home, with only a couple hundred dollars in court fees hanging over his head. When Tim saw his brother walking up the alley, he cried and clung to his leg. He tried to stay awake through the evening festivities but finally fell asleep with his head in Chuck's lap.

Over the next few months, Chuck patiently coaxed his brother to start speaking again. He stayed in most nights and played video games with Tim on the old TV in the living room. He even moved back up to Tim's room for a while, so Tim wouldn't be alone at night. He extended his bed with a folding chair, propping his legs up on it and cursing when they fell through.

"He'll get it back," Chuck said. "He just needs some QT [quality time]."

Tim nodded hopefully.

The following fall, Chuck tried to re-enroll as a senior, but the high school would not admit him; he had already turned nineteen. Then the judge on his old assault case issued a warrant for his arrest, because he hadn't paid $225 in court fees that came due a few weeks after his assault case ended. He spent a few months on the run before going downtown to the Warrant and Surrender Office of the Criminal Justice Center to see if he could work something out with the judge. It was a big risk: Chuck wasn't sure if they'd take him into custody on the spot. Instead, the court clerk worked out a monthly payment plan, and Chuck came home, jubilant, that afternoon.

That fall Tim started speaking again. He remained very quiet, preferring to communicate with a small smile or a shake of his head.

Tim's first arrest came later that year, after he'd turned eleven. Chuck was driving Tim to school in his girlfriend's car, and when a cop pulled them over the car came up as stolen in California. Chuck had a pretty good idea which one of his girlfriend's relatives had stolen the car, but he didn't say anything. "Wasn't going to help," he said.

The officer took both brothers into custody, and down at the police station they charged Chuck with receiving stolen property. They charged Tim with accessory, and later a judge in the juvenile court placed Tim on three years of probation.

With this probation sentence hanging over Tim's head, any encounter with the police might mean a violation and a trip to juvenile detention, so Chuck began teaching his little brother how to run from the police in earnest: how to spot undercover cars, how and where to hide, how to negotiate a police stop so that he didn't put himself or those around him at greater risk.

REGGIE

Chuck and Tim's middle brother, Reggie, came home for a few months then. He was an overweight young man of fifteen, and already developing a reputation as good muscle for robberies. Older guys in the neighborhood referred to him as a cannon, meaning a person of courage and commitment. Reggie had heart, they said. He wouldn't back down from danger. Miss Linda described her middle son as a goon. Unlike herself and her oldest son, Chuck, Reggie seemed utterly uninterested in neighborhood gossip. He didn't care if someone else was out there making money or getting girls—he only cared if *he* was.

"And he fearless," she said with some pride. "A stone-cold gangster."

Reggie also had a lesser-known artistic side: he wrote rhymes on the outside, and penned a number of "'hood" novels while he was locked up.

When Reggie came home this time, he planned a number of daring schemes to rob armored cars or big-time drug dealers, but he could rarely find anyone around 6th Street willing to team up with him. "Niggas be backing out at the last minute!" he lamented to me, half-jokingly. "They ain't got no heart."

Chuck tried to discourage Reggie from these robberies, but Reggie didn't seem to have the patience for making slow money selling drugs hand to hand, so he contributed only sporadically to the household. "My brother's the breadwinner," he acknowledged.

A month after he turned fifteen, Reggie tested positive for marijuana at a routine probation meeting. (This is referred to as a piss test, and when you test positive, it is called hot piss.) The probation board issued him a technical violation, and instead of allowing them to take him into custody, Reggie ran out of the building. They soon issued a bench warrant for his arrest.

That evening, Reggie explained that there was no point in turning himself in, because being in juvenile detention is much worse than living on the run.

"How long are you going to be on the run for?" I asked.

"Till I turn myself in."

"That's what you're going to do?"

"No, that's something I *could* do, but I'm not."

"Yeah."

"'Cause what happened last time I turned myself in? Time."

"Last time when you got locked up you had turned yourself in?"

"Did I."[1]

"How long did you sit before your case came up?"

"Like nine months."

During the time Reggie was on the run from this probation violation, he also became a suspect in an armed robbery case, so the police
issued a body warrant—an open warrant for those accused of committing new crimes—for his arrest. The robbery had been caught on tape,
and the footage was even aired on the six o'clock news. The cops began driving around the neighborhood with Reggie's picture and asking
people to identify him. They raided his mother's house in the middle
of the night, and the next morning Reggie told me:

> Yo, the law ran up in my crib last night talking about they had a body
> warrant for a armed robbery. I ain't rob nobody since I had to get that bail
> money for my brother last year. . . . They talking 'bout they going to come
> back every night till they grab me. Now my mom saying she going to turn
> me in 'cause she don't want the law in her crib. . . . I'm not with it. I ain't
> going back to jail. I'll sleep in my car if I have to.

In fact, Reggie did take to sleeping in his car, and managed to live on
the run for a few months before the cops caught him.

*　*　*

Some people in the neighborhood said that Chuck and his younger
brothers got into so much trouble because their fathers weren't around,
and their mother failed to set a good example. By virtually all accounts,
Miss Linda was an addict and had not raised her boys well. One had
only to step foot inside her house to know this: it smelled of piss and
vomit and stale cigarettes, and cockroaches roamed freely across the
countertops and soiled living room furniture. But many of Chuck's
friends had mothers who hadn't succumbed to crack, who worked two
jobs and went to church. These friends, too, were spending a lot of their
time dealing with the police and the courts.

MIKE AND RONNY

Mike was two years older than Chuck and had grown up just a block
away in a two-story home shared with his mother and uncle, who had

inherited the house from Mike's grandfather. His mother kept an exceptionally clean house and held down two and sometimes three jobs.

Mike's first arrest had come at thirteen, when the police stopped, searched, and arrested him for carrying a small quantity of marijuana. He was put on probation and managed to stay out of trouble long enough to finish high school by taking night classes, as the large graduation photo on his mother's mantel attested.

The two jobs Mike's mom worked meant that he had more money growing up than most of the other guys—enough for new school clothes and Christmas gifts. Chuck and Alex sometimes joked that as a result of this relatively privileged upbringing, Mike had too strong an appetite for the finer things in life, like beautiful women and the latest fashion. His elaborate morning routine of clothes ironing, hair care, body lotion, and sneaker buffing was the source of much amusement. "Two full hours from the shower to the door," Chuck quipped. Mike defended these habits and affinities, claiming that they came from an ambition to make something more of himself than what he was given.

At twenty-two, Mike was working part time at a pharmaceutical warehouse and selling crack on the side for extra cash. His high school girlfriend was about to give birth to their second child.

A few weeks after his daughter was born, Mike lost the job at the warehouse. Complications with his daughter's birth had caused him to miss work too many days in a row. He spent the first six months of his daughter's life in a fruitless and humiliating attempt to find work; then he persuaded a friend from another neighborhood to give him some crack to sell on credit.

Mike had no brothers or sisters but often went around with his young boy Ronny, whom he regarded as a brother and in more sentimental moments as a godson.[2] Ronny was a short and stocky boy who wore do-rags that concealed a short Afro, and hoodies that he pulled down to cover most of his face. His mother had gotten strung out on crack while he was growing up, and he spent his early years shuttling between homeless shelters. An adopted aunt on his father's side raised Ronny until he was twelve. When this beloved aunt died, his maternal grandmother took over his care. That's when the trips to detention centers started.

A self-proclaimed troublemaker, Ronny was repeatedly kicked out of school for things like hitting his teacher or trying to steal the princi-pal's car. When his grandmother asked him to be good, he smiled with one corner of his mouth and said, "I want to, Nanna, but I can't promise nothing. I can't even say I'm going to try." Daily she threatened to send him away to a juvenile detention center. Ronny began to carry a gun at thirteen, and at fifteen he shot himself in the leg while boarding a bus.

Ronny was also an excellent dancer and, in his words, "a lil' pimp." The first time we had a real conversation, we were driving to various jails in the city to find where Mike was being held, because the police had ar-rested him earlier that morning. We were sitting in my car, and Ronny asked how old I was. I told him my age at the time: twenty-one. After a moment he grinned and said, "I've been with women older than you."

Soon after we met, Ronny made a name for himself in the neighbor-hood by getting into a cop chase from West to South Philly, first by car and then on foot through a gas station, a Laundromat, and an arcade. He spent most of the next six years in juvenile detention centers in upstate Pennsylvania and Maryland.

ALEX

Alex had grown up a few blocks off 6th Street, but he hung out there all through his childhood and became good friends with Chuck and Mike in high school. He lived with his mother, but when he turned fifteen his father had reconnected with the family, which improved their cir-cumstances substantially. His dad owned two small businesses in the neighborhood, and Alex got to hang out there after school.

By twenty-three, Alex was a portly man with a pained and tired look about him, as if the weight of caring for his two toddlers and their mothers were too much for him to bear. He had sold crack and pills on the block in his teens and spent a year upstate on a drug conviction. By his early twenties, he was working hard to live in compliance with his two-year parole sentence. He worked part time at his dad's heating and air-conditioning repair shop, moving to full-time hours by the end of 2004. Sometimes Mike and Chuck grudgingly noted that if their dads owned a small business they'd have jobs, too, but mostly they seemed happy for Alex and hoped he could keep his good thing going.

ANTHONY

Anthony was twenty-two years old when we met, and living in an abandoned Jeep off 6th Street. The year before, his aunt kicked him out of her house because she caught him stealing from her purse, though Anthony denied this. He occasionally found day-labor work in light construction, sometimes getting on a crew for a few weeks at a time. In between, Mike sometimes gave him a little crack to sell, though he was never any good at selling it because he put up no defense when other guys robbed him. "Living out here [in a car], I can't just go shoot niggas up, you feel me?" Anthony explained. "Everybody knows where I'm at. I ain't got no walls around me."

When Anthony and I met, he had a bench warrant out for his arrest, because he hadn't paid $173 in court fees for a case that ended that year. He had spent nine of the previous twelve months in jail awaiting the decision. Soon after, two neighbors who knew that Anthony had this bench warrant called the police and got him arrested, because they said he had stolen three pairs of shoes from them.

"Where would I even put three pairs of sneaks?" Anthony asked, pointing to the backseat of the Jeep.

"He probably sold them," Mike said, "for food and weed."

When Anthony got sick with what looked to be pneumonia, Chuck started letting him sleep on a blanket on the floor next to his bed in the basement, sneaking him in through the back door after his grandfather was asleep. Chuck's mother, Miss Linda, let Anthony stay even after Chuck got locked up later that year, though Anthony's tax, she said, would have to go up. In angry moments Anthony complained bitterly that he would never be able to leave Miss Linda's for his own place, because she continually stole the money he was trying to save from his pockets when he was asleep.

* * *

The legal issues that Chuck and his friends on 6th Street struggled with seemed immense to me—too numerous and complex to keep straight without copious notes. Between the ages of twenty-two and twenty-seven, Mike spent about three and a half years in jail or prison. Out of the 139 weeks that he was not incarcerated, he spent 87 weeks on probation or parole for five overlapping sentences. He spent 35 weeks with a warrant out for his arrest, and had a total of ten warrants issued on him. He also had at least fifty-one court appearances over this five-year period, forty-seven of which I attended.

Initially I assumed that Chuck, Mike, and their friends represented an outlying group of delinquents: the bad apples of the neighborhood. After all, some of them occasionally sold marijuana and crack cocaine to local customers, and sometimes they even got into violent gun battles. I grew to understand that many young men from 6th Street were at least intermittently earning money by selling drugs, and the criminal justice entanglements of Chuck and his friends were on a par with what many other unemployed young men in the neighborhood were experiencing. By the time Chuck entered his senior year of high school in 2002, young women outnumbered young men in his classes by more than 2:1. Going through his freshman yearbook years later, when he turned twenty-two, he identified roughly half the boys in his ninth-grade class as currently sitting in jails or prisons.[3]

ON BEING WANTED

In 2007 Chuck and I went door to door and conducted a household survey of the 6th Street neighborhood. We interviewed 308 men between the ages of eighteen and thirty. Of these young men, 144 reported that they had a warrant issued for their arrest because of either delinquencies with court fines and fees or failure to appear for a court date within the previous three years. For that same period, 119 men reported that they had been issued warrants for technical violations of their probation or parole (for example, drinking or breaking curfew).

According to contacts at the Philadelphia Warrant Unit, there were about eighty thousand open warrants in the city in the winter of 2010. A small portion of these warrants were for new criminal cases—so-called body warrants. Most were bench warrants for missing court or for unpaid court fees, or technical warrants issued for violations of probation or parole.

Until the 1970s, the city's efforts to round up people with outstanding warrants consisted of two men who sat at a desk in the evening and made calls to the people on the warrant list, encouraging them to either come in and get a new court date or get on a payment plan for their unpaid court fees. During the day, these same men transported prisoners. In the 1970s, a special Warrant Unit was created in the Philadelphia courts to actively pursue people with open warrants. Its new captain prided himself on improving and updating the unit's tracking system, and getting the case files onto a computer.

By the 1990s, every detective division in the Philadelphia Police Department had its own Warrant Unit. Today, the Federal Bureau of Investigation, the Bureau of Alcohol, Tobacco, Firearms, and Explosives, and the US Marshals all run their own separate Warrant Units out of the Philadelphia force as well.

As the number of police officers and special units focused on rounding up people with warrants increased, the technology to locate and identify people with warrants improved. Computers were installed in police cars, and records of citizens' legal histories and pending legal actions became synchronized—first across the city's police force and then among police departments across the country. It became possible to run a person's name for any kind of warrant, from any jurisdiction in the country, almost instantly.

The number of arrests an officer or a unit makes had been a key indication of performance since at least the 1960s.[4] When technology improved, taking people in on warrants became a ready way for police to show they were actively fighting crime. Those officers or units who cleared more warrants or arrested more people were informally rewarded; those who cleared or arrested fewer people were encouraged to catch up.

In interviews, Philadelphia police officers explained that when they are looking for a particular man, they access social security records, court records, hospital admission records, electric and gas bills, and employment records. They visit a suspect's usual haunts (for example, his home, his workplace, and his street corner) at the times he is likely to be there, and will threaten his family or friends with arrest if they don't cooperate, particularly when they themselves have their own lower-level warrants, are on probation, or have a pending court case. In addition to these methods, the Warrant Units operating out of the Philadelphia Police Department use a sophisticated computer-mapping program that tracks people who have warrants, are on probation or parole, or have been released on bail. Officers round up these potential informants and threaten them with jail time if they don't provide information about the person the police are looking for. A local FBI officer got inspired to develop the computer program after watching a documentary about the Stasi—the East German secret police. With another program, officers follow wanted people in real time by tracking their cell phones.

*   *   *

On 6th Street, the fear of capture and confinement weighs not only on young men with warrants out for their arrest but also on those going through a court case or attempting to complete probation or parole sentences. The supervisory restrictions of probation and parole bar these men from going out at night, driving a car, crossing state lines, drinking alcohol, seeing their friends, and visiting certain areas in the city. Coupled with an intense policing climate, these restrictions mean that encounters with the authorities are highly likely, and may result in a violation of the terms of release and a swift return to jail or prison. The threat of confinement similarly follows men on house arrest or living in halfway houses. Those out on bail understand that any new arrest allows a judge to revoke the terms of their release and return them to confinement, even if the charges are later dropped. And many young men, with and without legal entanglements, worry about new charges. At any moment, they may be stopped by police and their tenuous claim to freedom revoked.

When Mike, Chuck, and their friends assembled outside in the mid-mornings, the first topics of the day were frequently who had been taken into custody the night before, and who had outrun the cops and gotten away. They discussed how the police identified and located the person, what the charges were likely to be, what physical harm had been done to the man as he was caught and arrested, what property the police had taken, and what had been wrecked or lost during the chase.

Police, jail, and court language permeated general conversation. Chuck and Mike referred to their girlfriends as Co-Ds (codefendants) and spoke of catching a case (to be arrested and charged with a crime) when accused of some wrong by their friends and family. Call list, the term for the phone numbers of family and friends one is allowed to call from prison or jail, became the term for close friends.

The first week I spent on 6th Street, I saw two boys, five and seven years old, play a game of chase in which one boy assumed the role of the cop who must run after the other. When the "cop" caught up to the other child, he pushed him down and cuffed him with imaginary handcuffs. He then patted down the other child and felt in his pockets, asking if he had warrants or was carrying a gun or any drugs. The child then took a quarter out of the other child's pocket, laughing and yelling, "I'm seizing that!" In the following months, I saw children give up running and simply stick their hands behind their back, as if in handcuffs; push their body up against a car without being asked; or lie flat on the ground and put their hands over their head. The children yelled, "I'm going to lock you up! I'm going to lock you up, and you ain't never coming home!" I once saw a six-year-old pull another child's pants down to do a "cavity search."

By the time Chuck and Mike were in their early teens, they had learned to fear the police and to flee when they approached.

TWO

The Art
of Running

A young man concerned that the police will take him into custody comes to see danger and risk in the mundane doings of everyday life. To survive outside prison, he learns to hesitate when others walk casually forward, to see what others fail to notice, to fear what others trust or take for granted.

One of the first things that such a man develops is a heightened awareness of police officers—what they look like, how they move, where and when they are likely to appear. He learns the models of their undercover cars, the ways they hold their bodies and the cut of their hair, the timing and location of their typical routes. His awareness of the police never seems to leave him; he sees them sitting in plain clothes at the mall food court with their children; he spots them in his rearview mirror coming up behind him on the highway, from ten cars and three lanes away. Sometimes he finds that his body anticipates their arrival with sweat and a quickened heartbeat before his mind consciously registers any sign of their appearance.

When I first met Mike, I thought his awareness of the police was a special gift, unique to him. Then I realized Chuck also seemed to know when the police were coming. So did Alex. When they sensed the police were near, they did what other young men in the neighborhood did: they ran and hid.

Chuck put the strategy concisely to his twelve-year-old brother, Tim:

If you hear the law coming, you merk on [run away from] them niggas. You don't be having time to think okay, what do I got on me, what they going to want from me. No, you hear them coming, that's it, you gone. Period. 'Cause whoever they looking for, even if it's not you, nine times out of ten they'll probably book you.

Tim was still learning how to run from the police, and his beginner missteps furnished a good deal of amusement for his older brothers and their friends.

Late one night, a white friend of mine from school dropped off Reggie and a friend of his at my apartment. Chuck and Mike phoned me to announce that Tim, who was eleven at the time, had spotted my friend's car and taken off down the street, yelling, "It's a undercover! It's a undercover!"

"Nigga, that's Alice's girlfriend." Mike laughed. "She was drinking with us last night."

If a successful escape means learning how to identify the police, it also requires learning how to run. Chuck, Mike, and their friends spent many evenings honing this skill by running after each other and chasing each other in cars. The stated reason would be that one had taken something from the other: a CD, a five-dollar bill from a pocket, a small bag of weed. Reggie and his friends also ran away from their girlfriends on foot or by car.

One night, I was standing outside Ronny's house with Reggie and Reggie's friend, an eighteen-year-old young man who lived across the street. In the middle of the conversation, Reggie's friend jumped in his car and took off. Reggie explained that he was on the run from his girlfriend, who we then saw getting into another car after him. Reggie explained that she wanted him to be in the house with her, but that he was refusing, wanting instead to go out to the bar. This pursuit lasted the entire evening, with the man's girlfriend enlisting her friends and relatives to provide information about his whereabouts, and the man doing the same. Around one in the morning, I heard that she'd caught him going into the beer store and dragged him back home.

It wasn't always clear to me whether these chases were games or more serious pursuits, and some appeared more serious than others. Regardless of the meaning that people ascribed to them at the time or afterward, these chases improved young men's skill and speed at getting away. In running from each other, from their girlfriends, and in a few cases their mothers, Reggie and his friends learned how to navigate the alleyways, weave through traffic, and identify local residents willing to hide them for a little while.[1]

During the first year and a half I spent on 6th Street, I watched young men running and hiding from the police on 111 occasions, an average of more than once every five days.[2]

Those who interact rarely with the police may assume that running away after a police stop is futile. Worse, it could lead to increased charges or to violence. While the second part is true, the first is not. In my first eighteen months on 6th Street, I observed a young man running after he had been stopped on 41 different occasions. Of these, 8 involved men fleeing their houses during raids; 23 involved men running after being stopped while on foot (including running after the police had approached a group of people of whom the man was a part); 6 involved car chases; and 2 involved a combination of car and foot chases, where the chase began by car and continued with the man getting out and running.

In 24 of these cases, the man got away. In 17 of the 24, the police didn't appear to know who the man was and couldn't bring any charges against him after he had fled. Even in cases where the police subsequently charged him with fleeing or other crimes, the successful getaway allowed the man to stay out of jail longer than he might have if he'd simply permitted the police to cuff him and take him in.[3]

A successful escape can be a solitary act, but oftentimes it is a collective accomplishment. A young man relies on his friends, relatives, and neighbors to alert him when they see the police coming, and to pass along information about where the police have been or where and when they might appear next. When the police make inquiries, these friends and neighbors feign ignorance or feed the police misinformation. They may also help to conceal incriminating objects and provide safe houses where a young man can hide. From fieldnotes taken in September 2006:

Around 11 a.m., I walked up the alleyway to the back of Chuck's house. Before I reached the porch, Chuck came running down the iron stairs, shouting something to a neighbor. Reggie followed him, also shouting. Their mother, Miss Linda, came to the top of the second-floor balcony and told me the law was on the way, and to make sure that Reggie in particular did not come back until she gave the green light. I recalled that Reggie had a warrant out for failure to pay court fees, and would doubtless be taken in if the cops ran his name.

I watched Chuck and Reggie proceed up the alleyway, and then Chuck turned and yelled at me to come on. We ran for about three blocks, going through two backyards and over a small divider. Dogs barked as we went by. I was half a block behind and lost sight of Chuck and Reggie. Panting, I slowed to a walk, looking back to see if the police were coming. Then I heard "psst" and looked up to see Chuck leaning out the second-floor window of a two-story house. A woman in her fifties, who I immediately guessed to be a churchgoer, opened the door for me as I approached, saying only, "Upstairs."

Chuck and Reggie were in her dressing room. This quite conservative-looking woman had converted what is usually the spare upstairs bedroom into a giant walk-in closet, with shoes, purses, and clothing arranged by color on the kind of white metal shelves that you buy and install yourself.

Our getaway had produced a mild euphoria. Reggie brushed past Chuck to examine the shoe collection, and Chuck wiped his arm off dramatically, teasing his younger brother about how sweaty he was.

"Look at yourself, nigga! You don't run for shit now with that little bit of shell in your shoulder," Reggie responded, referring to the partial bullet that had lodged just below the back of Chuck's neck when he was shot the month before.

Chuck laughed. "I'm in the best shape of my life." He explained that his shoulder hurt only when he played basketball.

Reggie sat on a small leopard-print stool and said, "Name a fat motherfucker who runs faster than me. Not just in the 'hood but anywhere in Philly."

"Oh, here you go," Chuck complained.

Chuck joked about the extensive shoe collection, saying you'd never know Miss Toya was like that. Reggie pulled out a pair of suede high heels and attempted to get one onto his foot, asking me to do up the straps. He got on her computer and started browsing pit bull websites, then

YouTube videos of street fights. Chuck cringed and exclaimed loudly as Kimbo, a well-known street fighter, hit his opponent repeatedly in the eye, revealing bloody and battered tissue that Chuck called "spaghetti and meatballs."

I asked Chuck why he made me run, and consequently dirty my sneakers, when I'm not even wanted.

"It's good practice."

Reggie grinned and said, "You be taking your fucking time, A."

"You're no track star," I replied.

"What!? I was haul-assing."

Chuck got on the phone with his mother and then a neighbor to find out how many police were on his block and for whom they had come. Apparently they were looking for a man who had fled on foot after being stopped on an off-road motorbike. They didn't find this man, but did take two others from the house next door: one had a bench warrant for failure to appear, and the other had a small amount of crack in his pocket. Into the phone Chuck was saying, "Damn. They got Jay-Jay? Damn."

About an hour later, his mother called to tell Chuck that the police had gone. We waited another ten minutes, then left for Pappi's, the corner store. Chuck ordered Miss Toya a turkey hoagie and BBQ chips and brought them to her as thanks. We then walked back to the block with Dutch cigars and sodas.

Running wasn't always the smartest thing to do when the cops came, but the urge to run was so ingrained that sometimes it was hard to stand still.

When the police came for Reggie, they blocked off the alleyway on both ends simultaneously, using at least five cars that I could count from where I was standing, and then ran into Reggie's mother's house. Chuck, Anthony, and two other guys were outside, trapped. Chuck and these two young men were clean, but Anthony had the warrant for failure to appear. As the police dragged Reggie out of his house, laid him on the ground, and searched him, one guy whispered to Anthony to be calm and stay still. Anthony kept quiet as Reggie was cuffed and placed in the squad car, but then he started whispering that he thought Reggie was looking at him funny, and might say something to the police.

Anthony started sweating and twitching his hands; the two young men and I whispered again to him to chill. One said, "Be easy. He's not looking at you."

We stood there, and time dragged on. When the police started searching the ground for whatever Reggie may have tossed before getting into the squad car, Anthony couldn't seem to take it anymore. He started mumbling his concerns, and then he took off up the alley. One of the officers went after him, causing the other young man standing next to him to shake his head in frustrated disappointment.

Anthony's running caused the other officer to put the two young men still standing there up against the car, search them, and run their names; luckily, they came back clean. Then two more cop cars came up the alley, sirens on. About five minutes after they finished searching the young men, one of the guys got a text from a friend up the street. He silently handed me the phone so I could read it:

Anthony just got booked. They beat the shit out of him.

At the time of this incident, Chuck had recently begun allowing Anthony to sleep in the basement of his mother's house, on the floor next to his bed. So it was Chuck's house that Anthony phoned first from the police station. Miss Linda picked up and began yelling at him immediately.

"You fucking stupid, Anthony! Nobody bothering you, nobody looking at you. What the fuck did you run for? You a nut. You a fucking nut. You deserve to get locked up. Dumb-ass nigga. Call your sister, don't call my phone. And when you come home, you can find somewhere else to stay."

* * *

When the techniques young men deploy to avoid the police fail, and they find themselves cuffed against a wall or cornered in an alleyway, all is not lost: once caught, sometimes they practice concerted silence, create a distraction, advocate for their rights, or threaten to sue the police or go to the newspapers. I occasionally saw each of these measures dissuade the police from continuing to search a man or question a man on the street. When young men are taken in, they sometimes use the grate in the holding cell at the police station to scrape their fingertips down past the first few layers of skin, so that the police can't obtain the prints necessary to identify them and attach them to their already pending legal matters. On four separate occasions I saw men from 6th Street released with bloody fingertips.

AVOIDING THE POLICE AND THE COURTS WHEN SETTLING DISPUTES

It's not enough to run and hide when the police approach. A man intent on staying out of jail cannot call the police when harmed, or make use of the courts to settle disputes. He must forego the use of the police and the courts when he is threatened or in danger and find alternative ways to protect himself. When Mike returned from a year upstate, he was rusty in these sensibilities, having been living most recently as an inmate rather than as a fugitive. His friends wasted no time in reacquainting him with the precariousness of life on the outside.

Mike had been released on parole to a halfway house, which he had to return to every day before curfew. When his mother went on vacation, he invited a man he had befriended in prison to her house to play video games. The next day, Mike, Chuck, and I went back to the house and found Mike's mother's stereo, DVD player, and two TVs gone. Later, a neighbor told Mike that he had seen the man taking these things from the house in the early morning.

Once the neighbor identified the thief, Mike debated whether to call the police. He didn't want to let the robbery go, but he also didn't want to take matters into his own hands and risk violating his parole. Finally, he called the police and gave them a description of the man. When we returned to the block, Reggie and another friend admonished Mike about the risks he had taken:

REGGIE: And you on parole! You done got home like a day ago! Why the fuck you calling the law for? You lucky they ain't just grab [arrest] both of you.

FRIEND: Put it this way: they ain't come grab you like you ain't violate shit, they ain't find no other jawns [warrants] in the computer. Dude ain't pop no fly shit [accused Mike of some crime in an attempt to reduce his own charges], but simple fact is you filed a statement, you know what I'm saying, gave them niggas your government [real name]. Now they

got your mom's address in the file as your last known [address]. The
next time they come looking for you, they not just going to your uncle's,
they definitely going to be through there [his mother's house].

In this case, their counsel proved correct. Mike returned to the halfway house a few days later and discovered that the guards there were
conducting alcohol tests. He left before they could test him, assuming
he would test positive and spend another year upstate for the violation.
He planned to live on the run for some time, but three days later the police found him at his mother's house and took him into custody. We had
been playing video games, and he had gone across the street to change
his clothes at the Laundromat. Two unmarked cars pulled up, and three
officers got out and started chasing him. He ran for two blocks before
they threw him down on the pavement. Later, he mentioned that their
knowledge of his mother's new address must have come from the time
he reported the robbery, and he bemoaned his thoughtlessness in calling them.

Young men also learn to see the courts as dangerous. A year after
Chuck came home from the assault case, he enrolled in a job training
program for young men who have not completed high school, hoping
to earn his high school diploma and gain a certificate in construction.
He proudly graduated at twenty-two and found a job apprenticing on a
construction crew. Around this time he had been arguing with his baby-
mom, and she stopped allowing him to see their two daughters, ages
one and a half and six months. After considerable hesitation, Chuck
took her to family court to file for partial custody. He said it tore at
him to let a white man into his family affairs, but what could he do? He
needed to see his kids. At the time, Chuck was also sending thirty-five
dollars per month to the city toward payment on tickets he had received
for driving without a license or registration; he hoped to get into good
standing and become qualified to apply for a driver's license. The judge
said that if Chuck did not meet his payments on time every month, he
would issue a bench warrant for his arrest.[4] Then Chuck could work off
the traffic tickets he owed in county jail (fines and fees can be deducted
for every day spent in custody).

Five months into his case for partial custody in family court, Chuck
lost his construction job and stopped making the payments to the city

for the traffic tickets. He said he wasn't sure if he had actually been issued a warrant, and unsuccessfully attempted to discover this. He went
to court for the child custody case anyway the next month, and when
his baby-mom mentioned that he was a drug dealer and unfit to get
partial custody of their children, the judge immediately ran his name in
the database to see if any warrants came up. They did not. As we walked
out of the courthouse, Chuck said to me and to his mother:

> I wanted to run [when the clerk ran his name], but it was no way I was get-
> ting out of there—it was too many cops and guards. But my shit came back
> clean, so I guess if they're going to give me a warrant for the tickets, they
> ain't get around to it yet.

The judge ruled in Chuck's favor and granted him visitation on Sun-
days at a court-supervised day-care site. These visits, Chuck said, made
him anxious: "Every time I walk in the door I wonder, like, is it today?
Are they going to come grab me, like, right out of the day care? I can just
see [my daughter's] face, like, 'Daddy, where you going?'"

After a month, the conditions of his custody allowed Chuck to go
to his baby-mom's house on the weekends to pick up his daughters. He
appeared thrilled with these visits, because he could see his children
without having to interact with the courts and risk any warrant that
might come up.

*   *   *

If, in the past, residents of poor Black communities could not turn to
the police to protect themselves or settle disputes because the police
were so often absent and uninterested, now it seems that residents face
an additional barrier: they cannot turn to the police because their legal
entanglements prevent them from doing so. The police are everywhere,
but as guarantors of public safety, they are still out of reach.

The hesitancy of legally precarious men to turn to the authorities has
some important implications. First, steering clear of the police and the
courts means that young men tend not to use the ordinary resources of
the law to protect themselves from crimes committed against them.[5]
While those on probation or parole may make tentative use of these resources (and sometimes regret it later, when the police arrest them us-

ing new information they provided), men with warrants typically stay away. During my first year and a half on 6th Street, I noted twenty-four instances of men contacting the police when they were injured, robbed, or threatened. These men were either in good standing with the courts or had no pending legal constraints. I did not observe any person with a warrant call the police or voluntarily make use of the courts during the six years of the study. Indeed, these young men seemed to view the authorities only as a threat to their safety.

Ned, age forty-three, and his longtime girlfriend Jean, age forty-six, lived on Mike's block. Jean smoked crack pretty heavily, although Chuck noted that she could handle her drugs, meaning she was able to maintain both a household and her addiction. Ned was unemployed and for extra money occasionally hosted dollar parties—house parties with a dollar entrance fee offering drinks, food, and games for a dollar each. He also engaged in petty fraud, such as intercepting checks in the mail and stealing credit cards. The couple's primary income came from taking in foster children. When Ned and Jean discovered they might be kicked out of their house because they owed property taxes to the city, Jean called Reggie's cousin, telling him to come to the house because she had some gossip concerning his longtime love interest. When he arrived, a man in a hoodie robbed him at gunpoint. Reggie later remarked that his cousin should have known better than to go to Ned and Jean's house: as the only man on the block with a warrant out for his arrest at the time, he was an easy target for a couple under financial strain.

If young men known to have a warrant become the target of those looking for someone to exploit or even to rob, they may resort to violence themselves, for protection or for revenge.

One winter morning, Chuck, Mike, and I were at a diner having breakfast to celebrate that the authorities hadn't taken Mike into custody after his court appearance earlier that day. Chuck's mother called to tell him that his car had been firebombed outside her house, and that firefighters were putting out the blaze. According to Chuck, the man who set fire to his car had given him drugs to sell on credit, under the arrangement that Chuck would pay him once he sold the drugs. Chuck hadn't been able to pay, however, because the police had taken the money from his pockets when they searched him earlier that week.

This was the first car that Chuck had ever purchased legally, a 1994 Bonneville he had bought the week before for four hundred dollars from a used-car lot in Northeast Philadelphia. He didn't speak for the rest of the meal. Then, as we walked to Mike's car, he said:

> This shit is nutty, man. What the fuck I'm supposed to do, go to the cops? "Um, excuse me, officer, I think boy done blown up my whip [car]." He going to run my name and shit, now he see I got a warrant on me; next thing you know, my Black ass locked the fuck up, you feel me? I'm locked up because a nigga firebombed my whip. What the fuck, I'm supposed to let niggas take advantage?

Chuck and Mike discussed whether Chuck should take matters into his own hands or do nothing. Doing nothing had the benefit of not placing him in more legal trouble, but as they both noted, doing nothing set them up to be taken advantage of by people who understood them to be "sweet."

A few days later, Chuck drove over to 8th Street with Mike and another friend and shot off a few rounds at the home of the man who he believed was responsible for blowing up his car. Although no one was injured, a neighbor reported the incident, and the police put out a body warrant for Chuck's arrest for attempted murder.

Hesitant to go to the police or to make use of the courts, young men around 6th Street are vulnerable to theft or violence by those who know they won't press charges. With the police out of reach, they sometimes resort to more violence as a strategy to settle disputes or defend themselves.[6]

THE NET OF ENTRAPMENT

It isn't difficult to imagine that a young man worried that the police will take him into custody learns to avoid both the cops and the courts. But young men around 6th Street learn to fear far more than just the legal authorities. The reach of the police extends outward like a net around them—to public places in the city, to the activities they usually involve themselves in, and to the neighborhood spots where they can usually be found.

Three hospitals serve the mixed-income Black section of the city within which 6th Street is located. Police officers crowd into their waiting rooms and hallways, especially in the evenings and on the weekends. Squad cars and paddy wagons park outside the hospital, officers in uniform or in plain clothes stand near the ambulances, and more officers walk around or wait in the ER. Some police come to the hospitals to investigate shootings and to question the witnesses who arrive there; others come because the men they have beaten while arresting them require medical care before they can be taken to the precinct or the county jail. Sitting in the ER waiting room, I often watched police officers walk Black young men out the glass double doors in handcuffs.

According to the officers I interviewed, it is standard practice in the hospitals serving the Black community for police to run the names of visitors or patients while they are waiting around, and to take into custody those with warrants, or those whose injuries or presence there constitutes grounds for a new arrest or a violation of probation or parole.

Alex experienced this firsthand when he was twenty-two years old and his girlfriend, Donna, was pregnant with their first child. He accompanied her to the hospital for the birth and stayed with her during fourteen long hours of labor. I got there a few hours after the baby was born, in time to see two police officers come into Donna's room to place Alex in handcuffs. As he stood with his hands behind him, Donna screamed and cried, and as they walked him away, she got out of the bed and grabbed hold of him, moaning, "Please don't take him away. Please, I'll take him down there myself tomorrow, I swear—just let him stay with me tonight." The officers told me they had come to the hospital with a shooting victim who was in custody, and as was their custom, they ran the names of the men on the visitors' list. Alex came up as having a warrant out for a parole violation, so they arrested him along with two other men on the delivery room floor.

I asked Alex's partner about the warrant, and she reminded me that the offense dated from Christmas, when the police had stopped Alex as he pulled up to a gas station. Since his driver's license had been revoked, driving constituted a violation of his parole.

After the police took Alex into custody at the maternity ward, it became increasingly clear to his friends on 6th Street that the hospital was a place to be avoided at all costs. Soon after Chuck turned twenty-one, his twenty-two-year-old girlfriend was due with their second child. Chuck told her that he would be at the hospital, even though he had a detainer out for a probation violation for breaking curfew. He stayed with her up until the point that she was getting in her aunt's car to go to the hospital. Then at the final moment, he said she should go ahead without him, and that he would come soon.

Later, Chuck sat with me on the steps and discussed the situation. "I told her I was on my way," he said. "She mad as shit I ain't there. I can hear her right now. She going to be like, "You broke your promise." I'm not trying to go out like Alex [get arrested], though. You feel me?"

As we spoke, his girlfriend called his cell phone repeatedly, and he would mute the sound after one ring and stare at her picture as it came up on the screen.

Just as a man worried the police will pick him up avoids the hospital when his child is born and refuses to seek formal medical care when he is badly beaten, so he won't visit his friends and relatives in prison or jail. Some prisons make it a general practice to run the names of visitors; others employ random canine searches of visitors' cars, and run the plates and names from the parking lot.

Funerals also become risky for men worried that the police may take them. Each of the nine funerals I attended for young men who had been killed in the 6th Street neighborhood featured police officers stationed outside with a tripod camera to film the mourners as they filed in. More officers stood across the street and parked on the adjacent blocks. When I asked an officer of the Warrant Unit about funerals, he replied that they were a great place to round up people for arrest. "But we try to stay a block or two away, so we don't get our picture in the paper."

Like hospitals and funerals, places of employment become dangerous for people with a warrant. Soon after Mike got released on parole to a halfway house, he found a job through an old friend who managed a Taco Bell. After two weeks, Mike, twenty-four at the time, refused to return to the house in time for curfew, saying he couldn't spend another night cooped up with a bunch of men like he was still in jail. He slept at his girlfriend's house, and in the morning found that he had been issued a violation and would likely be sent back to prison, pending the judge's decision. Mike said he wasn't going back, and they were going to have to catch him. Two parole officers arrested him the next day as he was leaving the Taco Bell, where he had gone to pick up his paycheck. He spent a year back upstate for this violation.

When Mike got booked at the Taco Bell, Chuck chewed him out thoroughly. Didn't he remember the time Chuck got taken?

Chuck started working at the local McDonald's when he was nineteen. Later that year he caught a probation violation for driving a car, his driving privileges having been revoked as part of his probation sentence. Though he had a warrant, Chuck kept working, saying that if the police came he would simply run out the back door.

A couple of weeks later, a former employee got into a fight with three other workers, and the police shut the McDonald's down while they questioned witnesses and looked for the women involved. When the fight began, Chuck had been in the storeroom, talking on the phone to his girlfriend. He came out, he said, and saw six police officers staring at him. At this point he phoned me to come pick up his house keys, fairly certain he would be taken into custody. When I got there, it was too late—Chuck was leaving in the back of a squad car.

A man worried that the police are hunting him—or at least may take him into custody should they come upon him—also comes to see friends, neighbors, and even family members as dangerous. First, he must avoid people who are "hot." After Reggie robbed a convenience store and the security camera footage appeared on the nightly news, the cops came looking for him with much more determination than when he only had a warrant out for a probation violation. He became so hot that other men on the block didn't want to be seen with him, worried that he'd bring heat on them. Mike gave me this advice:

> I'll only tell you this one time, A. Do not be around Reggie. He's hot right now, he's on the run. Don't get caught up in it. They're going to come for that nigga, and I don't want you nowhere around there. Don't let him get in your car, don't even talk on the phone. If he calls you, bang on [hang up on] that nigga. They probably tracing the calls, and you could fuck around and catch a ya'mean [be arrested on conspiracy charges, for harboring a fugitive, etc.] or something. Don't come through the block, don't even wave

at the dude. I already told that nigga don't call your phone no more, but just in case.

Young men's distrust extends beyond those who are particular targets of the police. Cops may exert significant pressure on a man's relatives or partner to provide information about him. Out of frustration and anger at his failures as a father, spouse, brother, or son, his partner or family members may freely call the police on him, taking advantage of his wanted status to get back at him or punish him.

Whether a man's friends, relatives, or girlfriend bring him to the attention of the authorities because the police pressure them to do so or because they leverage his wanted status to control or punish him, he comes to regard those closest to him as potential informants. Like going to the hospital or calling the police, spending time with friends, family, or romantic partners places men at risk.

CULTIVATING AN UNPREDICTABLE ROUTINE

Mike, Chuck, and their friends came to see danger and risk in the routine doings of everyday life. They learned to fear the police, and to regard the courts, the hospitals, their workplaces, their residences, and even their own family members as potential paths to confinement. To limit the risks that mundane places, relations, and people posed, they learned to practice concerted avoidance: to run and hide from the police, steer clear of hospitals, skip work, and hang back from their families and close friends.

Another strategy that young men on 6th Street adopt is to cultivate a secretive and unpredictable routine. I first noticed this strategy when Ronny shot himself in the leg when he was fifteen. Six police officers were occupying the ER lobby when he arrived; two of them quickly handcuffed the young man who had brought him in.

Ronny's grandmother, aunt, cousin, and sister sat in the lobby and waited for news. Some of the young men from 6th Street who had warrants at the time didn't show up at all, explaining to others that they couldn't take the chance, even though they "loved that lil' nigga" and wanted to be there. The men who did come, including Mike, stayed outside the hospital, hovering at the edge of the parking lot. They discussed which local police officers were inside, and what their chances were of going in to see Ronny without being spotted. One of Ronny's friends waited for a few minutes some yards away from the emergency room doors, heard the status report, and left. He returned periodically throughout the night, motioning through the doors for someone in the waiting room to come out and give him an update. Mike asked me to stay and keep in touch with him via cell phone:

MIKE: Yo, just stay here till you hear something. I'm about to leave out.
ALICE: Okay.
MIKE: I'm not trying to get locked up off of Ronny and then they run my record and I got, like, three warrants out for me, you feel me?

When Ronny's cousin was shot and killed later that year, the men from 6th Street attended his funeral in the same fashion that they had gone to the hospital—quickly and quietly, ducking in and out:

REGGIE: We couldn't really stay, you know, at the funeral or whatever, you know they're on my ass [the cops are looking for him]. But we ducked in and out and saw the body and everything. We ain't go to the gravesite though, but we saw his [the dead man's] grandmom, and she saved us a plate [of food] from after [the get-together at her house]. Lucky it was so many people at the church, because the cops was definitely out, boy.[7]

Cultivating unpredictability not only helps with evading the police; it also helps to reduce the risk of friends and family informing. Simply put, a man's neighbor, girlfriend, or mother cannot call the police on him if she doesn't know where he is.

Chuck, twenty at the time, explained the dipping and dodging sensibility to his thirteen-year-old cousin:

The night is really, like, the best time to do whatever you got to do. If I want to go see my moms [mother], see my girl, come through the block and holla at my boys, I can't be out in broad day. I got to move like a shadow, you know, duck in and out, you thought you saw me, then *bam*, I'm out before you even could see what I was wearing or where I was going.

Young men are so wary that their relatives, girlfriend, or neighbors may set them up that they may take any request from those close to them to show up or stop by as a potential threat. Mike noted:

> Nine times out of ten, you getting locked up because somebody called the cops, somebody snitching. That's why, like, if you get a call from your girl, like, "Yo, where you at, can you come through the block at a certain time," that's a red flag, you feel me? That's when you start to think, like, "Okay, what do she got waiting for me?"

When Chuck's nineteen-year-old neighbor had a bench warrant out for failure to appear in court, he was determined, he said, never to go back to jail. He slept in a number of houses, staying no more than a few nights in any one place. On the phone, he would lie to his family members, girlfriend, and fellow block members about where he was staying and where he planned to go next. If he got a ride to where he was staying, he requested to be dropped off a few blocks away, and then waited until the car was out of sight before walking inside. For six months, nobody on the block seemed to know where he was sleeping.

Young men looking over their shoulder for the police find that a public and stable daily routine becomes a path to confinement. A stable routine makes it easier for the police to locate a man directly, and makes it easier for his friends and family to call the police on him. Keeping a secret and unpredictable schedule—sleeping in different beds, working irregular hours, deceiving others about one's whereabouts, and refusing to commit to advance plans—serves as a generalized technique of evasion, helping young men avoid getting taken into custody through many of the paths discussed here.

PAYING TO PASS UNDETECTED

When Mike and Chuck and their friends had a little money, they spent some of it securing an array of underground goods and services that would help protect them from the authorities or postpone their admission to jail and prison.

One major item they sought was a clean ID.

Many readers may not be aware of how often they are asked to present some form of ID, or to hand over a credit card or proof of address, throughout the course of a day. Those who have these things, and who are free from the threat of the police, tend not to think about it when these documents are required of them. For young men around 6th Street concerned that the police are tracking them or will take them into custody on the spot, legitimate identification is the source of considerable concern.

On the one hand, Mike and Chuck and their friends feared discovery and didn't want their identity known. They hesitated to carry ID, to tell people their real name, or to write that name down. Around 6th Street, it is considered improper for even close friends to ask each other their last names, and young men routinely give fake names to people they meet, just to be on the safe side. Close male friends sometimes go years without knowing each other's last names. Yet at the same time that young men wish to conceal their identity, and fear using it, they need proof of it for all kinds of life's necessities, but can't get it. The formal documents needed to apply for a job, enter a building with a guard in the lobby, buy a cell phone, or put a car in the shop elude them through a complex combination of their poverty, residential instability, and legal entanglements and fears.

For the eleven years that I have known Reggie, he has been sitting in jail or prison, dealing with a pending court case, a warrant, or a probation or parole sentence, or working through some combination of the three. During a rare month that he was newly paroled from prison and had no pending court cases or warrants, he asked me to help him obtain a state-issued ID. Not a driver's license, which seemed an almost unattainable goal, but a non-driver's state-issued identification card. In addition to allowing him to apply for jobs, visit family and friends in jail, and check into hotel rooms, this ID would mean that when Reggie got stopped by the police, they could run his name immediately and verify that he had no pending warrants.

We first needed to apply for his birth certificate, which his mother had only a vague memory of possessing before she left the homeless shelter in which the family had spent the first few years of Reggie's life. Obtaining this document required many trips to the government offices downtown and other proofs of identity: a social security card and two pieces of mail (not letters but something more formal, such as a bill). After three weeks of collecting these items and two long days spent in fruitless trips to the Division of Vital Records downtown, Reggie shook his head, noting that ID is basically for rich people. "Because you have to have ID to get ID," he said. "Just like money."

Having gotten nowhere, we found a man in the 6th Street neighborhood who specialized in applications for birth certificates and other ID. People showed him their proofs of identity and he sent away for their birth certificates from the downtown office, taking forty dollars for this service. Ultimately, this man wasn't satisfied with any of the documents Reggie could come up with to apply for the birth certificate, and finally suggested we use a close relative's death certificate to prove his identity and residence. His mother at first refused to allow Reggie to take the death certificate out of the house, so we were stalled once again.

After six weeks of hard effort and considerable expense, Reggie had a birth certificate, two pieces of mail that would count for his proof of address, and a social security card. With these precious documents in hand, we drove to the Pennsylvania Department of Transportation.

As we approached the parking lot adjacent to the building, Reggie began to move around in his seat, fidgeting and adjusting his clothing. Once I'd parked the car, he made no move to get out. I turned to him and asked if he wanted me to go in first and get a ticket for the line. He sat silently for a while and then began to explain his concerns. Showing up and applying for this ID would lead employees to run his name and bring up some outstanding ticket or warrant. He eyed the security guards warily, saying that undercovers probably hung out at the Department of Transportation as well. "It's like, I'm home now, you feel me? I don't want to be back in there tomorrow . . ."

We sat in the DMV parking lot for over ten minutes while Reggie attempted to get up the courage to walk through the door. In the end, he couldn't go through with it, so we drove back to the block.

Like Reggie, a great many people living in the 6th Street neighborhood don't have government-issued ID, fear using their ID if they do have one, or have ID but can't do much with it because of their unpaid tickets, outstanding warrants, or the restrictions of their probation or parole. Local entrepreneurs recognize this core problem of poor and legally compromised people, and attempt to solve it in two ways: first by selling fake IDs and documents, and second by supplying the goods and services that typically require ID as part of the sales transaction, with no questions asked.

In the early 2000s, Mike and his friends bought fake licenses, social security cards, car insurance and vehicle registrations, and birth certificates. Merchants around 6th Street offered these goods under the table, if customers made the request appropriately. Salesmen on foot also offered these items as they made their rounds at bars, barbershops, and corner stores.

Mike used fake registration and car insurance documents when he got stopped in the early 2000s. The police didn't run his real name and so didn't discover that he had no license or registration for the car. Nor did they find out that he was on probation and prohibited from driving a car in the first place. Chuck was once able to get through an entire court case using a fake name and identification he had purchased from a man operating a stand outside a sneaker store. This fake identity allowed him to be tried for the case at hand without his previous cases coming into play.

Improved law enforcement technology has made it more and more difficult to use a fake identity to get through police stops. Indeed, giving a false name to the police has become all but impossible: beginning in the mid-2000s, squad cars were equipped with computers for running IDs. Philadelphia police around 6th Street now refuse to accept a driver's license or non-driver's state ID, asking instead for the man's photo number. This number is issued at a person's first arrest, and as one officer told me, "Any guy who says he doesn't have one is lying." Through the photo ID number, the officer can pull up an extensive description of the man, along with pictures of his face and body, from the computer in the police car. Some police cars in Philadelphia are now also equipped with finger print machines, so that a man's prints can be run quickly and on the spot without the trouble of taking him down to the police station.

As another strategy for passing under the radar, young men around 6th Street pay those with legitimate identities to put things in their name, such as apartment leases, utility bills, even accident claims. This makes it significantly harder for the police to track them. Before Mike was sentenced to a year and half in prison, he was doing very well financially. He had two used cars in two different women's names, lived in an apartment in a friend's name, had a gun registered to a friend of his uncle, had a cell phone in his children's mother's name, owned a dirt bike in the name of the previous owner, and rented furniture in his mother's name. In exchange for borrowing their identities, he gave these relatives and neighbors cash, food, drugs, and DVDs. Some also had occasional use of the items.

Five times over the six years I spent in the neighborhood, I observed people stopped by the police successfully use the name of another person they knew to be "clean." Once Mike gave a friend's name to get through a traffic stop and then went to court to pay the tickets for the moving violation, still using the man's identity. As compensation, Mike lent this man his leather Eagles jacket for a season.

A number of neighborhood businesses allow people to make purchases with no questions asked. Wanted people seek places to shop that don't require any documentation, because getting an ID in the first place could lead to an arrest; buying things using an ID would make it easier for the police to track them; and their dealings with the criminal justice system have rendered unusable the identification they have (for example, their licenses are suspended). These places where items ordinarily requiring identification may be bought without showing ID, signing one's name, or showing proof of insurance are known as ducky spots.

A man concerned that he may be taken into custody also fears using the hospitals, and so purchases a variety of medical goods and services from people in the neighborhood who work in health care and who supply drugs, medical supplies, and their general expertise to legally precarious community members. Chuck paid a neighbor working as a custodian at the local hospital around forty dollars for antibiotics when his foot got infected after he ran through some debris during a police chase. After two weeks of severe tooth pain, Chuck's neighbor, a twenty-year-old man, pulled his own molar with a pair of pliers and paid his cousin, who worked at a doctor's office, eighty dollars for a course of antibiotics. Reggie broke his arm when he tripped over the curb while running from a man trying to stab him. His neighbor brought over ma-

terial for a cast from his job at the VA hospital, heated it in a pan of water on the stove, and made a hard splint that Reggie wore for five weeks.
Reggie gave him a large bag of marijuana as compensation.

Mike and Chuck and their friends around 6th Street also paid friends
and neighbors for their silence and cooperation, and for news about the
police. In a community filled with suspects and fugitives, every resident is a potential conduit of information, either for the police or for
the men they're after. Mike and his friends tried to ensure that neighbors who could alert the authorities to their whereabouts or activities
were instead helping them hide.

In the same way that payments for sex can be placed on a continuum
from prostitution to marriage, the money that legally entangled people
pay others in the neighborhood to help protect them from the authorities ranges from explicit, short-term, quid pro quo exchanges, in which
a set fee is paid for a single piece of information or a single refusal to
talk to the police or testify as a witness, to longer-term relationships, in
which the arrangement is largely tacit, and the legally precarious party
provides extended financial support in exchange for silence, watchful-
ness, and general help in evading the authorities.[8]

The most extended relationship of this kind that I observed on 6th
Street involved two brothers who sold marijuana in the area. The pair
had grown up in the neighborhood but had long since moved away.
They didn't mention their business or anybody else's illicit doings over
the phone, they came and went quickly, and to my knowledge, no person on 6th Street had ever been to their house—or even knew where
it was.

When the two brothers came around in their dark SUV to drop off
drugs or pick up payments, they gave back to the community. They
helped pay for the funerals of three young men who were shot and
killed during my time there. They also contributed grocery money
to the mothers of the deceased, rent money to their girlfriends, and
haircut money for their sons. They gave cash to people who had recently come home from prison: a kind of get-started money. They put
money on the books of neighborhood men who were fighting cases in
county jail.[9]

As these two brothers coached and mentored younger guys on the
block, they often discussed the importance of giving as a core obliga-

tion to those less fortunate. But they also occasionally mentioned that their generosity encouraged others to protect them from the authorities. In particular, they made sure that those neighborhood residents with frequent dealings with the police didn't feel angry or resentful toward them. The older brother explained it like this to a younger boy on the block:

> What makes a nigga call the cops? Hate [jealousy]. It's only a matter of time before they see your picture or your name comes up [during a police questioning]. You want them to pass right by [the picture], you want them to choose the other guy, the guy who never did nothing for them.

Mike and Chuck regarded this practice with admiration, acknowledging that it's smart to send money to a man in jail who, if he gives you up, will see his commissary account quickly dry up. But like a marriage, this relationship requires consistent income, and most men in the neighborhood have only sporadic work in either the formal or the informal economy, with quite uneven and low returns.

Mike and Chuck certainly couldn't afford to maintain long-term relationships in which a steady flow of cash or other resources guaranteed the ongoing cooperation of neighborhood residents. But they did occasionally scrape together enough money for one-time payments, mostly to witnesses during trials.

According to Mike, about two years before we met, he had been walking home from a dice game with a large wad of cash when a man put a gun to his head and ordered him to give up his money.[10] Mike told me that he refused, and attempted to draw his own gun when the man shot him. Other accounts have it that Mike attempted to run away and shot himself by accident, whereupon this man took his money and then stripped him of his sneakers and watch. Whatever the details of this encounter, Mike emerged from it with a bullet lodged in his hip. His mother looked after him for five months while he was unable to walk, and then drove him to the outpatient clinic twice a week for months of physical therapy.

By the time we met, Mike could walk normally, though he said his leg hurt when he ran or stood for long periods, or when the weather changed. He believed this man had left the neighborhood, but about a month later he thought he spotted him driving around in a Buick. Mike told me that the man looked at him, he looked at the man, the man tensed, and Mike opened fire. Mike said, "I ain't know if he was going to start chopping [shooting], you know, thinking I was going to come at him. Better safe than sorry."

Two days later Mike saw him again, this time while driving with Chuck and another friend. Although I wasn't present, Chuck told me immediately afterward that the men in both cars opened fire, shooting at each other as they drove by in opposite directions. I couldn't confirm the shots that Mike, Chuck, and another friend fired, but the glass in the side and back windows of Mike's car was shattered, and I counted seven bullet holes in the side doors. Mike quickly towed the car to a friend's garage, worried that the police would see it if they hadn't been alerted to the shootout. This was around noon.

That afternoon, Chuck and this friend came to my apartment, took some wet (PCP), and lay on the couch and floor with covers over their heads.[11] They didn't eat, drink, or get up for almost twenty-four hours, occasionally murmuring curses at Mike about how close they had come to death.

Two nights later, the police came to Mike's old address, his uncle's house, to arrest him for attempted murder. Mike's uncle phoned his mother to let her know they were coming for him, so Mike left her place and hid out in various houses for the next two weeks, including my apartment for four days. The police raided his mother's house twice, then his grandmother's house, and then his children's mother's house. After two weeks he scraped together what money he could, found a lawyer, and turned himself in. He didn't know who had called the police, but the lawyer showed us the testimony of the man who had robbed him, explaining that this man would be the main witness at the trial.

When Mike made bail, the man got in touch with him through a mutual acquaintance. He explained that he wanted only three hundred dollars, which was what it would cost him to repair the shattered windows in his car. Mike considered this a very low sum to get out of an attempted murder charge and happily paid him. He also paid for a hotel room for this man to stay in on the appointed court dates, in case the police came to his house to escort him to court.[12] This man then failed to show up as a witness for three court dates, and the judge dismissed the case. To my utter astonishment, Mike and this man now appeared to be "cool." The night after the case ended, we had drinks with the man and played pool together at a local bar.

People in legal jeopardy can pay others *not* to show up as a witness at a trial; they can also pay people in the neighborhood to alert them if the police are coming, or can pay those who know of their whereabouts, activities, or identity not to give this information to the police. With such a large number of wanted people in the neighborhood (as well as people committing illegal acts who are liable to be arrested should those acts be brought to the attention of the authorities), 6th Street engages in a brisk trade in this kind of information and cooperation.

It should be noted that the payments legally precarious people make to the purveyors of false documents, or to those who might inform or testify, are in addition to the money they pay to lawyers and to the state directly in court fees and fines, bail, probation and parole costs, and tickets. These payouts for their continued freedom represent no small portion of their income.

INFORMING

If a young man exhausts the avenues discussed above, he may attempt to avoid confinement by giving the police someone they want more than they want him. In contrast to fleeing, avoidance, cultivating unpredictability, or paying to pass undetected, this strategy carries heavy social judgment. Indeed, informing is understood to be such a lowly way to get out of one's legal problems that men tend not to admit when they have done it. Since young men and women typically inform inside police cars or interrogation rooms, behind closed doors, it was difficult for me to study.

Chuck and Mike were close friends with a young man named Steve, who was about a year older than Chuck and a year younger than Mike. He lived across the street from Chuck with his mother and grandmother, his father having moved down south when he was a small child. Steve's mother worked in administration at Drexel University, so the family was better off than many of the others on the block. With his small build, light skin, and light eyes, Steve looked sneaky, Chuck's mom said, someone to keep your eye on. He was also notoriously hot-headed, pulling out his gun at inappropriate moments, like birthday parties for Mike's children.

Chuck and Mike hadn't thought that anyone could make Steve give up the bachelor life, but after high school he fell in love with Taja, a young woman who had grown up a few blocks away. Their stormy romance lasted longer than anyone expected—longer than *they* expected, they sometimes laughed. For almost the entire time I knew Steve and Taja, they were trying hard to have a baby, but Taja would miscarry every time Steve got locked up: three times in their six-year relationship.

Steve was a drug user more than a drug seller; when we met he was nineteen, and under house arrest awaiting the completion of a trial for possession of drugs.

In the spring the police stopped Steve while he was carrying a gun, and charged him with possession without a license to carry. He made bail, but then got picked up soon after for drinking while driving, revoking his bail. Steve sat in county jail as the court dates dragged on.

To our great surprise, Steve came home on house arrest three months later, still in the middle of his trial dates. He explained that the court released him for the remainder of the proceedings because the jails were overflowing, and the judge determined that he didn't pose a flight risk.

In confidence, Mike admitted to me that he did not believe Steve, since he'd never heard of a person coming home on house arrest during a trial for a gun case. He suspected that Steve had likely cut a deal to be at home during the lengthy court proceedings, most likely by giving up somebody the police seemed more interested in.

A week later, a local man on trial for murder phoned Reggie and told him that his lawyer had shown him Steve's statement. Apparently, Steve had signed an affidavit that he had been present at the time of the murder. A younger friend of Reggie's was at his house when he got the phone call, and soon began spreading the news that Steve was a snitch.

Faced with the public and personal disgrace of his betrayal, Steve spent three days threatening violence against Reggie's young boy, and then he told him to come to his house so they could discuss it. As the young man entered, Steve began yelling, "Who the fuck told you I was a rat, nigga? Who?"

"You just going to sit here and act like you ain't say shit," the young man said coolly. "They got your statement on file."

Steve said he would kill him, and the young man made a move toward Steve. Mike attempted to pull the two apart, but Steve pulled his gun and pistol-whipped the young man in the face and then in the back of his head.

"You been home less than a week!" Chuck admonished, as the young man covered his bloody face with his hands. "You can't pistol-whip a nigga that calls you a snitch. Plus, that makes you look like you really did do that shit."

"You ain't mature in jail at all," Mike added.

Mike asked the young man if he could go to the hospital, and he replied that he had a couple of open cases, but no warrants. We took him to the ER for stitches. Mike, who had a bench warrant for failure to appear in court, hovered in the parking lot, checking in every half hour or so via cell phone.

To my knowledge, this young man never again mentioned that Steve had snitched. A few days later there was another shootout, and the whole affair took a backseat in the local gossip.

Most of the time, young men don't resort to violence to rebuild their reputations after they snitch. Instead, they attempt to regain the trust and goodwill of the person they wronged.

When he was sixteen, Ronny and a few other young men from 6th Street drove to Montgomery County late one night and tried unsuccessfully to break into a motorcycle store. When they couldn't get in, they returned to their '89 Bonneville, only to find that the car wouldn't start. Ronny called Mike to come get them.

When Mike got the call, he and Chuck and I were watching movies in the apartment. It was around 2:00 a.m. I heard Mike on the phone to Ronny as follows: "Where the fuck is that at? Okay. Gimme like, a hour [to get out there]."

Mike turned to me.

MIKE: This lil' nigga out in the middle of nowhere. Car ain't starting. We still got them cables [jumper cables]?

ALICE: No. Who is he with?

MIKE: The boy Dre, couple other niggas.

ALICE: Why is he out there?

MIKE: I don't fucking know—probably because he trying to steal something. I'ma beat his lil' ass to the ground when I see that nigga. Now I got to get up. [*shakes his head as he puts on his boots*] Fuck it. I'ma just wear my long johns.

ALICE: I'll see you later.

Mike cursed the boys but went out anyway to retrieve them, saying that he couldn't refuse his young boy anything. Chuck and I waited until around four. Mike didn't come back. The next afternoon, I got a call from a cop at a Montgomery County police station, asking if I knew a man named Keshon Jackson. After a beat I realized that this was likely the fake name that Mike had used when he got booked so that any outstanding warrants wouldn't come up.

Apparently, when Mike pulled up, the dealership's silent alarm had already gone off, and the cops were waiting behind a hill for the boys to try to break in again. The cops ran out from behind the hill and chased Mike and Ronny, along with the other boys, across covered pools and sandboxes and through bushes. Two of the boys got away; Ronny, Mike, and another young man were caught and taken into custody.

According to the signed affidavit that Mike's lawyer read to us later, Ronny and his friend, both sixteen, were separately interrogated and agreed to name Mike as the one who had put them up to it. In exchange, the police dropped the charges against the minors and drove Ronny and his friend home. Mike, who was twenty-one at the time, was charged with attempted breaking and entering, vandalism, and trespassing.

When Ronny got back home, he fervently denied that he had informed, claiming he would never betray Mike like the other boys had. But Mike had seen the police report. On the phone to me from jail, he said he was deeply hurt by Ronny's betrayal, since he considered Ronny a younger brother:

Even if they [the police] was telling him like, look, just say it was Mike and we'll let you go home tonight, he should have played his part [remained silent; done the right thing] just on the strength of everything I done been through for that lil' nigga. Almost everything he got on his back was shit

I passed off [gave to him], you feel me? Any time he need a couple dollars, who he coming to? He ain't going to his nut-ass pop, he ain't going to Nanna [his grandmother]. He come straight to me like, "Yo, Mike. Let me hold [borrow] this, let me hold that." I done broke him off, like, so much change. Who he think keeping him fed out here? Nigga, you ain't eating [making money] by yourself! Ain't no other motherfucker out here looking out.

Mike spread the word that Ronny had snitched. It was worse than that, in fact, because Ronny had blamed Mike for a crime that he didn't even commit. For almost two weeks, Ronny didn't come out of his grandmother's house except to go to school. Then he took Mike's gun and robbed a house in Southwest Philadelphia. He sold the TV, stereo, and jewelry, and paid Mike's bail.

Mike came home and still refused to speak to Ronny. He wouldn't allow Ronny to come to the apartment where he was staying, though Ronny came to the door a number of times.

By the time Mike drove out to Montgomery County for the preliminary hearing, he and Ronny appeared to be on better terms. In fact, Ronny accompanied him to all the subsequent court dates to show his support. As we were walking out of the courthouse on one of these occasions, Mike said to me:

I know, you know, he a snitch, but that's my little nigga. I raised that nigga from this tall. Plus, like, he don't have no real family, like, his pops gone, his mom out there in the streets. Nigga had to look out for himself.

The support Ronny gave Mike during his court dates, and the money he risked his life to obtain to pay Mike's bail, seemed to have prompted a reconciliation between them. Though Mike treated Ronny somewhat coldly in the following months, he stopped telling people that Ronny had snitched.

Two years later, Mike was in state prison for a gun case, and Ronny's botched motorcycle theft came up in conversation in the visiting room. Mike and I had a good laugh about how stupid Ronny and his friends had been to try to break into the motorcycle store, and Mike recalled that he had run across a covered pool for the first time in his life. Then

Mike cursed Ronny's friend for snitching on him. He said that if he ever saw the kid again, he'd beat the shit out of him. I didn't mention that Ronny had snitched, too, and Mike didn't, either.

Five years after this initial snitching incident, Mike was back home, and Ronny got into a fight with a young man who, after Ronny had beaten him soundly, began talking about how Ronny had snitched on Mike a while ago, though "a lot of niggas don't know that." Mike handed Ronny his T-shirt to clean himself off and said to the offending young man, "Get your fucking facts straight, nigga. Everybody knows Ronny ain't do that shit."

Ronny's strategy to repair his public persona and his relationship with Mike after he had informed on him was to post Mike's bail, attend his court dates, and slowly regain his trust and forgiveness. He also denied that he had snitched, and after a time Mike denied it along with him, even sticking up for Ronny when others tried to revisit this piece of history.

* * *

For young men around 6th Street who worry that the police will take them into custody, the everyday relations, localities, and activities that others rely on for their basic needs become a net of entrapment. The police and the courts become dangerous to interact with, as does showing up to work or to places like hospitals. Instead of a safe place to sleep, eat, and find acceptance and support, their mother's home is transformed into a last known address, one of the first places the police will look for them. Close relatives, friends, and neighbors become potential informants.

One strategy for coping with the risky nature of everyday life is to avoid dangerous places, people, and interactions entirely. Thus, a young man learns to run and hide when the police are coming. He doesn't show up at the hospital when his child is born, nor does he seek medical help when he is badly beaten. He doesn't seek formal employment. He doesn't attend the funerals of his close friends or visit them in prison. He avoids calling the police when harmed or using the courts to settle disputes. A second strategy is to cultivate unpredictability—to remain secretive and to dip and dodge. Thus, to ensure that those close to him won't inform on him, a young man comes and goes in irregular and unpredictable ways, remaining elusive and untrusting, sleeping in different beds, and deceiving those close to him about his whereabouts and plans. He steadfastly avoids using his own name. He also lays out a good deal of money to silence potential informants and to purchase fake documents, clean urine, and the like. If a man exhausts these possibilities and does encounter the police, he may flee, hide, or try to bargain for his freedom by informing on the people he knows.

The danger a wanted man comes to see in the mundane aspects of everyday life, and the strategies he uses to avoid or reduce these risks, have some larger implications for the way he sees the world, the way others view him, and consequently the course his life may take. At a minimum, his hesitancy to go to the authorities when harmed leads him to become the target of others who are looking for someone to prey upon. His fear of the hospital means that he doesn't seek medical care when he's badly beaten, turning instead to underground assistance of questionable repute.

More broadly, a man in this position comes to see that the activities, relations, and localities that others rely on to maintain a decent and respectable identity become for him a system that the authorities exploit to arrest and confine him. Such a man finds that as long as he is at risk of confinement, staying out of prison and maintaining family, work, and friend relationships become contradictory goals: engaging in one reduces his chance of achieving the other. Once a man fears that he will be taken by the police, it is precisely a stable and public daily routine of work and family life, with all the paper trail that it entails, that allows the police to locate him. It is precisely his trust in his nearest and dearest that will land him in police custody. A man in legal jeopardy finds that his efforts to stay out of prison are aligned not with upstanding, respectable action but with being a shady and distrustful character.

THREE

When the Police
Knock Your Door In

To round up enough young men to meet their informal quotas and satisfy their superiors, the police wait outside hospitals serving poor Black communities and run the IDs of the men walking inside. They stop young men sitting on the stoop and search their pockets for drugs. But the police also deploy a less direct strategy to make their stats: they turn to girlfriends, mothers, and relatives to provide information about these young men's whereabouts and activities.

The reliance on intimates as informants is not the dirty dealing of a few rogue cops or the purview of a few specialized officers. Police don't reserve this treatment for the families of those few men who make their most wanted list. In our 2007 household survey of the 6th Street neighborhood, 139 of 146 women reported that in the past three years, a partner, neighbor, or close male relative was either wanted by the police, serving a probation or parole sentence, going through a trial, living in a halfway house, or on house arrest. Of the women we interviewed, 67 percent said that during that same period, the police had pressured them to provide information about that person.

As the police lean on women to help round up their partners, brothers, and sons, women face a crisis in their relationship and their self-image. Most help the police locate and convict the young men in their lives, and so must find a way to cope publicly and privately with their betrayals. A rare few manage to resist police pressure outright, garnering significant local acclaim. A greater number work to rebuild themselves and their relationships after they have informed, which is sometimes successful and sometimes not. These cases are considered at the end.

GETTING THE NEWS

The journey from intimate to informant (or, in rarer cases, from intimate to resister) often begins when a woman discovers that the man in her life has become wanted by the police, or has become more legally precarious than he had been.[1]

On an unusually warm Sunday afternoon in March, Aisha and I sat on the wide cement steps of her four-story subsidized apartment building. Her boyfriend, Tommy, leaned on the railing beside her, chatting with a neighbor who had stopped on his way home. Aisha's aunt and neighbor sat farther up the steps, waiting for their clothes to finish at the Laundromat across the street. We passed around a bag of jalapeño sunflower seeds and kept our eye out for Aisha's cousin, who was supposed to be coming back with a six-pack from the corner store. Time dragged on, and Tommy remarked that she'd probably taken our pooled money and gone to the bar.

As we sat watching the kids play and spitting the shells into little piles beside us, Tommy unfolded a notice he had received that day from family court, a notice that he must appear before a judge because the mother of his two-year-old son was asking for back payments in child support. If he came to court empty handed, he told us, the judge might take him into custody on the spot. If he didn't show up, a warrant might be issued for his arrest for contempt.

"She just mad you don't mess with her no more," Aisha said. "She knows you pay for all his clothes, all his sneaks. Everybody knows you take care of your son."

"When is the court date?" I asked.

"Next month," Tommy answered, without looking up.

"Are you going to go?"

"He don't have six hundred dollars!" Aisha cried.

We tried to calculate how many days in jail it would take to work off this amount, but we couldn't remember if they subtract five dollars or ten dollars for each day served. Aisha's aunt said she thought it was less than that. Aisha concluded that Tommy would lose his job at the hospital whether he spent two weeks or two years in jail, so the exact amount he would work off per day was of little consequence.

Tommy looked at Aisha somberly and said, "If I run, is you riding?"

"Yeah, I'm riding."

A neighbor's five-year-old son started to cry, claiming that an older boy had pushed him. Aisha yelled at him to get back onto the sidewalk.

"If they come for me, you better not tell them where I'm at," Tommy said quietly.

"I'm not talking to no cops!"

"They probably don't even have your address. They definitely coming to my mom's, though, and my baby-mom's. But if they do come, don't tell them nothing."

"Shoot," Aisha said. "Let them come. I'll sic Bo right on them."

"Yeah?" Tommy grinned appreciatively and nudged Aisha with his shoulder.

Aisha's aunt turned and eyed her skeptically, shaking her head.

"I'm not letting them take him," Aisha fired back. "For what? So he can just sit in jail for four months and lose his job? And don't see his son?"

Aisha and Tommy began dating shortly after I first met her, when she was a high school freshman. What she liked about him then was that he was gorgeous, for one, and dark skinned, even darker than she was. Tommy, she said later, was not only her first; he was also her first love. They kept in touch for years afterward, though Tommy had a child with another woman, and Aisha began seriously seeing someone else. When Aisha turned twenty-one, this second man was sentenced to fifteen years in a federal penitentiary in Ohio. About six months later, Aisha and Tommy got back together. Soon after that, Tommy began working as a custodian at the Hospital of the University of Pennsylvania. When he got the call for the job, they cried and hugged in the living room. Aisha had never dated a guy with a real job before, and became the only woman in her extended family with this distinction.

* * *

"If they lock me up, you going to come see me?" Tommy asked her.

"Yeah, I'ma come see you. I'ma be up there every week."

"I know that's right," Aisha's neighbor said. "Them guards up there going to know your name. They going to be like, 'You *always* coming up here, Aisha!'"[2]

We laughed quietly.

Later that evening, two of Aisha's girlfriends came by. She told them about her conversation with Tommy: "He talking about, 'if I run, is you riding?' Shoot, they ain't taking him! They're going to have to kill me first."

For Aisha, the news that Tommy may be taken came as a crushing personal blow. But it was also an opportunity to express her devotion, meditate on their relationship, and contemplate the lengths she would go in the future to hold it together.

Other women considered their family member's pending imprisonment in more political terms. Mike's mother, Miss Regina, was in her late thirties when we met. A reserved and proper person, she had made good grades in high school and got accepted to a local college. She became pregnant with Mike that summer. The way she told it, Mike's father was the first person she had ever slept with, and she hoped they would get married. But the man became a heavy crack user, and was in and out of jail during Mike's early years. By the time Mike was ten, Miss Regina told his father to stop coming around.[3]

By all accounts, Miss Regina worked two and sometimes three jobs while Mike was growing up, and she raised him with little help from her own parents. Mike got into a lot of trouble during his high school years, but managed to get his diploma by taking night classes.

By the time Mike came of age, the drama with the mother of his two children and his frequent brushes with the authorities had caused Miss Regina "a lifetime of grief." By twenty-two, Mike had been in and out of county jail and state prison, mostly on drug charges.

When we met, Miss Regina was working for the Salvation Army as a caretaker to four elderly men and women whose homes she visited for twelve- or eighteen-hour shifts three times a week. She had moved to Northeast Philadelphia a few months before we met, noting that the 6th Street neighborhood had become too dangerous and dilapidated. The house she was renting was spotless; she even had a special machine to clear away the smoke from her cigarettes.

Miss Regina had just gotten home from work, and had started a load of laundry in the basement. Her mother and I were watching the soap opera *Guiding Light* on the plush loveseat in the living room when the phone rang. From the kitchen Miss Regina yelled, "I don't believe this." She passed me the phone; it was Mike, who told me his PO (probation officer) had issued him a warrant for breaking curfew at the halfway house last night. He had come home from prison less than a month ago; this violation would send him back for the remainder of his sentence, pending the judge's decision. When we hung up, Miss Regina lit a ciga-rette and paced around the living room, wiping down the surfaces of the banister and TV stand with a damp rag.

"He's going to spend two years in prison for breaking curfew? I'm not going to let them. They are taking all our sons, Alice. Our young men. And it's getting younger and younger."

Miss Regina's mother, a quiet, churchgoing woman in her sixties, nodded and mumbled that it is indeed unfair to send a man to prison for coming home late to a halfway house. Miss Regina continued to pace, now spraying cleaning solvent on the glass table.

> Let me ask you something, Alice. When you go up the F [local slang for the Curran-Fromhold Correctional Facility (CFCF), the county jail], why do you see nothing but Black men in jumpsuits sitting there in the visiting room? When you go to the halfway house, why is it nothing but Black faces staring out the glass? They are taking our *children*, Alice. I am a law-abiding woman; my uncle was a cop. They can't do that.

On seventy-one occasions between 2002 and 2010, I witnessed a woman discovering that a partner or family member had become wanted by the police. Sometimes this notice came in the form of a battering ram knocking her door in at three in the morning. But oftentimes there was a gap between the identification of a man as wanted and the po-lice's attempts to apprehend him. Before the authorities came knock-ing, a letter would arrive from the courts explaining that a woman's fiancé had either missed too many payments on his court fees or failed to appear in court, and that a bench warrant was out for his arrest. Or a woman would phone her son's PO and learn that he did indeed miss his piss test again, or failed to return to the halfway house in time for cur-few, and an arrest warrant would likely be issued, pending the judge's decision. At other times, women would find out that the man in their lives was wanted because the police had tried and failed to apprehend him at another location.

In fifty-eight of the seventy-one times I watched women receive this news, they reacted with promises to shield their loved one from arrest. In local language, this is called riding.

Broadly defined, to ride is to protect or avenge oneself or someone dear against assaults to person or property. In this context, to ride means to shield a loved one from the police, and to support him through his trial and confinement if one fails in the first goal of keeping him free.[4]

It may come as a surprise that the majority of women I met who learned that a spouse or family member was wanted by the police initially expressed anger at the authorities, not the man, and promised to support him and protect him while he was hunted. In part, I think these women understood how easy it was to get a warrant when you are a Black young man in neighborhoods like 6th Street; they understood that warrants are issued not only for serious crimes but for technical violations of probation or parole, for failure to pay steep court fines and fees, or for failure to appear for one of the many court dates a man may have in a given month.[5] A second and related reason for women's anger is that the police have lost considerable legitimacy in the community: they are seen searching, questioning, beating, and rounding up young men all over the neighborhood. As Miss Regina often put it, the police are "an occupying force." A third reason is more basic: no matter what a woman's opinion of the police or of the man's actions, she loves him, and does not want to part with him or see him subjected to what has been referred to as the pains of imprisonment.[6]

Riding is easy to do in the abstract. If the authorities never come looking, a woman can believe that she will hold up under police pressure and do her utmost to hide the man and protect him. So long as the threats of police pressure and prison are real but unrealized, a woman can believe in the most idealized version of herself. The man, too, can believe in this ideal version of her and of their relationship.

A few days after Tommy received the notice from family court, he went to the police station and turned himself in. The police never came to question Aisha. They did come for Miss Regina's son, Mike.

WHEN THE POLICE COME

I'd spent the night at Miss Regina's house watching *Gangs of New York* with Mike and Chuck for maybe the hundredth time. I had fallen asleep on the living room couch and so heard the banging in my dream, mixed in with the title page music, which the DVD played over and over.

The door busting open brought me fully awake. I pushed myself into the couch to get away from it, thinking it might hit me on the way down if it broke all the way off its hinges. Two officers came through the door, both of them white, in SWAT gear, with guns strapped to the sides of their legs. The first officer in pointed a gun at me and asked who was in the house; he continued to point the gun toward me as he went up the stairs. I wondered if Mike and Chuck were in the house somewhere, and hoped they had gone.

The second officer in pulled me out of the cushions and, gripping my wrists, brought me up off the couch and onto the floor, so that my shoulders and spine hit first and my legs came down after. He quickly turned me over, and my face hit the floor. I couldn't brace myself, because he was still holding one of my wrists, now pinned behind me. I wondered if he'd broken my nose or cheek. (Can you break a cheek?) His boot pressed into my back, right at the spot where it had hit the floor, and I cried for him to stop. He put my wrists in plastic cuffs behind my back; I knew this because metal ones feel cold. My shoulder throbbed, and the handcuffs pinched. I tried to wriggle my arms, and the cop moved his boot down to cover my hands, crushing my fingers together. I yelled, but it came out quiet and raspy, like I had given up. My hipbones began to ache—his weight was pushing them into the thin carpet.

A third cop, taller and skinnier, blond hair cut close to his head, entered the house and walked into the kitchen. I could hear china breaking, and watched him pull the fridge away from the wall. Then he came into the living room and pulled a small knife from its sheath on his lower leg. He cut the fabric off the couch, revealing the foam inside. Then he moved to the closet and pulled board games and photo albums and old shoes out onto the floor. He climbed on top of the TV stand and pushed the squares of the drop ceiling out, letting them hit the floor one on top of the other.

I could hear banging and clattering from upstairs, and then Miss Regina screaming at the cop not to shoot her, pleading with him to let her get dressed. All the while, the cop with his foot on me yelled for me to say where Mike was hiding. It would be my fault when Miss Regina's house got destroyed, he said. "And I can tell she takes pride in her house."

TECHNIQUES OF PERSUASION

If the police decide to go after a man, chances are they will ask his relatives and partner where he is. Because these intimates are immersed in the lives of their legally precarious family members and partners, they tend to have considerable knowledge about their activities and routines. They know where a young man shops and sleeps, where he keeps his possessions, and with whom he is connected.

These days it isn't difficult, expensive, or time consuming for the police to identify family members who may have information about the whereabouts or incriminating activities of a man they are after. Nor does it require direct knowledge of the neighborhood or its inhabitants gained through close association. Rather, information about a man's relatives, children, partner, and relationship history can now be easily retrieved with a few keystrokes.

When the police arrest and process a man, they ask him to provide a good deal of information about his friends and relatives—where they live and where he lives, what names they go by, how to reach them. The more information he provides, the lower his bail will be, so he has a significant incentive to do this. By the time a man has been arrested a number of times, the police have substantial information about where his girlfriend works, where his mother lives, where his child goes to school.

Once a man has become wanted, the police visit his mother or girlfriend, and try to persuade her to give him up. In the words of one former Warrant Unit officer, "We might be able to track people with their cell phones or see every guy with a warrant in the neighborhood up on the computer screen, but when it comes down to it, you always go through the girlfriend, the grandmother, because she knows where he is, and she knows what he's done."[7]

After the police locate a family member or partner, they employ a series of techniques to gain the woman's cooperation. These begin when the police are searching for a man or arresting him, but may continue through his trial and sentencing as they attempt to gather information that will facilitate a conviction.[8]

The most direct pressure the police apply to women to get them to talk is physical force: the destruction of their property and, in some cases, bodily injury. From what I have seen around 6th Street and nearby neighborhoods, police violence toward women occurs most frequently during raids. During these raids and also during interrogations, they deploy a number of less physical tactics to get uncooperative women to talk. The major three are threats of arrest, eviction, and loss of child custody.

Threats of Arrest

During raids and interrogations, the police threaten to arrest women for an array of crimes. First, they explain to a woman that her efforts to protect the man in her life constitute crimes in their own right. When Chuck's mother, Miss Linda, blocked the police's entrance to her home and waved an officer away as he pulled up her carpet and opened up her ceiling, the officers explained that they could charge her with assault on an officer, aiding and abetting a fugitive, and interfering with an arrest. They also told her that she would face charges for the gun they found in her house, since she didn't have a permit for it. (In fact, in Philadelphia a permit is required only for carrying.) When Aisha's neighbor said she would refuse to testify against her son, officers told her that she would go to jail for contempt. Once she agreed to cooperate, they informed her that if she changed her statement she would be jailed for lying under oath.

Beyond her efforts to protect the man in question, the police make it clear to a woman that many of her routine practices and everyday behaviors are grounds for arrest. Over the course of raids and interrogations, the officers make women realize that their daily lives are full of crimes, crimes the police are well aware of, and crimes that carry high punishments, should the authorities feel inclined to pursue them. When the police came for Mike's cousin, they told his aunt that the property taxes she hadn't paid and some long-overdue traffic fines constituted tax evasion and contempt of court. The electricity that she was getting from her neighbor two doors down, via three joined extension cords trailed through the back alley (because her own electricity had long been cut off, and for the use of which she was babysitting her neighbor's two children three times a week), constituted theft, a public hazard, and a violation of city code.

The police also explain to a woman that she can be charged for the man's crimes. Mike's girlfriend told me she was sure she would be charged for possessing the gun or the drugs if she didn't give Mike up, since the police found them in her house and car. The police also threatened to bring her up on conspiracy charges, claiming that they had placed a tap on her cell phone and so had proof that she was aware of Mike's activities.

Police raids also place a woman's other male relatives in jeopardy. When Mike had a warrant out for his arrest and the police were showing up at his mother's house, she became very worried that her fiancé, who was driving without a license and who was also selling small quantities of marijuana as a supplement to his job at the hospital, would come under scrutiny. Because it is very likely that the other men in a woman's life are also facing some violation or pending legal action (or engaged in the drug trade or other illegal work), the police's pursuit of one man represents a fairly direct threat to the other men a woman holds dear.

Finally, the police tell a woman that if her present and past behavior is insufficient grounds for arrest, they will use every technology at their disposal to monitor her future activities. Any new crimes she commits will be quickly identified and prosecuted, along with any future crimes committed by her nearest and dearest. If she drives after she has been drinking, if she smokes marijuana, if her son steals candy from the store—they will know, and she or he will go to jail.

The threat of arrest and imprisonment is a powerful technique of persuasion, and perhaps more so when deployed on women. Fewer women than men go to prison or jail, making it a scarier prospect. Women don't receive the same degree of familial support available to men, as visiting people in prison is considered women's work, done for men by their female partners and kin, and men are less able to visit.[9] In the 6th Street neighborhood, people tend to regard imprisonment as more of an indictment of a woman's character and lifestyle than a man's, partly on the grounds that police routinely stop and search men, while women must do something more extreme to get the police's attention.

Threats of Eviction

In addition to threats of arrest and imprisonment, the police threaten to evict women who do not cooperate.[10] They told my next-door neighbor that if she didn't give up her nephew, they would call Licensing and Inspection and get her dilapidated house condemned. And when the police came to Steve's grandmother's house looking for him, they noted that the electricity and gas weren't on, the water wasn't running, and the bathtub was being used as an outhouse. These violations of the municipal health and building codes would easily constitute grounds for the city to repossess her property. The officers also informed her that the infestation of roaches, mice, and fleas in the house were sufficient grounds for the landlord to revoke her lease. Further, since she had placed the bail for Steve in her name, his running meant that the city could go after her for the entire bail amount—not just the 10 percent she put up, which meant the city could also take her car and her future earnings. When the police came to Aisha's neighbor's house looking for the neighbor's on-again, off-again boyfriend, they informed her that if she didn't give him up, they would come back late at night in a full raid. Since her apartment was subsidized, she could be immediately evicted for harboring a fugitive and putting her neighbors at risk. She would lose her present accommodations and all rights to obtain subsidized housing in the future.

Child Custody Threats

Another tactic that the police use to persuade women to talk is to threaten to take away their children. When the police raided Mike's neighbor's house, they told his wife that if she didn't explain where to find him, they'd call Child Protective Services and report that the windows were taped up with trash bags, that the heat had been cut

off and the open stove was being used as a furnace, and that her children were sleeping on the sofa. Officers also found marijuana and a
crack pipe in the house. If she continued to be uncooperative, this evidence would build a powerful case for child neglect and unfit living
conditions. That evening, the woman packed up her three children and
drove them to Delaware to stay with an aunt until the police activity
died down.

Most of the threats police make to women over the course of a raid,
a stop, or an interrogation are never realized. Consequently, when a
woman attempting to protect a man from the authorities does get arrested or evicted, or loses custody of her children, the news spreads
quickly. Anthony had a cousin who lived in Virginia; she was sentenced
to five years in prison for conspiracy to sell drugs and possession of an
illegal firearm after she refused to serve as a witness for the case against
the father of her child. With both her parents in prison, the four-year-
old daughter was sent to Philadelphia, where she was passed from relative to relative. Two of Miss Linda's neighbors got evicted from their
government-subsidized housing for harboring a fugitive and interfering with an arrest when the police entered their home searching for a
man who had robbed a bank. Families around 6th Street often recalled
such stories when they anticipated a raid, or after some interaction
with the police.

Presenting Disparaging Evidence

In order to get her to provide information, the police may injure a
woman or destroy her property. If she persists in protecting the man,
they threaten to arrest her, to publicly denounce her, to confiscate and
appropriate her possessions, to evict her, or to take her children away.
We might call violence and threats *external forces of attack*, as they operate from the outside to weaken the bonds between the woman and the
man the police are after.

The authorities also work within the relationship, by presenting the
woman with information about the man that shatters her high opinion
of him and destroys the positive image she has of their relationship. We
might call this an *internal attack*, as it works to break the bonds between
men and women from the inside.

The police's presentation of disparaging evidence operates as a complex, two-way maneuver. First, they demonstrate to the woman that the man she is trying to protect has cheated on her. They show her his cell phone records, text messages, and statements from women in the neighborhood. The improvement of tracking technologies means that no large effort need be made to furnish these pieces of evidence: they can be quickly gathered at a computer. If the police have no concrete evidence, they suggest and insinuate that the man has been unfaithful, or at least that he doesn't truly care about her but is simply using her. At this point the officers explain that at the first opportunity, this man who does not love her will give her up to save his own skin, will allow her to be blamed for his crimes. Perhaps he has already done so.

Just as the officers are explaining to the woman how her partner has been unfaithful and duplicitous, and would easily let her hang for his crimes, so they present the man with evidence of *her* betrayals. They show him statements she signed down at the precinct detailing his activities, or the call sheet filled out at the Warrant Unit, where, after repeated raids on her house, she phoned to tell authorities where he was hiding. They may also show him evidence that she has cheated on him, which they collect by tracking her cell phone, bills, and purchases, or from statements given by other men and women who are part of the couple's circle.

In short, the police denigrate the man and the relationship to the point that a woman cannot protect him and continue to think of herself as a person of worth. In anger and hurt, and saddled with the new fear that this man who doesn't love her may try to blame her for his misdeeds, leaving her to rot in prison, a woman becomes increasingly eager to help the police.

Moral Appeals

The previous techniques of persuasion work by weakening the bonds between the woman and the man the police are pursuing. Moral appeals to the value of imprisonment operate on the opposite principle: they rely on the strength of the woman's attachment, and play on her resolve to help and protect him. Specifically, moral appeals involve adjusting what the woman believes to be the right thing to do concerning the man she loves.

Before the police come knocking, a woman may believe that it is best for the man in her life to stay out of prison. He will go crazy in his cell, he will get stabbed, or get AIDS, or have an unhealthy diet. The prison won't see to his medical needs, like his diabetes or the worrisome bullets lodged in his body.[11] He will lose his job if he has one, or find it more difficult to find work once he comes home. Being in a cell day after day, cut off from society, with guards barking orders at him, he will become dehumanized, and normal life will become unfamiliar to him. To keep him from this fate, sacrifices must be made.

The police explain to the woman that this logic is flawed. In fact, the man would benefit from a stay in prison. He needs to make a clean break from his bad associates. It is not safe for him on the streets; he might be killed if he continues to sell drugs, or may overdose, if his proclivities run that way. He is spiraling deeper and deeper into dangerous behavior; jail will be a safe haven for him. Going to prison will teach him a lesson; he will emerge a better man, one more capable of caring for her and the children. The drama must end, they tell her, his drama and the drama that comes because of all the police activity. He has too many legal entanglements, too many court cases, warrants, probation sentences. He will be better able to find work without the warrants. It would be better if the man simply got it over with and began his life afresh. She can help him; she can save him before it is too late. He will thank her one day for this tough love.

A variant on this line of persuasion is that while it may not be best for the man to go to prison, it will be best for the family as a whole. Protecting the man means that she risks losing her children and her home; the bail in her name means that she could go into debt to the city and be jailed if she cannot pay it. His actions also expose her children to bad people and bad things. As a responsible mother, sister, or daughter, she should save her family and turn him in.

Promises of Confidentiality and Other Protections

The police's techniques of persuasion are often bolstered by promises that no information she provides will be shared with the man or with anyone else among her acquaintance. In twenty-one of the twenty-four raids that I witnessed, officers told family members that the man would never be made aware that they had given him up. During the two questionings I was involved in, the police assured me of my confidentiality, and when women recounted their own interrogations, they mentioned that the same promise was made to them the majority of the time.

The Multipronged Approach

Violence, threats, disparaging evidence, moral appeals, and promises of protection are analytically separable, but the police often deploy these techniques in tandem, each serving to strengthen and reinforce the other.

It was difficult for me to observe women's interrogations, because they were conducted behind closed doors at the police department, and women were reluctant to recount their experience once they got back home. For these reasons, I have used my own interrogation as an example.

This interrogation is notable because the police made use of many of the techniques described above, despite having very little to work with: they did not know what my relationship was to the men they were interested in; I was not living in public housing; I had no children; and neither I nor anyone in my immediate family had an arrest history or pending legal problems.

I had dropped Mike and Chuck off on 6th Street and was heading toward the airport to pick up a friend. Two unmarked cars come up behind me, a portable siren on top of the first one, and I pull over. A cop walks over to my window and shines a flashlight in my face; he orders me to step out of the car and show him my license. Then one of the cops tells me I am coming with them.

I leave the car on 2nd Street and get into the backseat of their car, a green Lincoln. The white cop in the back with me would have been skinny if not for the bulletproof vest, holster, gun, nightstick, and whatever else he had in his belt. He cracks bubble-gum hard and smells like the stuff Mike and Chuck use to clean their guns. On the way to the precinct, the white cop who is driving tells me that if I am looking for some Black dick, I don't have to go to 6th Street; I could come right to the precinct at 8th and Vine. The Black cop in the passenger side grins and shakes his head, says something about how he doesn't want any of me; he would probably catch some shit.

At the precinct, another white guy pats me down. He is smirking at me

as he touches my hips and thighs. There is a certain look of disdain, or perhaps disgust, that white men sometimes give to white women whom they
believe to be having sex with Black men—Black men who get arrested,
especially.

They take me up the stairs to the second floor, the Detective Unit. I sit
in a little room for a while, and then the two white cops come in, dark-
green cargo pants and big black combat boots, and big guns strapped onto
their legs. They remove the guns and put them on the table facing me. One
cop leafs through a folder and puts pictures in front of me of Mike, then
Chuck, then Reggie. Most of the pictures are of 6th Street, some taken
right in front of my apartment. Some mug shots. Of the forty or so pictures
he shows me, I knew about ten men by name and recognize another ten.
They question me for about an hour and a half. From what I remember
many hours later:

Is Mike the supplier? Do you think he'll protect you when we bring him
in? He won't protect you! Who has the best stuff, between Mike and
Steve, in your expert opinion? We know you were around here last week
when all that shit went down. (What shit?) We saw you on 2nd Street,
and we know you're up on 4th Street. What business do you have up 4th
Street? I hate to see a pretty young girl get passed around so much. Do
your parents know that you're fucking a different nigger every night?
The good cop counters with: All we want to do is protect you. We are
trying to help you. We're not going to tell him you gave us any information. This is between us. No paper trail. Did you sign anything when
you came in? No. Nobody knows you are even here. The bad cop: If you
can't work with us, then who will you call when he's sticking a gun to
your head? You can't call us! He'll kill you over a couple of grams. You
know that, right? You better hope whoever you're fucking isn't in one of
the pictures you're looking at here, because all of these boys, see them?
Each and every one of them will be in jail by Monday morning. And
he'll be the first one to drop your name when he's sitting in this chair.
And then it's conspiracy, obstruction of justice, harboring a fugitive,
concealing narcotics, firearms. How do you think we picked you up in
the first place? Who do you think is the snitch? What is your Daddy going to say when you call him from the station and ask him to post your

bail? Bet he'd love to hear what you are doing. Do you kiss him with that mouth?

* * *

To fully grasp the effect of these techniques of persuasion on women, we must understand the broader context of police violence in which they occur.

Between November 2002 and April of 2003, I spent a large part of every day with Aisha and her friends and relatives, who lived about fifteen blocks away from 6th Street. From the steps of her building or walking around the adjacent blocks, on fourteen occasions, a little more than twice a month, we watched the police beat up people as they were arresting them. Here is one account from the fall of 2007:

It is late afternoon, and Aisha and I are sitting on the stoop, chatting with her aunt and her older cousin. Aisha's mother sits next to us, waiting for her boyfriend to come with five dollars so that she can finish her laundry.

A white police officer jogs by, his torso weaving awkwardly, his breath coming loud enough for us to hear. Then I notice a young man running a little ahead of him, also out of breath, as if he had been running for a long time. The man slows to a walk, and leans down with his hands on his knees. The cop approaches him, running in this stilted way, and grabs the back of his neck with one hand, pushing him down to the ground. Drawing his nightstick, he straddles the man in a half crouch, and begins hitting him in the back and neck with it.

Two of Aisha's neighbors get up off the steps and quietly approach the scene, keeping some yards away. Aisha makes no move to get up; nor does her aunt or cousin. But we lean over to see.

Police cars pull up to the corner with sirens and lights on, first one then another, then another, blocking the street off. They handcuff the young man, whose face is now covered in blood, especially the side that had been scraped across the cement.

The police move the man to the cop car, and one cop places his hand on top of the man's head to guide him into the backseat. Then they look around on the ground, apparently searching the area for something. Two of the cops speak into walkie-talkies.

"He must have had a gun or drugs on him," Aisha's aunt says.

"I didn't see nothing," a neighbor replies.

When the police cars begin to pull off, a neighbor says that she saw one cop punch the man in the face after he was already cuffed.

Aisha's cousin, a stout young man of nineteen, gets up off the steps.

"Yo, I'm out, Aisha. It's too hot on your block."

"Okay," she laughs. "Tell your mom I said hi."

An elderly woman comes out after a few minutes with a bucket of bleach and water and pours it over the sidewalk, to clean the blood. Aisha and I go back to talking about her boyfriend, who has just received a sentence of fifteen years in federal prison. As the day goes on, I notice that Aisha and her family make no mention of what we have seen. Perhaps because they don't know the man personally, this event is not important enough to recount to those not present when it occurred.

That summer was punctuated by more severe police action. On a hot afternoon in July, Aisha and I stood on a crowded corner of a major commercial street and watched four officers chase down her older sister's boyfriend and strangle him. He was unarmed and did not fight back. The newspapers reported his death as heart failure. In August, we visited an old boyfriend of Aisha's shortly after he got to county jail. Deep lacerations covered his cheeks, and his eyes had swollen to tiny slits. The beating he took while being arrested, and the subsequent infection left untreated while he sat in quarantine, took most of the vision from his right eye.

In interviews, Warrant Unit officers explained to me that this violence represents official (if unpublicized) policy, rather than a few cops taking things too far. The Philadelphia police I interviewed have a liberal understanding of what constitutes reasonable force, and a number of officers told me that they have orders from their captains that any person who so much as touches a cop "better be going to the hospital."

In sum, the police apply a certain amount of violence to women to get them to talk, but substantially more to men as they chase them down and arrest them. The violence that women witness and hear about fixes what the police are capable of doing firmly in their minds. This knowledge likely spurs their cooperation, should the police desire it.

BECOMING A SNITCH OR AN ABANDONER

As the police roll out their techniques of persuasion, as they raid a woman's house and pull her in for questioning, the woman's public reckoning begins. Relatives, neighbors, and friends watch to see how she will hold up as the police threaten to arrest her, to evict her, or to take her children away.

When the raids and interrogations begin, many women find that they cannot live up to the hopes they and others had for their conduct. Rather than be the man's "ride-or-die chick," they implore him to turn himself in. Rather than hide him and help him survive, they kick him out of the house and cut off all contact, perhaps leaving him without food or shelter. Rather than remain silent in the face of police questioning, they give up all the information they can.

Shortly after Mike's baby-mom, Marie, had given birth to their second child, the police came to his mother's house looking for him on a gun charge. When Marie heard this news, she called me on the phone to discuss it and, in between her screams and cries, explained her concerns for him:

> You remember last time? He stopped eating! And then they put him in the
> hole [solitary confinement] for no reason. Remember how he was in the
> hole? I can't take those calls no more. He was really losing it. No sunlight.
> Nobody to talk to. Plus, he could get stabbed up, or get AIDS. How I'm sup-
> posed to take care of the baby? They don't care he got a bullet in his hip.
> Won't none of them guards pay attention to that, and I can tell it's getting
> ready to come out [push through the skin].

Firm in her conviction that Mike would suffer in jail, and determined to keep her growing family together, Marie promised to do whatever she could to protect him from the authorities.

Then the police paid a visit to Marie's house. They came early in the morning, waking up the baby. They didn't search the house, but sat and talked with her about the necessity of turning Mike in.

I came over that afternoon. Visibly shaken, Marie seemed to have adopted quite a different view of things:

MARIE: He needs to get away from these nut-ass niggas out here, Alice. It's not safe for him on the streets; he could get killed out here. He needs to go in there, get his mind right, and come out here—

MARIE'S MOTHER:—and act like a man.

MARIE: Yes. Because the drama has to stop, Alice. He has too much stuff [legal entanglements]. He needs to go in and get all that taken care of. How he supposed to get a job when he got two warrants on him? He needs a fresh start. He ain't going to like it, but he going. Soon as I see him [I'm calling the number on the card the police gave me].

In fact, Marie did not call the police on Mike right away; she tried to persuade him to turn himself in. Mike refused, and Marie continued to try to "talk some sense into him" over the next few days. She called the number on the card on the fifth day, after a second visit from the police. As they drove him off in handcuffs, we sat on the stoop and talked.

MARIE: I know he not going to take my visits right away but I don't care, like, it had to be done. It's too much drama, Alice. He can call me a snitch, I don't care. I know in my heart—

MARIE'S MOTHER:—that was the right thing to do.

After Marie got Mike taken away, he castigated her daily from jail and spread the word that she had snitched. This, she said, was nothing compared to the internal anguish she felt over betraying the father of her two children, and her most trusted friend. The pains of his confinement, she explained, rested on her shoulders:

Every time he hungry in there, or he lonely, or the guards is talking shit to him, that's on my head. Every time he miss his son—I did that to him.

THE TRUE RIDER

Overwhelmingly, women who come under police pressure cave: they cut off ties to the man they had promised to protect, or they work with the police to get him arrested and convicted. When this happens, women suffer public humiliation and private shame, and face the difficult task of salvaging their moral worth in the wake of their betrayals. Most often, the relationship is permanently ruined; to salvage her dignity, the woman may start over with a new man in a new social scene—perhaps a few blocks away, or better yet, in another neighborhood. Four times I observed women pack up and move after being publicly labeled a snitch.

I witnessed a number of situations in which the police pressure never materialized. The man turned himself in, or wasn't pursued after all, or the police caught up to him quickly and so didn't get around to putting pressure on his girlfriend or relatives. In these cases, the woman doesn't have to manage her spoiled identity or reconstruct her relationship, because she didn't have to resort to betraying her boyfriend, brother, or son.

In other cases, a woman is able to support and protect the man because the police don't connect her to him, and therefore don't put pressure on her or her family directly. Because a man's main girlfriend and close relatives tend to be known to the police and targeted for information, he often finds his inner circle untrustworthy, while someone with whom he has a weaker connection—a new friend, an old girlfriend, or a more distant cousin—turns out to be the true rider.

Most of the time, women who are identified by the police cave quickly under their pressure. But a few women around 6th Street showed remarkable strength in resisting them. Miss Linda's ability to resist police pressure was widely recognized in the 6th Street community. As Mike once proclaimed to a small crowd assembled on her steps after a raid, "She might be a thief and her house might be dirty as shit, but Miss L ain't talking. She don't care if they bang her door in, she don't give a fuck!"

Miss Linda would often say that she rode hard for her three sons because she had more heart than other women, but the truth of the matter was that she also had more practice. Chuck, Reggie, Tim, and their friends and associates brought the law to her house on at least twenty-three occasions during my six years on 6th Street.[12]

When her middle son, Reggie, was seventeen, the police stopped him for loitering on the corner, and he allowed them to search him. An officer discovered three small bags of crack in the lining of his jeans, and

Reggie started running. The cops lost him in the chase, and an arrest warrant was issued for possession of drugs with intent to distribute.

That evening, Miss Linda prepared her house for the raid she seemed sure was coming. She located the two guns that Reggie and his older brother, Chuck, had hidden in the ceiling, and stashed them at a neighbor's. She did the same with Chuck's bulletproof vest, his bullets, and the tiny plastic baggies he used to hold the small amounts of crack he was selling at the time. She took her marijuana stash, along with her various crack-smoking paraphernalia, to her boyfriend's house three blocks up. And after some effort, she secured accommodations for Chuck's close friend Anthony, who had been sleeping in their basement and had a bench warrant out for failure to appear. She let her neighbors know that the police were coming so that their sons and cousins could go elsewhere for the night. (This was in case the police got the wrong house, which had happened before, or in case they decided to search the houses nearby.) She dug out the sixty dollars Reggie had hidden in the wall, as the police typically take whatever cash they find. She persuaded her father, Mr. George, to sleep at his girlfriend's place that night, in case "the law gives him a coronary."

Though Miss Linda had instructed Reggie to leave the house before midnight, he fell asleep by accident, and was still there when a three-man SWAT team busted the door in at about four in the morning. (The door remains broken and unlocked to this day.) Miss Linda had slept on the couch in preparation and, unsure if Reggie was still in the house, launched into a heated argument with the officers to delay their going upstairs. This ruse proved successful. According to Reggie, he was able to leave through a window in his bedroom and run through the alley before they could catch him.

The next night, three officers returned and ordered Reggie's younger brother, Tim, and Mr. George to lie facedown on the floor with their hands on their heads while they searched the house. According to Tim, an officer promised Miss Linda that if she gave Reggie up, they would not tell him that she was the one who had betrayed him. If she did not give her son up, the officer said he'd call Child Protective Services and have her youngest son taken away, because the house was infested with roaches, covered in cat shit, and unfit to live in. On this night, she again refused to tell the police where Reggie was.

Shaken but triumphant, Miss Linda came out early the next morning to tell her friends and neighbors the story. We sat on her iron back-porch steps that look out onto the shared alleyway.

MISS LINDA: I do my dirt, I'm the first to admit it. Some people say I'm a bad mother. You can say what you want about me, but everybody knows I protect my sons. All three of them. These girls out here can talk all they want, but watch when the fucking law comes BAM! knocks they door in. Don't none of these girls know about that. They can talk, but won't none of them ride like me. Only some females is true riders, and I'm one of them females. [*Takes a drag from her cigarette, nods her head confidently. Grins.*] They can come back every night.

When her cousin came to sit with us, Miss Linda repeated the story, adding that she had deliberately worn her sexiest lingerie for the raid, and had proudly stuck out her chest and butt when the officer was cuffing her against the wall. She acted this out to shrieks of laughter. She said that she told a particularly good-looking officer, "Honey, you so fine, you can search me anytime!"

Later in the day, more police officers came to search the house, and while they were pulling it apart once again, Reggie phoned to see if they were still there and if his mother was alright. Sitting not two feet from one of the officers, she coolly replied, "Yeah, Mom-Mom. I got to call you back later, because the police are here looking for Reggie. You haven't seen him, have you? Okay, alright. I'll call you back later. I'll pick up the Pampers when I go food shopping."

When the police left, Miss Linda told me: "Big George [her father] is going to tell me to clean this shit up as soon as he comes in. But I'm not cleaning till next week. They're going to keep coming, and I'm not putting this house back together every fucking morning."

I was there two nights later when the police raided Miss Linda's house for the third time. On this night, three officers put plastic cuffs on us and laid us facedown on the living room floor while they searched the house. Despite her previous boasts of telling off the police and propositioning them with "I got three holes, pick one," Miss Linda cried and screamed when they dropped her to the floor. An officer mentioned that the family was lucky that Mr. George owned the house: if it were a

Section 8–subsidized building, Miss Linda and her sons could be immediately evicted for endangering their neighbors and harboring a fugitive. (Indeed, I had seen this happen recently to two other families.) Upstairs, the police found a gun that Miss Linda couldn't produce a permit for; they arrested her and took her to the police station. When Tim and I picked her up that afternoon, she said she was told that she would face gun charges unless she told the police where to find Reggie. They also promised her anonymity, though she said she didn't believe them for a second.

By her own and Tim's accounts Miss Linda had been quite stalwart up until this point, but the third raid and the lengthy interrogation seemed to weaken her resolve. When Reggie came around later to pick up the spaghetti she had prepared for him, she begged him to turn himself in. He refused.

A week later, Miss Linda was coming home from her boyfriend's house and found her TV and clothing dumped in the alleyway. Her father, Mr. George, told her that he would no longer allow her to live there with Tim if she continued to hide Reggie from the police:

> This ain't no damn carnival. I don't care who he is, I'm not letting nobody
> run through this house with the cops chasing him, breaking shit, spilling
> shit, waking me up out of my sleep. I'm not with the late-night screaming
> and running. I open my eyes and I see a nigga hopping over my bed trying
> to crawl out the window. Hell, no! Like I told Reggie, if the law run up in
> here one more time I be done had a stroke. Reggie is a grown-ass man [he
> was seventeen]. He ain't hiding out in my damn house. We going to fuck
> around and wind up in jail with this shit. They keep coming, they going to
> find some reason to book my Black ass.

Mr. George began calling the police whenever he saw Reggie in the house, and Miss Linda told her son that he could no longer stay there. For two months, Reggie lived in an abandoned Buick LeSabre parked in a nearby alleyway.

Here under extreme duress, Miss Linda nonetheless refused to tell the police where to find Reggie. And though she ultimately begged him to turn himself in, and then kicked him out of the house when her father threatened to evict her, she never gave her son up to the police. While Reggie was sleeping in the Buick, she kept in close touch with him, supplying him with food almost every evening. Her neighbors and family, and Reggie himself, seemed to believe that she had done the best she could, better than anyone else could have done. The evening the cops took Reggie in, I sat with Miss Linda and some of her neighbors. She poured Red Irish Rose wine into small plastic cups for us.

> MISS LINDA: Well, at least he don't have to look over his shoulder anymore, always worried that the law was going to come to the house. He was getting real sick of sleeping in the car. It was getting cold outside, you know, and plus, Reggie is a big boy and his neck was all cramped up. And he used to come to the back like: "Ma, make me a plate," and then he'd come back in twenty minutes and I'd pass him the food from out the window.

Brianna, Chuck's girlfriend, responded, "You ride harder than any bitch out here, and Reggie knows that."

THE RIDER REBORN

Veronica was eighteen when she met Reggie, who was nineteen. She had been dating one of Reggie's friends, though not seriously, and this man never had much time for her. He would leave her with Reggie while he was busy, and as Reggie put it, one thing led to another. Soon Veronica was spending most evenings at Reggie's. Chuck and Tim were starting to call her Sis.

"At first I couldn't fall asleep," she told me a few weeks into this relationship. "I was scared the bugs would crawl on me at night. You really have to love a Taylor brother to sleep in that house." Indeed, the kitchen crawled with roaches, ants, and flies; the floors themselves looked like they were moving, as if you were in some psychedelic bug dream.

One night, Veronica woke up thinking that the roaches were crawling on the bed again, only to see Reggie scrambling to make it out the window while yelling at her to push him through. This was not easy, as Reggie is a young man of substantial girth. Then two cops busted through the bedroom door and threw Veronica out of the bed. They cuffed her to the bed frame for an hour while they searched the house, she told me the next day, even though it should have been plain to them that Reggie had fled through the still-open window, which naturally would be shut in February. She said they told her they'd find out every illegal thing she did, every time she smoked weed or drove drunk, and they'd pick her up every time they came across her. They would put a special star in her file and run her name, and search her and whoever she was with whenever they saw her. They told her they had tapped her cell phone and could bring her up on conspiracy charges. Despite these threats, Veronica couldn't tell them where Reggie had run, because she simply did not know.

Later that day, Reggie called her from a pay phone in South Philly. Veronica pleaded with him to turn himself in. He refused, and she told him then and there that they were through.

Reggie put Veronica "on blast," telling his friends, relatives, and neighbors that she had cut him loose when the police started looking for him. He then began seeing Shakira, a woman he had dated in high school.

The next day, Veronica called me in tears: Reggie had told everyone on the block that she wasn't riding right, that she didn't really give a fuck about him, and that she was out as soon as shit got out of hand. He told her he would never have expected it, thought she was better than that.

As Veronica retreated from 6th Street, Shakira stepped up to help Reggie hide. She met him at his friend's house, and spent the next few days holed up in the basement with him. She arranged for a friend to bring them food. In the meantime, the police raided Miss Linda's house, Veronica's house, and Reggie's uncle's house. But they didn't visit Shakira's house or question her family, which seemed to allow her to preserve her role as a brave and loyal person. I went to see her and Reggie on the third day.

SHAKIRA: I been here the whole time, A. When they [the police] came to his mom's we was both there, and he went out the back and I been here this whole time.

REGGIE: She riding hard as shit.

ALICE: That's what's up [that's good].

REGGIE: Remember Veronica? When she found out the boys [the police] was looking for me, she was like: click [the sound of a phone hanging up]. She'd be like, "I see you when I see you." Shakira ain't like that, though; she riding like a mug [motherfucker, i.e. very hard]. She worried about me, too.

We didn't hear from Veronica for a few weeks, and then the police found Reggie hiding in another shed nearby. They came in cars and helicopters, shutting down the block and busting open the shed with a battering ram.

When Reggie could make a phone call, he let Veronica know that he wasn't seeing Shakira anymore. Veronica wrote him a letter, and then she started visiting him. It took three hours on the bus to get to Northeast Philadelphia where the county jails are, because the routes don't line up well. Veronica had never visited a guy in jail before, and we'd often discuss what outfit she could wear to look her best while complying with the jail's regulations.

As Veronica made the weekly trek to the county jail on State Road, Reggie's friends stayed home. They didn't write; they didn't put any money on his books.

Every day, Reggie voiced his frustration with his boys over the phone to me:

Niggas ain't riding right! Niggas ain't got no respect. G probably going to do it [put money on his books], but Steve be flajing [bullshitting; lying]. When I come home, man, I'm not fucking with *none* of these niggas. Where the fuck they at? They think it's going to be all love when I come home, like, what's up, Reggie, welcome back and shit. . . . But fuck those niggas, man. They ain't riding for me, I got no rap for them when I touch [get home]. On my word, A, I ain't fucking with none of them when I get home. I would be a fucking nut for that. Brandon especially, A. I was with this nigga *every day*. And now he's on some: "My bad, I'm fucked up [broke]." Nigga, you wasn't fucked up when I was out there! I banged on that nigga, A [hung up on him].

Despite their continued promises to visit and to send money, after three months not one of Reggie's boys had made the trip. Only Veronica came. She wrote him about two letters every week, with him writing two or maybe three letters back. Sometimes she and I would go together to visit him. On Reggie's birthday, Veronica wrapped a tiny bag of marijuana in a twenty-dollar bill and smuggled it to him in the visiting room.

One afternoon, Veronica and I were sitting on Miss Linda's second-floor porch playing Spades with her. Though usually quiet, Veronica spoke for the longest I'd heard:

> Ain't none of his boys go visit him, none of them. . . . The only people that
> visit is me and Alice. Like, that should tell him something. Your homies
> ain't really your homies—I'm the only one that's riding. I'm the only real
> friend he got. Who's putting money on your books? They said they was go-
> ing to put some on there, but they ain't do it. The only money he got on his
> books is from me and you.

It seemed that Veronica, who had dropped Reggie while he was on the run, who was humiliated as a weak and disloyal person, was now, through the work of visiting and writing letters, reborn a faithful and stalwart companion.

A woman can also salvage her relationship and self-worth by gradually letting the details of a man's confinement fade, and joining with him to paint her conduct in a more positive light. Eight times I noted that a woman visiting a man in custody would join with him to revise the events leading up to his arrest and trial in ways that downplayed her role in his confinement.

When Mike was twenty-four and his children were three and six years old, he began dating a woman from North Philly named Michelle. Within a month they had become very close: Michelle's three-year-old son started calling Mike Daddy, and Michelle's picture went up on Mike's mother's mantelpiece next to his graduation picture and the school photos of his son and daughter. He started spending most nights at her apartment.

Michelle was the first Puerto Rican woman Mike had ever dated, and he had high hopes that her ethnic background would signify strong loyalty. "With Spanish chicks," he said, "it's all about family. Family is everything to them. Black chicks ain't like that. They love the cops."

Michelle and Mike both explained to me that Michelle was nothing like the mother of Mike's children, Marie, who so frequently called the police on him. Since Michelle's father and brothers sold drugs, she was used to the police and the courts, and wouldn't cave under their pressure. With strong memories of her mother struggling with her father's legal troubles all through her childhood, Michelle told me that she was a second-generation rider. She also said that she loved Mike more than any man she had ever met, including her son's father, who was currently serving ten years in federal prison.

Michelle's loyalty would be tested three months into their relationship. Mike missed a court appearance, and a bench warrant was issued for his arrest. Upon hearing the news, Michelle assured me that nothing—not the cops, not the judge, not the nut-ass prison guards—would break them apart.

At around four o'clock the following Friday morning, she phoned me sobbing: the cops had knocked her door down and taken Mike. He tried to run, and they beat him out on the sidewalk with batons. She said they beat him so badly that she couldn't stop screaming. Why did they have to do that? They had already put him in handcuffs.

At the precinct, the police kept Mike cuffed to a desk for eighteen hours in the underwear they had found him in. The next morning, they brought Michelle down to the station and questioned her for three hours. Then they showed Mike Michelle's statement, which detailed his activities, his associates, and the locations of his drug-selling business. When he got to county jail, he wrote her a letter, which she showed me:

> Don't come up here, don't write, don't send no money. Take all your
> shit from my mom's, matter of fact, I'll get her to drop that shit off. You
> thought I wasn't going to find out that you a rat? They showed me every-
> thing. Fuck it. I never gave a fuck about you anyway. You was just some
> pussy to me, and your pussy not even that good!

Mike spread the word that Michelle was a snitch, and this news was the hot topic for a few days between his boys on the block and those locked up.

Incensed and humiliated, Michelle explained to me that Mike had no right to be angry with her. He clearly didn't care about her. In fact, despite all his claims to the contrary, the police had shown her the text messages and phone calls that proved he was still seeing Marie. Not only that, but Mike had tried to pin the drugs on her and to claim that the gun in the apartment belonged to her father. Michelle wrote him a scathing letter back:

I should have known that you were still messing with your baby-mom. I felt like a fool when they showed me your cell phone calls and texts at 2 and 3 in the morning. And don't even try to tell me that you were calling your kids, 'cause no 7 year old is up at 2 a.m. Did you think I wasn't going to find out you tried to put that shit on me? I read every word. That bitch can have you.

With concrete evidence of Mike's infidelity, Michelle came to see that Mike did not value or respect her: their relationship had been a sham. She began to regard her past association with him as sordid and shameful, and her present efforts to protect him humiliating. At the same time, the police were showing Mike that she had betrayed him. Injured and humiliated, he rebuffed and belittled her just as she faced indisputable evidence of his duplicity, and confronted the possibility that this man who didn't love her might let her hang for his crimes.

Two days later, the cops took Michelle out to the suburbs where Mike had been selling. According to the police report, she gave up his stash spot, his runner, and all the customers she knew about.[13]

A friend of Mike's explained it like this:

The girl said, "Fuck it, I've only known him for three months, I want to keep my kid." Plus, her mom is in a nursing home, and she has custody of her two little sisters, so you know they told her they was going to kick her out the spot (the Section 8 building) and take her son and her sisters and shit. She has too much on the line. That bitch ain't think twice. She was like: What do you want to know?

After Mike's mother and grandmother and I attended his court dates and saw Michelle's statement, Mike declared that she was a snitch, and stopped talking to her for a while. The news spread quickly to Mike's boys—both those on the block and those locked up.

Though at first Michelle was able to justify her actions by noting that the police had threatened to take her children away and that Mike had in fact been cheating on her, these details seemed to have been forgotten in the neighborhood's collective memory as the weeks dragged on, and she increasingly came to feel that she had betrayed a good man. As his trial dates came and went, she began visiting him more often, and sending money and letters. Slowly, Michelle and Mike began to reconcile.

Some months later, Mike and I were chatting in the visiting room. He mentioned that the girlfriend of one of his friends had recently testified against that man in court. "She's a fucking rat," Mike said. "She don't give a fuck about him." We debated the circumstances of this, and I commented on how difficult it is to remain silent when the police threaten to evict you or take your kids. As an example, I noted that while Michelle clearly loved Mike, she had informed on him under just this kind of police pressure.

At this point our weekly gossip turned into a heated argument. Other visitors in the room began to stare as Mike forcefully explained to me that Michelle had not snitched. In fact, it was the woman in whose house he had been renting a room that had given the statement against him.

"You supposed to be keeping tabs! Like, that's your *job*. You're getting stupid. You used to remember every fucking thing."

"I really thought it was Michelle," I replied limply.

"What the fuck good are you if you can't even get basic shit right?"

My confidence as the group's chronicler quite shaken, I apologized profusely. At his next court date a month later, I asked Mike's lawyer to show me the statement again. Checking over the lengthy police report, I realized that my notes were accurate. Michelle had informed on Mike, on three separate occasions. I wasn't sure whether she had convinced Mike that she had remained silent, or they were both simply trying to put it behind them, but I decided it would be best not to bring it up again.

On our next visit, Mike lamented that one of his boys was continuing to call Michelle a snitch.

"Niggas is gonna hate," he said. "That's been my whole life, since middle school. Everybody wants what I got."

I nodded my head in solidarity.

THE DIZZYING JOURNEY FROM RIDER TO SNITCH

Many women in the 6th Street neighborhood view the forcible and un-expected removal of a boyfriend, brother, or son to be, as Mike's girl-friend once put it, "the end of everything." When a woman gets the news that the police may be after the man in her life, she may take it as her obligation to help him hide from the authorities. Through protect-ing him, she makes a claim for herself as a loyal girlfriend or a good mother, an honorable and moral human being.

If the police never come looking for the man, she can continue to be-lieve that she would do her utmost to shield him from the authorities, should the occasion for bravery and sacrifice arise. But if the police do come, they typically put pressure on her to provide information.

For the police and the district attorney, the task of turning intimates into informants is mostly a technical problem, one of many that arise in the work of rounding up and processing enough young men to meet informal arrest quotas and satisfy their superiors. But the role the po-lice ask women to play in the identification, arrest, and conviction of the men they love presents deeper problems for women: problems for their sense of self.

To be sure, some of the women I came to know on 6th Street didn't seem to care very much whether their legally entangled family mem-bers or neighbors were in jail or not. Some even considered the confine-ment of these troublesome young men a far preferable alternative to dealing with them on the outside. But those who took these positions tended to keep their distance from the men the police were after, and consequently tended not to know enough about their whereabouts to be very useful to the authorities. It is the women actively involved in the daily affairs of legally precarious men who prove most helpful in bring-ing about their arrest, so those women who consider the possible con-finement of a son or boyfriend a grave event, a wrenching apart of their daily life, are the ones the police enlist to capture and confine them.

When the police begin their pressure, when they raid a woman's house or pull her in for questioning, a woman faces a crisis in her relationship and in the image she has of herself: the police ask her to help imprison the very man she has taken it as a sacred duty to protect. Not only do the police ask her, they make her choose between her own security and his freedom. For many of the women I have come to know on 6th Street, this choice is one they are asked to make again and again. It is part of what enduring the police and the prisons is about.

Relatives and neighbors looking in on this crisis from the outside may see a woman's options in stark terms: she can prove herself strong in the face of threats and violence and protect the man, or she can cave under the pressure and betray him. If she withstands the police, she will garner public acclaim as a rider. If she caves, she will suffer humiliation as an abandoner or an informant.

But as a woman comes under increasing police pressure, her perspective on right and wrong begins to shift. As the police roll out their techniques of persuasion, she finds herself increasingly cut off from the man she loves, and interacting more and more with the authorities. The techniques they use to gain her cooperation turn her basic understandings about herself and her significant others upside down. She learns that her children and her home aren't safe, nor are the other people she holds dear. She begins to see her daily life as an almost endless series of crimes, for which she may be arrested at any moment the police see fit. She learns that the man she loves doesn't care about her, and comes to see her involvement with him as sordid, shameful, and pathetic.

As the police show the woman that her boyfriend has cheated, or that her son may try to blame her for his crimes, she comes to realize that protecting him from the authorities may not be such a good idea after all. Threatened with eviction, the loss of her children, her car, or all future housing benefits, her resolve to shield him weakens. By the time the police assure her of confidentiality, she begins to see the merits of working with the authorities.

* * *

There is an excitement surrounding wanted men. They are, in a certain way, where the action is.[14] But wanted men also stop coming around as much or as routinely. Their contributions to the household, though perhaps meager to begin with, may cease altogether. Their life on the run may be exciting, but it is a holding pattern; it has no forward motion. To some degree, a man's wanted status demands that a woman live in the present, and this present is a dizzying and uncertain one.

Out of this morass, the police offer the woman a dubious path: she can turn against the man; she can come over to their side. As she begins to orient herself to the their way of thinking, she finds a way out of the dizzying holding pattern created by the man's evasion and the police's pressure. She is now able to chart some forward path, and leave the upside-down world the raids and interrogations have created. Maybe he will hate her and she will hate herself, but at least she is moving forward.

As the police make it harder for her to remain on the man's side, they construct a vision of what life would be like without him, independent of the involvement with crime and with the police that he requires. They create a distinctive path for the woman that involves a change in how she judges herself and others.

A woman who contemplates changing sides discovers that a number of lines of action become available to her. She may urge the man to turn himself in, or, if pressure persists, she may give him an ultimatum: give yourself up or I will. She may openly call the police on the man, in plain view of their mutual family and friends. She may turn him in secretly, and attempt to conceal that she has cooperated with the authorities. Alternately, she may cut off ties with him, refuse to speak to him anymore, or kick him out of the house.

During this process, the pressure imposed by the police allows the woman to reconcile herself to her behavior, and the police's techniques of persuasion come in handy as justifications for her actions. But when the man is taken into custody and the pressure from the police lifts, it becomes increasingly difficult for the woman and for the rest of the community to accept what she did. She must now deal head-on with the public humiliation and private shame that come with abandoning or informing on the man she professed to care for.

It is in the nature of policing that officers tend to interact most with those in whose behavior they find fault, such that the woman's encounters with the police begin when she refuses to comply and end when she comes over to their side. That is, her intense and intimate association with the authorities lasts only for the duration of their denigration and her resistance. Once she cooperates and gives the man up, the police abandon their interest in her. At the moment she changes sides, she finds herself surrounded by neighbors and family who mock and disdain her, who consider her actions immoral and betraying.

Throughout this process, the woman takes a journey rife with emotional contradictions. The news that the man in her life has become wanted prompts a renewal of her attachment, such that she strengthens her commitment to him just as he ceases to play an active role in her daily life, to furnish her with any concrete future, or to assist her financially. When the man is taken into custody and the pressure to inform on him lifts, a woman can pledge her devotion once more and make amends. Unlike life on the run, his sentence or trial has a clear end point. She can coordinate her life around the visiting hours, and the phone calls in the morning and evening. She can make plans for his return.[15] But since she has contributed to his confinement, her attempts to repair the relationship coincide with his most heated anger against her. Even if he forgives her, a woman can renew her commitment to him, and return to regarding him as good and honorable, only after he has left her daily life most completely, as he sits in jail or prison.

Once a woman's son or partner is incarcerated, she may come full circle. As she did when she first got the news that the authorities might come looking, she returns to thinking that the police, the courts, and the prisons are unjust, and she will do just about anything to protect and support the man she loves.

A few skilled intimates do not travel the path the police put forward, as they are able to resist the pressure in the first place. They learn to anticipate raids, and to mitigate the damage that a raid may cause. They learn to make a scene and become a problem for police by vocally demanding their rights, by attracting a large audience, or by threatening to sue or go to the newspapers. They practice concerted silence, learning how to reveal as little as possible. They distract the officers from the direction the man ran, or the box in which incriminating evidence may be found. They also make counteroffers, such as sexual favors, or provide information about someone else the police might be interested in. Their refusal to cave under pressure means that their conduct calls for little explanation, and their relationships need few repairs.

Though some women manage to redeem their relationships, their reputations, and their sense of self after they cooperate, and a rare few are able to withstand police pressure and garner some honor and acclaim, it must be said that the police's strategy of arresting large numbers of young men by turning their mothers and girlfriends against them goes far in creating a culture of fear and suspicion, overturning women's basic understandings of themselves as good people and their lives as reasonably secure, and destroying familial and romantic relationships that are often quite fragile to begin with.

FOUR

Turning Legal Troubles into Personal Resources

The police and the courts are certainly making life difficult for families in the 6th Street neighborhood: breaking loved ones apart, sowing suspicion and distrust. But residents aren't simply the unwilling pawns of oppressive authorities. Both men and women at times actively make use of the form this intervention takes, appropriating their legal entanglements for their own purposes. In their ongoing struggles to negotiate family and work, and to make claims for themselves as honorable people, young men and women turn the heavy presence of the police, the courts, and the prisons to their advantage in ways the authorities neither intended nor expected.[1]

JAIL AS A SAFE HAVEN

Prisons were designed to be so unpleasant that even those living in quite harsh conditions outside their walls would find them a deterrent from crime.[2] To be sure, young men around 6th Street usually take great pains to elude the police and stay out of jail. But confinement begins to look more attractive to them during times of sustained violent conflict. When the 6th Street Boys found themselves under threat from other groups of young men from neighboring blocks, they sometimes manipulated their legal entanglements so as to get taken into custody voluntarily, in effect using jail as a safe haven from the streets.

During a dice game one evening, Tino put a gun to Jay-Jay's head and demanded all his money. Tino had moved to 6th Street only a few months before, so Chuck and Mike considered him only a candidate member of the group—a recent transplant on probationary status. Jay-Jay, who was originally from 4th Street but a frequent guest on 6th, didn't think that Tino was seriously trying to rob him, and told him to stop playing. Tino had been "wetted" (that is, taking wet [PCP]) all weekend and was now humiliated by Jay-Jay's refusal to take his robbery seriously; he demanded again that Jay-Jay give him everything in his pockets. Jay-Jay again refused.[3] By this time, Chuck and Reggie were yelling at Tino to put down the gun. Steve, also wetted out that night, was laughing—he didn't think that Tino had what it took to rob Jay-Jay or to shoot him, and said so. Tino pulled the trigger and Jay-Jay fell to the pavement.

Later, sitting in the basement with Chuck, Reggie, Steve, and me, Tino held his knees and rocked back and forth, repeating, "My intentions wasn't to shoot him. My intentions wasn't to shoot him."

Steve fired back, "You was wrong. No two ways about it. You was wrong."

Reggie's phone rang three times that night with messages from the 4th Street Boys: "It's on."

Jay-Jay's death triggered what is called a war, a series of shootouts between members of one block and those of another. In this case, Jay-Jay's boys from 4th Street and the Boys Across the Bridge joined forces. They began driving up and down 6th Street and shooting at the 6th Street Boys.

At first the 6th Street Boys hesitated to go to 4th Street and shoot at the men attacking them. Steve mentioned many times that since Jay-Jay had been killed, the 4th Street Boys had every right to shoot at them. But Steve's and Chuck's families were in danger: Steve's brother had stopped going to baseball practice, and his sister, who slept on the living room couch right by the window, had to move down to the basement. A bullet went right past Tim's knee while he was watching TV. These young men wouldn't stop, the guys thought, until they fired back.

Most of the 6th Street Boys weren't present for this war. Mike, Ronny, and Anthony were in prison or jail, and Alex had moved off the block and was working at his dad's heating and air-conditioning repair shop. After he killed Jay-Jay at the dice game, Tino moved to North Philadelphia, where he went into hiding for three months. This meant that only

Chuck, Reggie, Steve, and Steve's younger cousin were left to fight two blocks of young men by themselves. After a couple of weeks, Chuck and Steve had both been shot—Chuck in the neck and Steve in the thigh. Fresh bullet holes dotted five houses on Chuck's street.

As the weeks went by, I watched the remaining members of the 6th Street Boys get taken into custody—not in connection with these shootings, but for quite minor probation and parole violations, or for bench warrants for not showing up at court or for failure to pay fines and fees.

A few days after he was shot, Steve paid an unscheduled visit to his probation officer and asked to be tested for drugs. His urine test came back positive for marijuana, a result he had skillfully evaded in many previous tests. The PO issued him a warning for the positive test, letting him know that the next time he failed the test he would go back to jail for the violation. Two weeks later, Steve returned and was again tested for drugs. This time the judge sent him back to jail for six months.

Steve's younger cousin went to the police station and turned himself in on a bench warrant he had been issued ten months earlier for not paying his court fees. The officer who took the report later told me that the judge had offered to release him and put him on a payment plan for the court fees, but he declared that he was never going to pay the money and that they might as well keep him until he worked off the court fees and costs in jail. (The judge had ruled that his fees would be reduced by ten dollars for every day he spent in custody.) Chuck had no warrants pending and wasn't on probation at the time, so he remained on the block a few weeks after Steve and his cousin got taken into custody. Then he drove a friend's off-road motorbike past the police station and allowed himself to be chased for two blocks before he stopped the bike and put up his hands. The police charged him with fleeing the police and driving an off-road bike on city streets, and took him in. This left Reggie, who had a body warrant out for his arrest for a robbery. After a week on his own, he went down to the local police station and turned himself in.

The four members of the 6th Street Boys who were present on the block during this war may have allowed themselves to be taken into custody for reasons having nothing to do with the conflict. It is also possible that they didn't elect to get taken into custody and were caught, but these alternative explanations seem unlikely. Steve's cousin freely turned himself in on a low-level bench warrant and then refused to accept the judge's offer that would have allowed him to remain out of jail. This was the first time I had known Steve's cousin to turn himself in. Steve appeared at his probation officer's without being asked, and then volunteered for a drug test—the only time he had done so in the three years I had known him. He had managed to pass all his drug tests and adhere to other requirements of probation in the previous eight months. Chuck, who rode an illegal motorbike past the police station, may have been doing so for the thrill of publicly evading the authorities. Mike, for one, delighted in outrunning the cops before an audience of neighbors, family members, and women. But Chuck had no history of driving off-road motorbikes near police officers, let alone driving by police stations on them.

I believe that Reggie was the last person to get himself taken into custody because he already had a body warrant out for his arrest for armed robbery; he worried that if he turned himself in, he'd sit in jail during a lengthy trial and then possibly serve a number of years in prison. Chuck, Steve, and Steve's cousin, who turned themselves in more quickly, faced only a few months in jail apiece for their less serious violations: just enough time to let the violence on the street subside. Reggie tried to stay out as long as he could, but with dwindling numbers of the group still out on 6th Street it became too dangerous to try to make it on his own. A few years of prison seemed like the better option.

Three members of the group who were already in custody admitted to me that they were glad to be locked up so that they didn't have to participate in this war. This also led me to think that Chuck, Reggie, Steve, and Steve's cousin got arrested deliberately, using their wanted status to get out of harm's way.

*   *   *

Sometimes women, too, used jail as a safe haven, calling the police on their sons or partners when they decided the streets had become too dangerous.

When Steve got into an altercation with a guy from 4th Street, his girlfriend, Taja, called the cops and told them where they could find Steve; he had a warrant out for violating his parole. Taja told me that she'd have called the cops on the men who were trying to shoot him but feared retaliation, so instead she told the police to come get Steve. In her mother's kitchen, she and I talked over her decision with her sister:

TAJA: I miss him or whatever, but better that than I get the call like, "Yo, come to the hospital." Right?

HER SISTER: Niggas is trying to get at him [kill him]. You did what you needed to do.

Though Steve's girlfriend may have saved his life, he refused to speak to her for over a month while he sat in jail, refusing her visits and returning her letters. This, she said, hurt her deeply. Still, she remained adamant that she had done the right thing, and after a few months in jail he began to forgive her.

While men may quietly turn themselves in to save themselves from mortal danger, women looking to prevent the men in their lives from getting killed find that jail isn't such an easy option. Even if a man would, in his heart, rather be locked up than face a gun battle in the streets, he cannot admit this openly, and so makes quite a public show of his displeasure with the woman who put him there. For women, using jail as a safe haven for partners or relatives in danger comes with a heavy price.

THE BAIL OFFICE AS A BANK

After a man's trial ends, he or his family are entitled to 80 percent of the bail they put up for his release. Bail money becomes available six months after the close of a case, and must be claimed within a year; otherwise it goes into the city's coffers.

Instead of recovering the bail money right away, people sometimes leave it at the bail office until they have a particular need for it, effectively using the bail office as a short-term bank.

Like most young men on 6th Street, Chuck didn't have a bank account. He attempted to squirrel away money in his mother's basement, in various holes in the walls, and on his person, but his mother would often find the wads of cash and spend them on drugs. When his girlfriend Brianna was pregnant with their first child, Chuck had three cases end within a span of a few months. Instead of collecting the bail money immediately, he kept it at the bail office, checking in on it periodically. When Brianna gave birth to their baby girl, he cashed it out, and spent the bulk of the twelve hundred dollars on a stroller, crib, breast pump, baby clothes, and groceries.

Young men around 6th Street also leverage their bail money to obtain informal loans. Mike once got a loan for one thousand dollars from the local marijuana dealer, under the arrangement that Mike would pay it back with interest when his bail came through a few months later. He used his bail papers as proof that this money was indeed coming to him, and on the day the money was available, he and the dealer went down to the office together to retrieve it.

Bail money accrues no interest while it sits at the bail office; what's more, 20 percent of the original amount paid cannot be recovered. Even so, leaving the money at the bail office often seems like a better alternative than withdrawing it, given how hard it is to keep money safe and to control how one's money gets spent. In this way, bail provides some banking privileges and even some informal credit to men who otherwise don't have access to conventional bank accounts.

BEING WANTED AS A MEANS OF ACCOUNTING FOR FAILURE

Once a man finds himself in legal jeopardy, being a dependable friend, spending time regularly with his partner and family, going to work, and calling the police when threatened or harmed are no longer safe options. These actions may expose him to the authorities and lead to his confinement. Yet when wanted men (or social analysts, for that matter) imply that being wanted by the police is the root cause of their inability to get a job, see their children, trust the police, or live in an apartment in their own name, they may be stretching the facts. Long before the rise in imprisonment rates, Black men distrusted the police and faced substantial difficulties in finding work and participating in their families' lives.[4] While a compromised legal status may exacerbate these difficulties, being wanted also serves as a way to save face and to explain personal inadequacies.

Urban anthropologist Elliot Liebow wrote that the unemployed men he spent time with in the late 1960s accounted for their failures with the theory of manly flaws.[5] Instead of admitting that their marriages failed because they couldn't support their spouses, they explained that they were too manly to be good husbands—they couldn't stop cheating, or drinking, or staying out late. This reasoning allowed them to save face in light of their failure to secure a job and provide for wives and children. For the young men of 6th Street, who also find themselves unable to secure a decent job, being on the run takes the place of, or at least works in concert with, the manly flaws described by Liebow as a means to retain self-respect in the face of failure. In this way, a warrant becomes a resource in addition to a constraint.

When Mike was twenty-one he had a bench warrant out because he did not show up to court for a hearing in a drug possession case. During this time he was not making what he considered to be decent money selling drugs, and he had been unable to pay his son's Catholic school fees for more than a month. Parents' Day at his son's school that year was a Thanksgiving fair, and Mike had been talking about the day for weeks. The night before the fair Mike agreed that he would pick up his baby-mom Marie and go to the school around ten the next morning.

Chuck, Mike, Steve, and I slept at Chuck's that night, and in the morning, Marie began calling Mike's cell phone at 8:30. She called around thirteen times between 8:30 and 9:30. I asked Mike why he did not pick up and he said that it was not safe to go, considering the warrant. At noon he finally answered her call. By then the fair was almost over and Marie had caught the bus back and forth herself. She was yelling so loudly we could hear her voice through the phone:

MARIE: What the fuck good are you on the streets if you can't even come to your son's fair? Why I got to do everything myself—take him to school, pick him up from school, take him to the doctor . . . And you on some "I'm falling back. I'm laying low. I can't be up at no school. I can't do this, I can't do that." What the fuck I'm supposed to tell your son? "Michael, Daddy can't come to the fair today because the cops is looking for him and we don't want him to get booked." Is that what you want me to say?

Mike called her some names and hung up. Before going back to sleep, he mentioned what a "dumb-ass" his baby-mom was.

MIKE: Do she want me to get locked up? How I'm going to be there for my kids if I'm locked up? She don't be thinking, like, she don't have to look over her shoulder, you know what I'm saying? She be forgetting I can't just do whatever I want, go wherever I want.

Mike seemed convinced that going to the fair would put him at risk, and at the time I believed this to be the reason he stayed home. But a few months later, while he was still wanted for the same bench warrant, he attended a parent-teacher conference.

ALICE: I thought you didn't want to go up there. Remember Marie was mad as shit the other time you didn't go.
MIKE: I'm cool now because I just paid the school fees. I ain't want dude to come at my neck [get angry], like, "Where the money at? Why you ain't pay?" I wasn't trying [didn't want] to hear that bullshit.

From this I gathered that Mike had stayed home from Parents' Day earlier in the year at least in part because he had not wanted to confront the school's administration. Once he paid the bill he proudly attended the next event, a parent-teacher conference.

If a warrant could help Mike avoid the shame of an unpaid school bill, a warrant could also serve as an important explanation for not having a job. Steve had a warrant out for a few weeks when he was twenty-one, for failure to pay $141 dollars in court fees, and repeatedly mentioned how he could not get work because of this warrant:

If I had a whip [car], I'd go get me a job up King of Prussia [a mall in a neighboring county] or whatever. But I can't work nowhere in Philly. That's where niggas be fucking up. You remember when Chuck was at McDonald's? He was like, "No, they [the police] ain't going to see me, I'm working in the back." But you can't always be back there, like sometimes they put you at the counter, like if somebody don't show up, you know what I mean? How long he worked there before they [the police] came and got him? Like, a week. They was like, "Um, can I get a large fry and your hands on the counter because your Black ass is booked!" And he tried to run like shit, too, but they was outside the jawn [the restaurant] four deep [four police officers were outside] just waiting for him to try that shit.

Though Steve often invoked his warrant as an explanation for his unemployment, the fact was that he didn't secure a job in the six years that I knew him, including the many periods during which he had no warrant out for his arrest.

Jamal, eighteen, moved into the neighborhood with his aunt, and after a while became Reggie's young boy. Like the other guys, he often talked about his court cases or mentioned that he had to go see his probation officer. One afternoon, Steve, Mike, Chuck, and I were sitting on Chuck's back-porch steps when Reggie drove up the alleyway and announced, "Yo, the boy Jamal, he *clean*, dog! He ain't got no warrant, no detainer, nothing. He don't even got, like, a parking ticket in his name." Reggie told us that he'd just been to see Jamal's mother across town, and she'd complained to him that her son hadn't yet found a job. She informed Reggie that Jamal had no pending cases or anything else "in the system that would hold him," so he should have had no problem finding employment.

Reggie then talked about what he would do if he had his warrant lifted, as the guys suspected Jamal had:

> I wish I would get my shit [warrant] lifted. I'd be bam, on my J-O [job], bam, on my A-P [apartment], bam, go right to the bank, like, "Yeah, motherfucker, check my shit, man. *Run* that shit. My shit is clean, dog. Let me get that account." I be done got my elbow [driver's license] and everything.

Here Reggie explains how his wanted status blocked him from getting jobs, using banks, obtaining a driver's license, and renting an apartment. Yet the things he thought a "clean" person should do weren't things that he himself did when he was in good standing with the authorities over the the years that I have known him; nor were they things that most of the other men on the block did. Alex, Mike, and Chuck sometimes got jobs when they didn't have warrants out for their arrest, and Chuck even got a job once when he did have one. But others, like Reggie and Steve, remained unemployed whether they had warrants or not. None of them obtained a valid driver's license in the six years of the study.[6] Only Mike and Alex secured their own apartments during this time, but they kept them for less than three months. None of the men opened a bank account, to my knowledge.

* * *

Being wanted, then, can work as an excuse for a wide variety of unful-filled obligations and expectations. Having a warrant may not be the reason why Steve, for example, didn't look for work, but police officers do in fact come to a man's workplace to arrest him, and some of the men, like Chuck, experienced this firsthand. In the context of their on-going struggles, the explanations young men give for their failures to find a job, see their families, secure an apartment, apply for a driver's license, or open a bank account amount to reasonable half-truths that can convincingly account for these failures, in both their minds and those of others who have come to see their own lives in similar terms.[7]

THE THREAT OF PRISON AS A TOOL OF SOCIAL CONTROL

Many women in the 6th Street neighborhood devote themselves to the emotional and material support of their legally compromised partners and kin, taking the protection of their partners and male relatives from the police as part of their sacred duty as mothers, sisters, partners, and friends. But these relationships don't always run smoothly. Sometimes men break their promises; sometimes they cheat, in plain view of the neighborhood gossips, bringing humiliation to women; sometimes they become violent. At this point women may find that a man's legal precariousness can come in handy as a weapon against him. In anger and frustration at men's bad behavior, women at times harness a man's warrant or probation sentence as a tool of social control, to dictate his behavior or to punish him for various wrongs.

When I met Alex, he was twenty-two and living with his girlfriend, Donna, who later became pregnant with his second child. Alex was serving a two-year parole term and had recently gotten a job at his fa-ther's heating and air-conditioning repair shop. He was spending less time on the block than he used to, when he was unemployed and selling marijuana.

The repair shop closed at five o'clock. Donna worked in a liquor store, which closed some hours later. On Thursday and Saturday nights, she also tended bar at the KatNip. This meant that after he got off work, Alex could go and visit his old friends from 6th Street before Donna had the chance to haul him back home. Sometimes he would stay on the block drinking and talking until late at night.

Donna frequently argued with Alex over what time he got home and his drunken condition. During these fights, she occasionally threatened to call his parole officer and claim that Alex had violated his parole. She also threatened to report him if he broke up with her or cheated on her, or if he didn't contribute enough of his money to the household. The 6th Street Boys often joked that Alex couldn't stay out past eight o'clock, because Donna would call the PO and report him for staying out past curfew.[8] As the night went on, Mike would say, "Okay, Alex, better get your fat ass home before your mizz [missus] pick up the phone!"

Aside from this ability to call the parole officer and notify him of a violation—which could easily send Alex back to prison—Donna also had the advantage that Alex was paroled to her apartment. This meant that she could phone the parole office and tell them she no longer wanted Alex to live there. In this case, he would be placed in a halfway house.[9]

In the early morning after a party, Mike and I drove Alex back to Donna's apartment. She was waiting on the step for him:

DONNA: Where the fuck you been at?

ALEX: Don't worry about it.

DONNA: You must don't want to live here no more.

ALEX: Come on, Don. Stop playing.

DONNA: Matter of fact, I'll give you the choice. You're going to sleep in a cell or you want to sleep in the halfway house.

MIKE: You drawling [acting crazy], Donna, damn!

DONNA [to Mike]: Ain't nobody talking to you, nigga!

ALEX: Come on, Don.

DONNA [to Alex]: Uh-unh, you not staying here no more. I'm about to call your PO now, so you better make up your mind where you going to go [either jail or a halfway house].

ALEX: I'm tired, man, come on, open the door.

DONNA: Nigga, the next time I'm laying in the bed by myself, that's a wrap [that's the end].

ALEX: I got you!

Later that day, Donna phoned me to vent. She listed a number of reasons why she needed to threaten Alex like this. If she didn't keep him on a tight leash, he'd spend all his money on lap dances or on drugs or alcohol. And, she explained, he might violate his probation and spend another year in jail:

> I can't let that nigga get locked up for some dumb shit, like he gets caught for a DUI or he gets stopped in a Johnny [a stolen car] or some shit. What the fuck I'm supposed to do? Let that nigga roam free? And then next thing you know, he locked up, and I'm stuck here by myself with Omar [their son] talking about "Where daddy at?"

Donna seemed to view her threats as necessary efforts to rein Alex in. Threatening to call the police gave her some chance of keeping him home with her instead of out in the street, where he might get into trouble. His presence in the house also meant that she'd have more help with their two-year-old son. And the more time he spent at home with her, the less money he would be spending on beer or marijuana or other women. If his paycheck got diverted to other expenses, it would be difficult for her to pay the bills. Donna also indicated that she missed Alex and wanted to spend more time with him.

To Alex, her threats seemed manipulative and underscored the unfair balance of power:

> I fucking hate my BM [baby-mom]. Just because she can call the law she think she in control, like she can just run all over me. One day she's going to get it, though. She's going to see [she will lose me to this poor treatment and regret it].

Yet Alex was determined to complete his probation, and believed that in order to do this, he must comply with Donna's demands. He remarked, "It's better for me to be locked up in her house than locked up in that house [jail]." With her power to call the police and land him in prison, he also thought there was little he could do to fight back when she did things like take his house keys, put holes in his tires, or throw his clothes out the second-story window: "I can't do nothing, you understand. I just got to wait."

Mike and Chuck were sure that Alex would continue to live with Donna even after finishing his parole, but he proved them wrong. A week after he completed that two-year term, he left her house and rented his own apartment.

Marie, the mother of Mike's two children, lived on Chuck's block in a house with her mother, grandmother, and five other relatives. She, too, used the threat of the police to gain some measure of control over her partner. The couple had started dating in high school; their son was born during their senior year, and their daughter two years later.

A few years after their second child was born, Mike began openly seeing a woman named Chantelle. He claimed that he and Marie had broken up and he could do as he wished. Marie, however, hadn't agreed to this split, and maintained that they were still together and that he was in fact cheating. "He don't be telling me we not together when he's laying in the bed with me!" she lamented.

Mike began riding past Marie's block with Chantelle on the back of his ATV motorbike. Marie was infuriated by the insult of her baby-dad riding through her block with another woman for all her family and neighbors to see, and told him that he could no longer come to visit their two children. Mike and Marie spent many hours on the phone arguing over this. Mike would plead with her to see the children and she would explain that in order to do this, he'd have to tell Chantelle that it was over.

Chantelle wanted to fight Marie, and almost did so one afternoon. Marie was standing outside her house with seven relatives behind her, waving a baseball bat and shouting, "Get your kids, bitch. I got mine" (meaning that she had more claim to Mike than Chantelle did, because they shared two children). One of Chantelle's girlfriends and I held Chantelle back while she took off her earrings and screamed, "I got your bitch, bitch!"[10] and "I'ma beat the shit out this fat bitch."

Marie began threatening that she would call the cops on Mike if he continued to see Chantelle, since he had a bench warrant out for his arrest. For a time, Marie and Mike's conversations on the phone would end like this:

> MARIE: Alright, nigga. In five minutes the cops is going to be up there.
> MIKE: You're not calling the cops.
> MARIE: You still fucking her?
> MIKE: I'm doing what I'm doing.
> MARIE: Do you see the [police] car outside? It should be there by now.

Despite her threats, Marie tried a number of tactics to get Mike to stop sleeping with Chantelle before she resorted to actually calling the police on him. She poured bleach on the clothes that he kept at her house so that he didn't have nice clothes to wear when he went out with the other woman. She took her house keys and drew a white line in the paint on his car, and then she threw a brick through his car window. She attempted to throw hot grease on him when he came into the kitchen, but he ducked, and most of it missed him. She began prank-calling his mother, Miss Regina, pretending to be Chantelle, in an attempt to find out how close Chantelle and Mike had become, and what this new woman's relationship was with Mike's mother.

After the hot grease and the prank phone calls, Mike consulted his mother and his friends Chuck and Steve. All agreed that Marie needed to be taught a lesson—even Miss Regina, who in Mike's words is "not a violent person."

Mike paid a woman who lived down the street a large bag of marijuana to beat up Marie. According to him, he and this woman drove to the bus stop and waited until Marie appeared. Then the woman got out of the car and beat Marie against a fence. Mike stayed in the car and called to her to hit Marie again and again. Mike said that Marie didn't fight back, only put her arms up to block the blows to her face.

A few days after the swelling around Marie's eyes and cheeks had gone down, Mike and I were sitting on a neighbor's porch steps. A police car pulled up, and two officers arrested him on the warrant. He didn't think to run, he told me later, because he only had a bench warrant and assumed they were coming for two young men sitting next to us, who had recently robbed a convenience store.

While Mike sat in the police car, Marie came out of her house and talked at him through the window in a voice loud enough for the rest of us to hear: "You not just going dog me [publicly cheat on or humiliate me]! Who the fuck he think he's dealing with? Let that nigga sit for a minute [stay in jail for a while]. Don't let me catch that bitch up there, either [coming to visit in jail]."[11]

During the first few weeks that Mike was in jail, he refused to speak to Marie or allow her to visit him. In a letter to his mother, he wrote, "I love Marie, but she loves the cops too much, so I think I'm going leave her and be with Chantelle."

Yet as the trial dragged on, Mike started asking me if Marie knew about the court dates and if she'd be there. On the dates that he wasn't brought out of the holding cell and into the courtroom, he'd call me later to ask if Marie had shown up. On the day of his sentencing a year and a half later, Marie appeared in the courthouse in a low-cut top with a large new tattoo of his name on her chest. When Mike came into the room, they locked eyes and both began to cry. On the way out of the courthouse, Miss Regina joked, "I don't know why I bothered to come today. I should have gone to work. All he was looking at was that damn Marie."

So Mike forgave Marie for calling the cops on him when he had a warrant, though he'd sometimes bring up this betrayal in later years when they were fighting.

* * *

Marie had gotten Mike taken into custody for a warrant on a case he *already* had pending, but at times I observed women going a step further: bringing new charges against a man because of some personal wrong.

Lisa was in her late thirties and lived on Mike's block with her two nieces. Her son was a car thief and typically spent only a couple of weeks in the neighborhood between stints in jail. Lisa had a crack habit, and sometimes allowed Mike and his friends to hang out or sell out of her house in exchange for money and drugs. She was also a part-time student at Temple University, though the guys joked that she'd been in school for nearly two decades.

Lisa and Miss Linda were such good friends that Miss Linda's sons Chuck and Reggie stayed overnight at Lisa's house many times when they were growing up, and considered her something of an aunt. Then, when he was eighteen years old, Reggie got Lisa's sixteen-year-old niece pregnant. He refused to help pay for her abortion or even to acknowledge that he had impregnated her. Lisa declared that she "wasn't fucking with Reggie no more," meaning that she was cutting off the long-standing relationship between their families. Her two nieces threatened to have him beaten up by various young men they were involved with. Because Reggie usually hung out on the corner only two houses away, this became a frequent conflict.

That same spring, the war with 4th Street was under way. The 4th Street Boys had united with the Boys Across the Bridge and were driving through 6th Street, shooting at Reggie and his older brother, Chuck. On one of these occasions, Reggie fired two shots back as their car sped away. These bullets hit Lisa's house, breaking the glass in the front windows and lodging in the living room walls. Although no one was wounded, Lisa's two nieces had been home at the time. They phoned their aunt, who called the police. She told them that Reggie had shot at her family, and the police put out a body warrant for his arrest for a double count of attempted murder.

After five weeks, the police found Reggie hiding in a shed and took him into custody. Miss Linda and Chuck tried to talk Lisa and her nieces out of showing up in court so that the charges would be dropped and Reggie could come home.[12] From jail, Reggie phoned Anthony, his mother, and me, and discussed this in a four-way conversation:[13]

REGGIE: The bitch [Lisa] know I wasn't shooting at them [her nieces]. She
   knows we're going through it right now [are in the middle of a series
   of shootouts with young men from another block]. Why would I shoot
   at two females that live on my block? She knows I wasn't shooting
   at them.

ANTHONY: You might have to pay her a couple dollars and put her up in
   the 'tel [to ensure that she won't be home if the police should try to
   drag her in to testify].

REGGIE: She just mad because her son locked up. She's hurting right now,
   so she's trying to take it out on me.

MISS LINDA: What you really need to do is call that bitch up and tell her
   that you apologize [for not taking responsibility for the pregnancy].

REGGIE: True, true.

Reggie did apologize to Lisa and her nieces—before the court date—and spread the word that he was responsible for getting Lisa's niece pregnant. Lisa and her nieces didn't show up for three consecutive court dates, and after five months Reggie came home from jail. Lisa seemed pleased with this result:

> You not just going get my niece pregnant, then you talking about that's not your child, you know what I'm saying? That nigga used to be over my house every day when he was a kid. [Meaning that because Reggie had known their family for so long, he should have shown more respect.] Fuck out of here. No. I mean, I wasn't trying to see that nigga sit for an attempt [an attempted murder conviction], but he needed to sit for a little while. He got what he needed to get. He had some time to sit and think about his actions, you dig me? He done got what he needed to get.

*   *   *

From these examples, we can see that young women and men around 6th Street sometimes reappropriate the intense surveillance and the looming threat of prison for their own purposes. Even as women endure police raids and interrogations, and suffer the pain of betraying the man they'd rather protect, they occasionally make use of a man's "go to jail" card to protect him from what they perceive to be mortal danger. In anger and frustration at men's bad behavior, they can sometimes use men's precarious legal status to control them, to get back at them, and to punish them for any number of misdeeds. In doing so, they get men taken into custody, not for the crimes or violations the police are concerned with, but for personal wrongs the police may not know or care about.

Perhaps more remarkably, the young men who are the targets of these systems of policing and surveillance occasionally succeed in using the police, the courts, and the prisons for *their* own purposes. They may check themselves into jail when they believe the streets have become too dangerous, transforming jail into a safe haven. When they come home from jail or prison, they may turn the bail office into a kind of bank, storing money there for specific needs later on, or using those funds as collateral for informal loans. Young men even turn their fugitive status into an advantage by invoking a warrant as an excuse for a variety of unmet obligations and personal failings.

In these ways, men and women in the neighborhood turn the presence of the police, the courts, and the prisons into a resource they make use of in ways the authorities neither sanction nor anticipate. Taken together, these strategies present an alternative to the view that 6th Street residents are simply the pawns of the authorities, caught in legal entanglements that constrain and oppress them.

FIVE

The Social Life of Criminalized Young People

In the neighborhood of 6th Street and others like it, boys begin in school, but many make the transition to the juvenile courts and detention centers in their preteen or teenage years. By the time many young men in the neighborhood have entered their late teens or early twenties, the penal system has largely replaced the educational system as the key setting of young adulthood. These boys and young men are not freshmen or seniors but defendants and inmates, spending their time in courtrooms instead of classrooms, attending sentencing hearings and probation meetings, not proms or graduations.

As the criminal justice system has come to occupy a central place in their lives and by extension those of their partners and families, it has become a principal base around which they construct a meaningful social world. It is through their dealings with the police, the courts, the parole board, and the prisons that young men and those close to them work out who they are and who they are to each other.

CHILDREN'S LEGAL WOES AS MOTHER'S WORK

When I first met Miss Linda, her eldest son, Chuck, was eighteen, her middle son, Reggie, was fifteen, and her youngest son, Tim, was nine. Chuck and Reggie were already in jail and juvenile detention centers, respectively, but I was around to watch Tim move from middle school to the juvenile courts as he turned twelve and thirteen. At this point

Miss Linda transferred much of her parental energies to this new setting. The following scene is an excerpt from field notes:

We are sitting in small wooden chairs lined up in rows in Room K of the
Juvenile Courthouse, located at 18th and Vine in downtown Philadelphia.
The room has high, recessed ceilings and paneled walls. It is 9:10 in the
morning, and the room begins to fill with boys and their mothers or guard-
ians. Miss Linda's youngest son, Tim, 13 now, is sitting to my left with his
elbows resting on his knees, his hands making a cup holding up his head.
He checked his cell phone at the entrance and so has little to do now but
watch the other people or try to sleep.

Miss Linda sits on his other side and fidgets, moving her legs up and
down in quick motion.

Tim asks her if she still has any gum, and she says no, unless you want
half of what I got in my mouth. He shakes his head emphatically. She says,
"Don't act like you don't be taking the gum out of my mouth just 'cause
Alice here."

My stomach is growling, and Tim turns to me and says, "That you?"

I nod. Miss Linda and I had split a 25-cent bag of corn chips this morning as we waited for Tim to shower and iron his clothes, but that was
hours ago.

We watch the other boys file in. They look to me to be 10, 11, and 12 years
old, a few of them, like Tim, in their early teens. Some of them are walking in with their mothers and are coming from home to attend probation
hearings or to be tried for various crimes. Others are accompanied by
caseworkers and come from juvenile detention facilities. These boys hope
to be released today, so they carry on their shoulders large white cloth bags
containing their clothing and other meager possessions. By 9:30 there are
about 50 boys in the room and 5 girls. Two of the boys look Latino to me;
all the others are Black. A sea of silent Black boys waiting to be tried.

A white uniformed guard moves down the aisle and tells two boys to
take off their baseball caps, which they do grudgingly. One of the boys
reveals hair that had been braided a couple of months ago and badly needs
to be taken out and redone; he tries to smooth it out with the palm of
his hand.

The guard tells the woman behind us that she can't eat those crackers
in the courthouse. She says, "This isn't the courthouse; this is the waiting

room." He says, "Ma'am, put the crackers away or go outside and eat them." She puts them in her pocket, and when the guard is a few rows behind us she mumbles that she's a diabetic and has to eat at certain times.

Mothers approach a middle-aged white man in khaki pants who sits at a desk in the front of the room. They ask questions which I can't quite hear from the middle row where we are sitting. After a while the man stands and says, "If you have court today, form a line to check in." He holds a thick printout with a long list of names and leafs through it, telling the boys in line which courtroom they will have. He pauses to listen to a mother who has approached him at the desk, who says her son was unable to come to court today. She says something else, and the man replies loudly that he doesn't decide who gets a warrant and has nothing to do with warrants. He looks up her son's name on the sheets of paper and tells her which court-room to go to. One of the boys in line has a heavy metal leg restraint that causes him to limp as he drags it along the floor. Another is handcuffed in the front with a white plastic band.

We move to a small courtroom now, where we sit on long benches and wait for a judge to appear and begin hearing the cases. In the rows around us sit mothers and their sons, some with their younger children also. A mother in front of us recognizes a woman in our row; they reach over the bench and talk about mutual friends and relations, one mother saying, "Yeah, he passed in May," the other responding, "I'm sorry to hear that."

Two guards stand at the front, and the public defenders and some case managers sit in the first row. A thin white woman, who I assume is a public defender, stands and turns toward us and calls a name; no one replies. She calls another name, and a boy and his mother or guardian approach her and speak in muffled voices. Miss Linda recognizes one of the public defenders as the lawyer who defended her middle son, Reggie, some years back. The judge emerges from a door behind the bench, and the guard asks us to stand and then to be seated.

Tim had caught this case last year when he attempted to leave school in the middle of the day; his teacher pursued him out of the school and into the street. Tim threw rocks at the teacher as he ran away, and though none of these rocks hit the teacher, he pulled a hamstring while in pursuit, and so the school police arrested Tim on charges of aggravated assault.[1]

Eventually, Tim's name is called, and he walks with his mother to the front of the desk. The judge asks if a certain person is here; I assume this is the teacher. The prosecutor says, "No, Your Honor, I do not believe he is here, but I did reach him last night, and he told me he was planning to be here." The public defender, the judge, and the prosecutor all look at their calendars and go back and forth for a while until they find a good date to continue the case. The court clerk passes a paper to Miss Linda, and it is all over. Tim and his mother move toward the door, signaling me to get up.

We walk quickly out of the room and through the building, past security, as if staying any longer might cause the judge to change his mind or find something in the file indicating that Tim should be detained. When you go to court, there's always a chance that they might take you; we will celebrate Tim's continued freedom when we get home.

As we drive back from the juvenile court building, Miss Linda is smiling and laughing. She calls her boyfriend on my cell phone, and says, "Yup. We on our way home now. I knew he wasn't coming." If Tim's teacher doesn't show up another two times, the case will be thrown out for lack of a witness to the crime. We all know this, and it's a very exciting prospect.

I drive up the back alley and park in the driveway Miss Linda shares with the house connected to hers. Miss Linda and Tim walk up the iron stairs to the balcony over the garage, and then into the house from the back kitchen entrance. The sun has come out, and I sit on the iron steps. From here you can see the backs of the houses from the next block over, which share the alleyway.

Miss Linda comes out with a cup of Irish Rose and smiles. "I'm celebrating!" she says. To a neighbor who has opened his back door she calls out, "You want some?" He nods, and she says he'll have to give her a dollar—a dollar per cup. He laughs, and she tells him that she isn't joking.

She hears the phone ring from inside the house and jumps up, saying it might be Chuck. It isn't, and I can hear her telling whoever it is that she's happy because she'll get to keep her son here with her, at least for the time being. "To keep it real," she says, "one is enough. At least if Chuck and Reggie are locked up, I know they good. When all three of my sons are home, I can't get no sleep. Let them come home when these streets cool down, you feel me?"

The day is getting warmer now, and Miss Linda's cat, named Rat, emerges from the garage and finds a place in the sun next to some empty Hugs bottles and chicken bones and cigarette butts in the alleyway.

Tim comes out of the kitchen and down the back steps with two paper cups and passes me one, saying *hum* to get my attention.

Miss Linda hears the phone ring again—it is inaudible to me—and jumps up to get it. She is rewarded this time, as it is Chuck calling from CFCF (Curran-Fromhold Correctional Facility), the county jail. She talks with him for a few minutes and then calls Tim over to speak to his brother. Chuck is waiting to start trial for a case he caught for possession with intent to distribute.

Tim sprints up the stairs. I can hear him laugh, and I assume he's telling Chuck about the good news today in court.

Tim talks to his brother for a few minutes and then calls me over to the phone. I walk up the steps and through the kitchen, which smells of cigarette smoke, cooking oil, and animal urine. In the living room, Miss Linda is lying on the two-seater sofa, sipping her drink and watching court TV. Tim says, "I love you, too" to Chuck before passing me the phone.

With a heavy addiction to crack and alcohol, Miss Linda was by many accounts not an ideal mother. But she took pride in staying abreast of her sons' legal developments. This was no small or finite task, as at least one of her sons was in juvenile detention, jail, or prison at any given time during the six years I spent with the family—save for a two-month period in 2007 when all three sons were at home.

In contrast to Miss Linda, Mike's mother, Miss Regina, worked two jobs and kept an exceptionally clean house. She also spent much of her time dealing with her son's legal affairs. When Mike was in his early twenties, he caught a series of cases for drugs as well as gun possession. In addition to attending Mike's court dates and managing his probation and parole, Miss Regina visited him in jail and prison, arranged for his two children to visit, sent him packages and money regularly, accepted his phone calls, and wrote him letters.[2] As his sentencing date in the federal courts approached, she also organized Mike's friends, relatives, and past employers to write letters on his behalf, and to attend the trial:

It is the day of Mike's sentencing in federal court. He has been awaiting trial in a federal holding cell for the better part of a year and had been in county jail for another year before that.

This morning, Miss Regina drove his uncle and aunt, and the mother of his children, Marie, to the courthouse downtown. Also, she has arranged for Mike's grandmother to pick up Mike's girlfriend and his girlfriend's mother, who live way out in the greater Northeast. I have come in my own car.

In the weeks before the sentencing, Miss Regina had succeeded in persuading nine family members and friends to send letters on Mike's behalf. She gave us each a stamped envelope and typed up the letters that his grandmother and uncle had written by hand.

Walking into the courthouse, Miss Regina gets a call from Mike's lawyer, who says there has been a last-minute time change—the sentencing will now take place at 3 p.m. Frustrated but resolute, Miss Regina tells the assembled group that we'll be going to her house in North Philly to wait it out. There she makes chicken and rice and salad, and entertains us with pay-per-view. She practices what she'll say if the judge calls on her.

At the sentencing, Mike emerges wearing the suit that Miss Regina sent him. She remarks on how well it fits and how it was right for her to go with a size smaller than he had suggested. He smiles when he sees so many of his family assembled. I haven't seen him in over a year, since only direct relatives were permitted to visit him in the federal holding cell. He looks older, his beard grown out.

The judge, a middle-aged Black man with a stern gaze, asks the parole officer (PO) to stand. He asks if the PO has been in touch with anyone in Mike's family about his upcoming release. Because the time that Mike has sat awaiting trial will be counted toward his federal sentence, he'll serve only eight months in the Federal Detention Center. So, he'll be home within the year. The PO says that Mike's mother phoned him to give all her contact information, and that she kept calling to check in and let him know that she wanted to be "part of the process." Miss Regina nods fervently as he is explaining this.

The judge says that it is clear that Mike is a good person who has done some bad things. He says the letters from Mike's children made the biggest impact on him; he could tell how much his children loved him and that they actually wrote the letters themselves. Then he got out the letter from Mike's ten-year-old son and read it aloud to us. The last line was "So please let my daddy come home, because my mother does not know how to raise a boy, and I need my daddy." Miss Regina mouths the words as the judge reads the letter; she has read it so many times, she knows it by heart.

The judge says that the maximum sentence for Mike's offense is 16 years. Given the two years he has already served awaiting trial and given that he has such support from his family, Mike will receive only six months in prison and six months in a halfway house, followed by three years on federal probation. The judge asks Mike if he has anything to say, and Mike says he is sorry for his actions and that he is glad to be given this chance. Then the judge asks Miss Regina to stand as he tells Mike, "Now turn around, and thank your mother for everything she has done for you." Mike is caught a bit off guard by this, and the judge tells him again to thank his mother.

Mike turns to her, sobbing. She says, "It's okay, baby."

Like Miss Linda and Miss Regina, many women around 6th Street find that their son's legal proceedings structure their days, which are punctuated by court hearings, bail payments, jail visits, and phone calls to public defenders. Their days are also marked by the good or bad news they receive concerning his fate with the courts, the parole board, and the prisons. Staying on top of a son's legal matters and supporting him through the legal process can be a heavy burden, but it can also be a rewarding way for women to spend their time. It is partly through their efforts to keep their sons out of jail and to support them once they have been taken that women fulfill their obligations as mothers.

PENAL TRANSITIONS AS SOCIAL OCCASIONS

A young man's movement through the criminal justice system happens in a series of phases: the police stop him, search him, and run his name in their database; he catches a case, gets taken into custody, gets a bail hearing, attends months or years of court dates, gets sentenced; serves time, pays fees, and comes home on probation or parole. Along the way, he may violate the terms of his supervision, for example by drinking or staying out late, or get accused of a new crime, or fail to pay his court fees and fines, or fail to attend a court date, and be issued a warrant. As he ages, he moves from juvenile detention centers to adult facilities, and from shorter sentences in county jail to longer ones in state or perhaps even federal prison.

Over the course of a young man's passage through these stages, a number of events present themselves: bail hearings, trial dates, and returns home after long stints locked up. These events serve as key social occasions, for which a young man's friends and family dress up and argue over who should pay. People watch carefully to see who is in attendance, who is sitting with whom, who organizes the event or sits in the first row. If the mother of the man's children is missing from the benches of the courtroom, talk begins to circulate that she has indeed left him for a man down the street. If a new woman is sitting next to his mother in the first row, people acknowledge her as his main partner. At these public criminal justice proceedings, the members of a man's social circle deduce where they stand in his life and where he stands in the eyes of those around him.

One of the first significant social occasions that the criminal justice system provides occurs when a young man gets booked. With a young man suddenly taken from his home and placed in confinement, the question arises as to what will happen to the belongings he has left behind. Who will care for these items? Who will take responsibility for them or be allowed to use them? In the first hours or days of a young man's confinement, a tremendous redistribution of his material possessions takes place, and his partner, family, and friends watch to see whom he chooses to manage this movement of goods and to whom they will be given.

* * *

Mike's mother, Miss Regina, usually coordinated his legal matters, organized the attendance of his court cases, and kept the schedule for jail visits, letting those who wished to see him know what his visiting hours were and which dates had already been spoken for by others.[3] Often, she also undertook the management of her son's affairs while he was away, and when he was first taken, she typically spent a number of days taking care of what he left behind: cleaning out the apartment he could no longer pay rent on, canceling his cell phone and paying the cancellation fees, taking over his children's school fees, and securing his various possessions—cars, motorbikes, sneakers, speakers, jewelry, CDs—or selling them to pay his bills.

But when Mike went back to prison on a parole violation in 2004, he appointed his new girlfriend, Tamara, to handle his affairs, mind his possessions, and give some of them to specific people. His mother called me to discuss his decision:

MISS REGINA: I got no problem with Tamara; she's a good person. But he's known her for *two months*, Alice. I've been taking care of his stuff for years. Last time, the only thing I didn't have here was the bike.

ALICE: Yeah, Marie [the mother of his children] had it.

MISS REGINA: And what happened to it?

ALICE: The cops took it.

MISS REGINA: Yup. Because her cousin was riding it around. You can't ride those bikes in town! Those are off-road bikes. Or if you do, you better be faster than the cops!

ALICE: Right!

MISS REGINA: Me and you are the only ones that make sure everything is still here when he comes home.

ALICE: Yep.

MISS REGINA: When he got locked up for that gun case, everything stayed right here. Every shirt was ironed and waiting for him. Sneakers still in the box. But like I said, if he wants Tamara to do it, that's fine. She can pay all his bills and clean out that apartment and find somewhere to put his car that don't even run. Let her tow that car somewhere, that's fine with me. I already told him I don't want anything in that apartment. Anything. And when he comes home and his TV gone and he sees Ant wearing his clothes up and down the street, he better not come complaining to me.

In some communities, the event that makes clear to a young man's family that he's in a serious relationship is a school dance or graduation ceremony to which he takes his new partner. Later, it might be a family wedding out of town, a vacation, or a nephew's christening. But for Mike, the first event indicating to his mother that he had a serious girlfriend came when he got taken into custody and designated Tamara to handle his affairs.

Not only does the distribution of his possessions become a key task for a trusted friend or family member, but the people to whom a newly jailed man bestows his belongings are recognized by loved ones as his inner circle, the people he trusts and cares for the most. When Mike violated his parole by drinking alcohol and got sent back to prison a few years before, he phoned me shortly after his arrival to explain who should get what:

> MIKE: I told Chuck he can hold the AP [apartment] down for me till I get back, so can you give him the key? I know his pops ain't letting him sleep at the crib no more. And he already got the keys to the Bonnie [Pontiac Bonneville]. I told him to just ride out with that.
>
> ALICE: Okay.
>
> MIKE: Can you give my cell phone to Shanda? I told her you were going drop it off to her—you know hers got cut off.
>
> ALICE: Yeah. Probably tomorrow.
>
> MIKE: My moms might want that car, though. If she call you about the car, just tell Chuck I got to give it to her, you know.
>
> ALICE: Okay.
>
> MIKE: Ronny going to come by for my Xbox; I told him to call you before he come to make sure you there.

The events marking a young man's passage through the system thus become times when private relationships are made public; when a young man makes careful decisions about the relative ranking of his social relations. But these occasions are not only times when private relationships are made public, they are also times when a man's general social standing or level of familial and neighborhood support is made manifest. For example, young men on 6th Street took the number in attendance at another man's sentencing as indication of his social standing, a demonstration of how much "love" he has in the streets. From field notes taken in 2009:

> There was a big showing in room 405 today for Reggie's Must Be Tried.[4] I drove his mother, Miss Linda, and their neighbor Anthony, who has two bench warrants and took a real risk showing his support today. Reggie's older brother, Chuck, drove their youngest brother, Tim, who skipped class today at his new school in order to come. Victoria, Reggie's sometime girlfriend, met us there. The judge, a stern-faced Italian man, dropped all the charges—conspiracy, drug possession (when he arrived at the hospital

he had some work [drugs to sell] on him), possession of a weapon—so now it's just attempted murder. On the way back, we heard from Reggie's cousin Keisha, who said she had gone to the neighborhood courthouse instead of the courthouse in Center City. She met us back at the house and brought some weed. All in all, it was quite festive and solidary. Reggie called from jail and discussed the showing with me proudly, comparing it to Rocky's sentencing last month, where none of the people who had promised to attend actually showed up.

PENAL EVENTS AS ROMANTIC SHOWDOWNS

As important social occasions, the events marking a man's movement through the criminal justice system can become public stages for run-ins between women competing for his affections.

When a man is on the outside, he has some chance of keeping the women in his life from finding out about each other. When he gets booked, such a balancing act becomes much more difficult. At his sentencing, his longtime girlfriend comes face to face with his "jump-off"—a woman she didn't know existed. In the first days that he is permitted to have visits in county jail, the mother of his child confronts his new girlfriend, who had arrived fifteen minutes before she did and took up his visiting hour. Women also look through the sign-in book at the visitor's desk to determine whether other women have been there.

These meetings can become dramatic events in which women size each other up, try to determine where they stand in relation to each other, and even demand that the man make a public statement about their respective places. It is in the jail visiting room, the courthouse, and the bail office that women triumph as a man's main partner, or get humiliated and cast aside.

* * *

When Mike was released from prison, he was sentenced to a halfway house in North Philly, and there he met Tamara, a caseworker for the residents. She was in graduate school as well, working on her master's degree. Tamara and Mike started dating, and when Mike later went back to prison on a violation for breaking curfew, Tamara started coming to visit him. He was careful to ensure that she visited on separate days from his baby-mom, Marie, who came once a week with his two children. But a couple of weeks into his sentence, Tamara came on an off day, ostensibly to visit her younger brother, who was also serving time at Graterford:

There was an important incident at Graterford today. Marie and I drove up there to see Mike, and Tamara is sitting two tables over, playing chess with her brother. So Marie and I are sitting there, and Tamara comes over and says, "What's up, Mike, how you doing?" and he says to Marie, "This is Tamara, she works at the halfway house." To Tamara he says, "This is Marie, my kids' mom." At this Marie stands up and says, "Is that all I am to you? That's all I am? I ain't drive five fucking hours for this shit."

In almost a whisper Mike says, "Shut up and sit down before they cancel this visit."

"Who is she?"

"Nobody, just a friend."

"You fucked her, didn't you."

"Oh, here you go. Why you always assume that?"

"Because I know you. I know you."

"We don't mess with each other, we just cool."[5]

The rest of the visit, Marie is touching Mike and playing with his hair. Tamara starts talking loudly to her brother so that we can hear, telling him that she really likes Mike and hopes he isn't still messing with his baby-mom. Mike starts talking louder so that Marie can't hear what Tamara is saying, and looks at me pleadingly to do something about the situation.

When the guard indicates that the time is up, Marie stands and holds on to Mike's waist, looking up at him and leaning in for a kiss. Mike hesitates and grins sheepishly, and then hugs her back and kisses her.

By the time we are waiting in the holding cell outside the visiting room to be released, tears are streaming down Tamara's cheeks.

A similar public reckoning took place when Aisha attended her boyfriend Trey's sentencing in the federal courts in 2009. In this case, she clearly lost to Trey's baby-mom:

Aisha called me today, sobbing loudly. I left class and came over right away. Second time I've seen Aisha cry in seven years, the first time being at the funeral of her sister's boyfriend, whom the police strangled to death in front of us. Trey's sentencing was today, and to the heavy news of his 15-year bid in federal prison was added the injury of his baby-mom showing up and sitting with Trey's mother. When Aisha got there, his BM was already there in the second row, talking quietly with his mom and aunt. Aisha said his mom didn't even greet her, acted as if she didn't know her, like they hadn't been talking every day this whole year he's been away.

Given her anger and hurt, I am surprised by how sensitive Aisha is to Trey's mother's position. She said that his mother probably just didn't know what to do with the two of them in the same room.

Aisha said she wasn't sure if she should leave, but in the end she decided to stay, sitting in the back row. His BM ignored her the whole time he was up there, making all the sounds and gestures when he came out that women make to indicate that it is their man standing up there. Then his BM spoke to her as they took the stairs down.

"She asked me right to my face if I was a dyke," Aisha told me.

"Why would she think that?"

"Because that's what Trey told her. He said we was just cool, I just be sending him money and stuff."

"What did you say?"

"I told her: I'm not a dyke; he told me he don't mess with you anymore."

Aisha said that the woman responded by showing Aisha her ring, saying, "We are getting married as soon as he comes home." Aisha looked at Trey's mother for confirmation, and Trey's mother refused to meet her eyes, as if she were trying to be careful getting down the steps.

To Trey's BM Aisha replied, "Well, better you than me, because I am not waiting no 15 fucking years for him."

Today, Trey has called twice and is trying to tell Aisha that he didn't even know that his BM would be there, and that he keeps telling her not to come. He will take her off his visitor's list wherever they take him. But Aisha isn't listening anymore. She tells Trey that she knows he is lying and that he never would have told his baby-mom that she was a lesbian unless he wanted to preserve his relationship with her. If he was really done with her, he would have openly acknowledged that Aisha was his girlfriend. In addition, there was the indisputable evidence of the seating arrangements in the courtroom. If Aisha had been his girlfriend, then his mother would have sat with her in the first row, and the mother of his children would have been sitting in the back, not the other way around. "Your mom was sitting with her," she says to him on the phone. "You can't tell me they didn't come together."

"All the months I wrote him and visited him and put money on his books, and took his collect calls," Aisha says to me. "I'm done."

By way of neutralizing Aisha's threat to the mother of his children, Trey had told this woman that Aisha was a lesbian and hence they were "just friends." Meanwhile, he had been telling Aisha that things were over between him and his baby-mom, and he simply saw her because she had been bringing the kids to visit. When Aisha and Trey's baby-mom ran into each other at his sentencing, these separate narratives collided: his baby-mom found out that Aisha was a genuine competitor, while Aisha discovered that Trey and his baby-mom were still very much romantically involved.

* * *

To say that the events accompanying a man's movement through the criminal justice system have become key social occasions isn't to say that the community has no other ways of going public with a new relationship, sizing up rivals, or coming together. Cookouts and block parties continue, as do funerals and christenings. Many young women and a much smaller number of young men still graduate from high school. But court sentences, bail hearings, and homecomings from a long sentence have become frequent enough, and for enough people, that they now exist alongside these older occasions, serving as significant social events not just for young men and their immediate families but sometimes for their larger networks of family, friends, neighbors, and acquaintances.

LEGAL WOES AS THE BASIS OF PERSONAL HONOR

Just as the criminal justice system now furnishes the social events around which young people work out their relationships to one another, it has provided the social material with which young people construct themselves as brave and honorable. Contact with the criminal justice system is almost universally understood as something to be avoided. The institution is, generally speaking, one that grants dishonor and shame rather than pride or standing to those who pass through it. Even so, the looming threat of prison, the movement of young men through the courts and the jails, the assignment of a diminished and precarious legal status to these young men, and the pressure on their loved ones to provide information about them, all provide some opportunity for bravery and honor.

*   *   *

In these field notes from the spring of 2007, Chuck's friend Anthony describes a number of his legal entanglements and brushes with law, taking considerable pride in his own conduct:

> Around 1 in the morning last night, Chuck and Anthony are sitting on Chuck's front stoop, passing a blunt (a cigar hollowed out and filled with marijuana) back and forth. We have just been to the bar, and Anthony, having had more than a few shots of Hennessy, begins to pace around and talk about his warrants.
>
> "I ain't sweating them, man," he says. "I went to court with ya'll, I be driving around." Here he refers to Reggie's latest court date, which he risked arrest to attend in solidarity.
>
> Chuck tells Anthony that if he keeps talking loudly he'll wake up Pop George, Chuck's grandfather.
>
> "If the law come," Anthony says, ignoring Chuck, "I'm out. You ain't going to see me no more."
>
> I tell Ant that if he has bench warrants, he should go to the Warrant and Surrender Unit and get them taken care of. Chuck nods his head in agreement. A few weeks ago Chuck had missed a court date, and he and I had spent seven and a half hours in the basement of the Criminal Justice Center getting the warrant lifted and a new date.
>
> Anthony says, "I ain't turning myself in. They going to have to come get me. I ain't making their job easier."
>
> Chuck tells him that as long as his warrants are only for failure to appear, not a probation violation, he won't get taken into custody; they'll just issue him a new date. Anthony asks how many men who came to the War-

rant and Surrender office that day for a new date wound up getting taken into custody on the spot. Chuck doesn't answer, and Anthony repeats the question.

Chuck laughs and says, "Three."

Anthony acts out how surprised the men must have looked to see the guards coming up behind them with the handcuffs.

Still pacing, Anthony says, "If they do grab me, I ain't calling niggas, like, I need this I need that, put bread on my billzooks [books— commissary], write me, and all this. I'm just calling niggas like: what's going on out there?"

Chuck replies that Anthony will so call for money when he gets to jail, just like everybody else.

Anthony shakes his head no, insisting, "I bids, nigga, I bids!" By this he means that he handles his time in jail without complaint, like a pro.

Talk turns to the two women we'd seen at a bar earlier that night, one of whom used to date Mike, and then Anthony brings it back to his legal matters.

"All my cases was gun cases," he says. "I never caught a drug case."

I take this to mean that he is normally quite skilled at evading the police, and only gets arrested when he is caught carrying a gun because of the various beefs between 4th Street and 6th Street, which are beyond his control.

Anthony continues: "I beats cases. [The *s* is for extra emphasis.] I'm 27 now, and I been in jail like four, five years, and I ain't got NO convictions."

He turns to me. "How many motherfuckers you know that's my age, A, and don't got no convictions?"

I shrug.

"I'm old as *shit* not to have convictions."

Anthony is now quite drunk and bragging about all kinds of things: the women at the bar whom he could have slept with if he had wanted to, all the free drinks the bartender gave him, his performance on the basketball court earlier today. Chuck keeps telling him to keep quiet, because Pop George will hear him. "As soon as he calls my name," Chuck says, "it's over."

Ant starts saying, half-jokingly, that he is going to rob the next guy to come up the block.

Chuck says, "Just don't put my name in it. Don't put me on your call

list"—by which he means that when Ant gets booked, he better not mention that Chuck had anything to do with the robbery.

Anthony replies, "I'm not getting booked!!"

Chuck repeats that he doesn't want his name in it.

"You crazy," Anthony says. "I never got locked up on 6th Street. When ·
I get locked up, I'm getting locked up on 4th and Castor, 6th and Elms-
worth . . ." By this I take him to mean that he knows his neighborhood and
its alleys so well that the cops would never catch him here. He also implies
that the 6th Street neighborhood contains so many people willing to help
him hide that he will always be safe.

Chuck laughs and tells Anthony to take his ass in the house.

Anthony replies, "When did I ever get booked on the 6?!"

Chuck says, "Yo, pipe down."

Anthony nods emphatically, his point made.

A neighbor pulls up with a woman in his car, and the talk turns to who
is out creeping, that is, cheating on their spouse.

On this night, Anthony took pride in how he approached his time on
the run, and how he typically handled the months or years in jail awaiting trial. He also boasted about his lack of convictions, the first time I'd
heard someone bring this up. His account of his conduct throughout
his legal woes was offered as a testament to his good character, but also
as an indirect way of indicating his respect in the community. Because
Anthony's ability to evade the police depended on the willingness of
others to open their doors to him and to keep silent in the face of police questioning, the length of his time on the run, the number of his
cases that got thrown out for lack of witnesses, and the rarity of his
arrests occurring in the 6th Street neighborhood showed the esteem
with which neighbors and friends held him.

Getting arrested is nothing to be proud of, but news may travel of
a young man's bravery during the beating that sometimes accompanies the arrest—like it did when Ronny neither cried nor begged when
the police broke his arm with their batons. An arrest warrant is certainly bad news, but surviving on the run requires skill and cunning,
for which a person can be admired and granted some degree of respect.
Given the number of restrictions a man on probation or parole has, and

the frequency in which these supervisory sentences result in a violation and a subsequent return to jail or prison, merely continuing to live on the outside can be seen by others as a significant accomplishment.

COMMITMENT AND SACRIFICE IN A FUGITIVE COMMUNITY

Just as young people work out their social relations in the courtroom or construct an honorable identity by handling their legal woes with dignity, so too do they demonstrate their devotion by taking legal risks on one another's behalf. With police stops and searches a daily occurrence, and many residents either going through court cases or risking arrest on sight, there is simply not enough safety from the authorities to go around. Saving oneself may mean giving up a brother, son, or best friend. In the context of legal insecurity, people show their love and commitment to one another by protecting those close to them from the police, sometimes at the cost of their own safety. Some of these gestures are as small as telling a cop that they didn't see which way a man went. Some are bigger, like when a man with a warrant risks an encounter with the police to attend the birth of his child. And some are as big as offering oneself up for another's arrest. Small or large, all these gestures carry deep meaning, becoming rituals that people perform to show respect, to demonstrate love or intimacy, to uphold the revered status of others, and to identify themselves as good people. In this way, people construct a moral world through the looming threat of prison, finding opportunities for acts of protection and sacrifice that bind them to others.

One major risk young men take on behalf of those they hold dear is to attend the funerals of close friends who have been shot. Police usually show up at these services to videotape the mourners with a tripod camera.

Recall that when Ronny's cousin was shot and killed, Reggie attended the funeral although he had a warrant out for his arrest. Reggie phoned me afterward specifically to let me know he had taken this risk on behalf of his deceased friend.

Indeed, a certain amount of this kind of legal risk-taking is expected in very close relationships, such that when a man fails to sacrifice his personal safety to fulfill his social obligations, it is taken as an indication of selfishness, or a sign that he isn't sufficiently invested in the relationship.

*   *   *

When Brianna, Chuck's girlfriend, was due with their first child, he promised to attend the birth despite having a low-level warrant out for his arrest. In the end he stayed home, later sitting with me and lamenting how angry Brianna would be that he had failed to show up as he had promised. He wasn't wrong about her reaction—when I arrived at the hospital to see her and the new baby, her mother and aunt were sitting next to her bed, discussing his failures as a father and partner:

BRIANNA: He don't care. I mean, he care, but he don't care *enough*. He going to say [he was saying], "If I get locked up, how I'ma take care of the baby?" It's not like they got him on a body [a murder case] or something—if they did come grab him [arrest him at the hospital], all he would do is sit for a quick three months [the minimum for a probation violation]. The longest it would be would be like six months. Plus, it's not even a guarantee that they would come grab him.

BRIANNA'S AUNT: Keisha baby-dad was up here last month [for the birth of their baby] and he came home. That nigga had a couple jawns [warrants] on him.

BRIANNA: He just don't want to be up there no more [in jail] because he was there like all last year.

BRIANNA'S MOTHER: But think about it, like, in ten years when he looks back, he's going to wish he saw his baby born, he's not going to care that he was sitting [was in jail] for a couple months.

BRIANNA: Exactly.

Chuck's decision to stay home hurt his baby-mom, not only because he had failed to attend the birth of their daughter, but also because he had refused to risk his own safety on behalf of his new family. For Brianna, his willingness to take this risk stood as a folk test of his attachment to her. His failure to show up was a hurtful act, a demonstration of his lack of commitment.

Though young men with warrants or under court supervision are expected to risk their own safety for the people they love, a man may also measure his feelings for a woman according to how little legal risk he allows *her* to take on his behalf. Mike and Chuck agreed that they'd ask only "hood rats" to smuggle drugs into the visiting room when they were in county jail, never a relative or a real girlfriend, as the risk of arrest was too great. They looked down on other, younger men who thought nothing of having their main girlfriend or baby-mom run balloons of marijuana or pills into the visiting room.[6]

Protecting a loved one from arrest could serve as an apology as well, healing the breach of past wrongs. Chuck and Reggie's mother, Miss Linda, was a consistent user of crack, and would periodically take the money from their pants pockets while they slept (this is called "digging in pockets"). It got to the point that the brothers came up with a series of hiding places in the house, including a hole in the wall and a loose floorboard. Typically, they had only small sums, but one winter night, their mother discovered four hundred dollars in Chuck's back pocket.

Chuck told Mike and me that when he woke up and found the money gone, he confronted Miss Linda, who flatly denied taking it. Chuck declared that he was finished with her, that this was the last time— he would be sleeping at friends' houses or his girlfriend's house from now on.

At the time, Chuck was buying drugs with Mike and Steve; they were pooling their money so they could buy a larger amount at a lower price. They were buying on consignment, receiving the drugs first and making payment after the sales. The four hundred dollars was Chuck's portion of the money they owed their supplier or "connect." This meant that Mike, Steve, and Chuck couldn't pay him back—and worse, couldn't get any more drugs to sell. They were concerned about what their connect would do to them, and also how they'd make any money in the future.

MIKE: I told you not to sleep at your mom's, nigga! You a nut for that. You a fucking nut. Who she give it to [which drug dealer did she give the money to]? I'ma fuck that nigga up, man. I told those niggas from John Street don't go around there, don't serve her [sell drugs to Chuck's mother]. How many times I got to tell them don't serve her?

True to his word, Chuck stopped sleeping at Miss Linda's and didn't answer when she called his cell phone. This went on for two weeks, until the police showed up at Miss Linda's door, looking for Chuck's younger brother Reggie. The officers came to the house four times over the next two weeks. Each time, Miss Linda refused to give them any information, though she said they threatened to take her youngest son, Tim, away and cut off her welfare. Chuck began phoning to check on her and see how she was doing. When the police stopped coming, he moved back home.

It seemed as if by protecting Reggie from the police, and by withstanding the violence of the raids, Miss Linda made amends for the money she'd stolen. The first night that Chuck was back sleeping at her house, she beamed: "I *always* protect my sons. You can say a lot of things about me, but I'm not letting them take my babies."

Just as protecting someone from arrest is considered an act of commitment and affection, carelessly putting others at risk is taken to be a sign of negligence, an indication of a person's bad character.

It is a warm spring day, and Anthony and I are sitting on Miss Linda's steps along with a few neighbors and friends. Miss Linda pokes her head out the kitchen door and says her stomach is talking; she asks Ant to go and get hoagies. She tells him she also wants three bags of pork rinds. Her youngest son, Tim, who is fifteen now, gives Anthony two dollars for loosies (single cigarettes) and says that he wants his change back, and that Ant better not smoke any of them before he gets back. I get up and say, "I'll go with you," and Miss Linda jokes, "Yeah, you better go, 'cause Ant ain't got no money." As we get up to go, Miss Linda starts trying to persuade a neighbor to play spades with her, a dollar a hand. He is protesting that he has to go to work soon.

Anthony and I walk down the alley and over to Pappi's store. Ant puts the pork-rind chips on the counter and says, "Let me get three." Pappi's son passes him three single cigarettes, which cost a dollar fifty. I pick up the hoagies from the back counter where Pappi's youngest daughter is on the grill, and she hands them to me silently.

As Anthony and I walk out of the store, we see two cop cars stopped about fifty yards to the left. Two people, a young man and a young woman who look no older than 15, stand facing the side of one of the cars, with their arms up over their heads and their forearms leaning on the car. A Black, heavy-set cop in his forties is patting down the young man while a thinner white cop in his midthirties stands nearby.

As he crosses the street in front of me, the white cop looks at Ant, who immediately starts running toward Miss Linda's house. The cop starts off after him and by the time I catch up, Anthony is walking out of Miss Linda's house in handcuffs, followed by the cop. The cop is on the radio asking for someone to search the bushes in the front of the house; he thinks Anthony threw a gun there.

Anthony is yelling that his lip is busted and bleeding. Then he turns to me and says, "It's cool, A, I'ma be home in a minute. It's cool," to which Miss Linda replies, "Shit. He ain't staying *here*."

The cop puts Anthony into the backseat, placing his hand on top of Ant's head as he gets into the car. Anthony is talking at me through the closed window, but I can't hear him; I shrug at him and shake my head. Two more squad cars pull up into the alleyway with sirens blaring and lights flashing. Neighbors are coming outside or leaning out of their windows to look.

The cop who chased down Anthony asks Miss Linda her name, whether this is her house, and what her relationship is to Anthony. She flatly denies that he lives with her and says he is just someone she knows from around the neighborhood. The cop asks her for his name, and she says, "Ask *him* what his name is." The cop asks her who I am to her, and Miss Linda replies, "That's my fucking white girl. Is it a problem?" The cop tells her not to use profanity and to take a seat.

Miss Linda begins yelling at Anthony through the closed window of the police car: "Don't you ever bring the law to my house! That's what you get, nigga! That's what the fuck you get. Don't think I'ma take your calls, either; don't even bother putting this number on your list!"

The cop tells us not to go back inside, and I wonder where Tim is. It seems to take a long time for the police to fill out the paperwork, and a small crowd has now gathered at the end of the alley.

When the police leave, Miss Linda goes inside and calls to Tim, who has been hiding in a fallen wall of the basement. "Ain't nobody looking for you," she says as he crawls out.

Miss Linda is now convinced the police will come back that night and raid the house. She grabs her glass pipes and her marijuana stash from the top shelf of the glass china cabinet in the dining room and phones Mike, asking him to come for Chuck's gun. She leaves to put her contraband in her secret hiding spot and returns a few minutes later, looking calmer, though she continues to say over and over how this has messed up her whole day. Then Reggie calls from jail, and she picks up the phone and says:

"This dickhead runs into the house! Brings the cops all in here. They found the holster, the bullets. Don't ask me which fucking bullets; I don't know which bullets. Mike needs to get back here and get all the shit out of here, before they come back again. Because they definitely coming back—if not tonight, tomorrow night."

After pouring another drink and taking a drag from a neighbor's cigarette, she starts talking about past raids on her house. Then she says, "Anthony's problem is he is selfish. He don't think. They almost took my son today, and I just got him back two fucking weeks ago [from juvenile detention]. Not even two weeks."

And so the giving and taking of legal risk becomes a way that people in the neighborhood of 6th Street define their relationships, honor or dishonor someone, and draw moral distinctions among one another. Giving up another person under pressure is seen as a shameful act of betrayal. Doing so voluntarily is considered an act of retribution, or the start of an open conflict. The unintentional bringing of "heat" is taken as a sign of negligence or of bad character.

*   *   *

From these examples, we can see that the heavy presence of the police and the looming threat of prison enter into the rituals of gift-giving that unite people. Like the giving of food, shelter, or child care,[7] protecting loved ones from the police, or risking arrest on their behalf, becomes part of an ongoing give-and-take that creates and sustains social relationships.

This brings us to an interesting wrinkle. Despite the norm of silence and the high value placed on protecting others, doing so—particularly at personal expense—doesn't always reflect well on the person making the sacrifice. Someone can put herself at risk too freely, or for people with whom she is not perceived to be on terms intimate enough to merit the gesture, thus diminishing the value of the protection and that of the giver. Sometimes people are perceived to protect others in a desperate or manipulative way, to increase their intimacy with someone who may not otherwise be interested in a closer connection. Such was the case when Chuck's ex-girlfriend allowed him to stay at her place for a month while he was on the run, without asking for anything in return but his company.

Protecting others, or risking one's safety for their wellbeing, is hazardous to the giver not only because of the risk of arrest or other harm, but also because either action signals a strength of attachment that may later be mocked. For instance, a woman may risk arrest on behalf of her boyfriend by sneaking drugs into jail, only to find out that this man has cheated on her, or has told others that she means little to him. A man may protect a friend with whom he has been arrested, only to learn later the friend gave him up quickly when the police offered him a deal. Hence, protecting others opens a person up to the humiliation of being scorned or used.

THE MORAL AMBIGUITY OF ENCOUNTERS WITH THE LAW

We have seen how the looming threat of prison can provide opportunities for someone to demonstrate love, affection, or antagonism toward others; make claims about his own character or sentiments; or draw conclusions about other people's.

When Anthony ran into Miss Linda's house as the police chased him, he had clearly placed others at risk, and Miss Linda's anger was understood to be an appropriate reaction to his thoughtless actions. But often it is not so clear who has placed whom at risk, or how much risk an individual had really added to what a person already faced. If someone has protected another and risked arrest to do so, disputes may arise concerning how much protection was given, or how serious the risk really was. The giver may feel that the recipient has undervalued the gesture, that he's squandered his safety on someone who didn't appreciate it. Or the recipient may feel that the giver is trying to claim credit for a gesture that wasn't intended to be benevolent. Because police encounters, court hearings, and probation meetings have unpredictable outcomes, it's not always obvious how a given brush with the authorities would have gone if a person had acted differently. The functionality of run-ins with the law as expressive opportunities in social relationships is complicated by the inherent ambiguity of these encounters.

The following extended excerpt from field notes reveals this ambiguity:

We are going OT—out of town. I am driving with a girlfriend of mine from school, who sits across from me in the passenger seat. Mike and Chuck are sitting in the backseat. They are smoking an L (a marijuana cigarette), passing it back and forth and ashing it out the window.

A cop car flashes us to pull over. My girlfriend yells, "Oh, shit!" and gets a bottle of perfume out of her purse; she begins spraying the car and the rest of us. "Grass," from the Gap. Mike throws the butt of the L out the window as we pull over onto the gravel.

Two white police officers come to the car and ask me for my license and registration. I ask them why I am being pulled over, and one says that I was going over the speed limit. They walk back to their car to run my name and the tags. As we are waiting, Mike asks how fast I'd been driving, and I feel that he's accusing me. Chuck says quietly, "She wasn't going more than like a pound," which means fifty.

One of the officers comes back to the window and says that he smelled marijuana when he approached the vehicle, and asks us all to get out of the car. They tell my girlfriend and me to stand over to the side, and they tell Mike and Chuck to face the car, put their hands up on the hood, and spread their legs. One officer is radioing for a female cop to come and search us, though in the end he never bothers with it. He pats Mike down as he is pressed up against the car.

The officer who had been on the radio begins searching the car. I watch as he pulls the contents out of the side door pockets and from under the seat. Mostly papers of mine from school. I think about what could incriminate us there. In the side door pocket on the driver's side, the officer finds some needle-and-tube contraption. He sort of chuckles and holds it up to the other officer like he's found something good. I explain that it is part of the kit Mike's baby-mom is learning from in her studies to become a nurse's assistant, which is in fact exactly what it is. He lets it go.

The officer searching Mike demands to know who was smoking marijuana, who it belonged to. Mike says loudly, "It was mine. It was mine." The

officer asks, "Where is it?" Mike says, "There ain't no more, I smoked it all."
As the officer turns toward us, Mike says to him, "They don't have nothing
on them, they don't even smoke weed."

After Mike declares that it was his marijuana, the officer searches
him again, opening the pockets of his jacket and jeans. A small bag of
marijuana falls out. The officer puts handcuffs on him and says that he
will be taken to the police station and charged. He tells the three of us
to go, without ever touching me or my girlfriend. I ask if we can stay and
wait to hear where they are taking Mike, but they say no, and order us to
drive away.

Later, Mike tells me that at the precinct they made him pull up his tes-
ticles and cough, and a small bag of cocaine dropped from his anus. Now
he's being charged with possession of marijuana and possession of cocaine,
though very small amounts of both. Later, I ask Chuck if he had drugs on
him, and he nods. In the lining of your jeans? He nods again. But they
hadn't searched him.

I know that Mike must be bailed out quickly if he's going to make it out
on bail at all, because he's on probation in Bucks County. At some point the
detainer from that probation will show up in the system, and then his bail
will be denied, because a person on probation isn't allowed to make bail in
another case.

Chuck falls easily asleep, not seeming concerned. My girlfriend and I
stay up all night, going to different houses and collecting money. When I
get the call from Mike the next morning that he has had the bail hearing
and we need to come to the courthouse with $500, we are ready, and post it
within the hour. I drive out to the county jail alone. I wait for many hours
for Mike to be released, twisting my hair in ringlets and trying to ignore
a young man who keeps asking if I am here for my boyfriend. Then Mike
comes out, and we drive home.

As soon as he walks out the door, I am full of descriptions of recent
events—how we found out what police station he was being held at, who
we got the money from, how we ran to the courthouse before anyone
found out about the detainer to post the bail, how quickly I drove to the
county jail to get him, how long I waited, who was in the waiting room,
how I dodged their advances, and so forth.

Mike stops me finally, telling me to be quiet, looking frustrated and
angry.

"What are you mad for? I spend two days making sure you come home, and now you have attitude?"

Mike explains that I don't appreciate the gravity of what has happened, of how close I'd come to being arrested. He had prevented this by taking the blame himself, which he didn't have to do.

I protest that since it was in fact his marijuana and cocaine, and he was the one who'd been smoking in the car, I shouldn't have to thank him for keeping me safe from an arrest.

He counters with the argument that his actions during this police encounter differed from his habitual practice. He says that when the cops come, people typically remove the drugs from their person and place them in the car if they can't toss them successfully from the vehicle. The drugs get found in the car, nobody admits guilt, and down at the police station the chips fall where they may. Most of the time, Mike explains, this means that the driver takes the fall, even if he wasn't the one carrying the drugs. By not placing the drugs in the car, and by vocally admitting his guilt at the start of the search, he'd spared the rest of us from arrest, and me—the driver—in particular.

Mike then explains that he wouldn't have done this for just anyone; in fact, if Chuck had been the only other person with him, he wouldn't have admitted to anything. But he felt like I had really been there for him, and so he wanted to do this thing for me, to show me that I was appreciated. He seems angry that I don't understand the weight of this gesture, and frustrated that he has to explain it to me.

The next day, Chuck and I discuss what happened, and when I mention that Mike had taken the blame on our behalf, Chuck frowns and says, "That's what he's saying?" He then explains that when Mike said he could have tossed the drugs in the car, leading me, the driver, to potentially take the blame, he was lying, because he hadn't actually thought of that at the time. Chuck claims that Mike hadn't remembered he was carrying the weed bag until it dropped out of his pocket while the cop searched him. He hadn't remembered he had the small bag of cocaine, either, until he was in the back of the police car. If he had remembered these items before he was searched, Chuck says, he probably would have tossed them both in the car, no matter what the consequences.

"But what about when he said that we didn't have anything on us, when he said it was his weed?" I ask. Clearly this was an instance of Mike's taking the blame squarely and gallantly on his shoulders, saving the rest of us from a potential arrest. Chuck then explains that Mike's speaking up actually didn't protect us. If he hadn't spoken up, we might all have been taken to the police station and questioned. But my girlfriend and I wouldn't have been charged with anything, Chuck says, since we were clean—we had no drugs on us, we didn't have any warrants, we weren't on probation (which we would be violating by driving), and no drugs were in fact found in the car. He says, "They was going to let you go regardless." He then explains that Mike probably figured that since I'd been questioned only once before, and wasn't practiced in withstanding threats from police, he couldn't count on my silence. Especially not my girlfriend's, Chuck points out. "Who is Mike to her?"

"Now he wants to act like he did that shit for you," Chuck says. "But think about it: like, if you going to get booked, it's better to get booked *alone*."

To work out whether Chuck's account is valid, I try to think of what my friend from school could have possibly told the police about Mike. Well, at least his real name. In the hope that his other cases wouldn't come into play and to make it harder for them to find him once he made bail, Mike had given the two officers a fake name and had scraped his fingertips off on a metal grate in the cell so that they couldn't find him through his prints.

After a few days, Mike still seems angry with me that I didn't express gratitude for the sacrifice he'd made on my behalf, and that I didn't accept his version of events. I speak to Aisha on the phone, relaying the events of the past days to her, describing what Mike had done and how close we had come to being arrested. I make sure Mike is within earshot while I talk to her, and this seems to patch things up between us. Chuck says nothing else to me about it.

From these field notes, we can see that it can be quite unclear who has taken the blame for whom, or how much risk there really was in the first place. I believed that Mike had taken blame that was rightfully his, but he felt that he had made a significant sacrifice for me, and that I didn't understand the situation enough to appropriately value his gesture. I began to be convinced by Mike's arguments until I talked with Chuck, who had a different interpretation from either of us. Chuck agreed with Mike that keeping drugs on you instead of throwing them in the car should be understood as a gesture of sacrifice, protecting the driver at your personal expense. That is, he didn't dispute that passengers in a car ordinarily drop the drugs, leaving the driver holding the bag. What Chuck was disputing was whether Mike had *remembered* that he had drugs on him. If he'd actually forgotten, then he'd kept the rest of us safe unintentionally and was now trying to get credit for it. Furthermore, by quickly admitting to the police that he was carrying the marijuana and we weren't, Mike actually wasn't preventing our arrest. According to Chuck, what he was preventing was the possibility that we'd talk. Mike was trying to avoid putting us in a position where we'd compromise his freedom.

Added to these interpretations is a fourth, which I came up with while rereading my field notes a few days later. The person who actually may have benefited from Mike's impromptu confession was not me or my friend from school but Chuck, who did have drugs on him, and likely would have been searched next if Mike hadn't spoken up and claimed responsibility when he did. Chuck would have been in a much more vulnerable position to inform on Mike to reduce his own charges, so Mike's taking the blame prevented that from happening. Neither Chuck nor Mike mentioned this, at least not while I was present. In fact, Mike specifically told me that he wouldn't have taken the blame if only Chuck had been in the car.

From this single police stop, a great many interpretations of the risks involved and the motivations behind the actions of the parties present can be put forth. One reason it may have been important for Mike to provide a version of the events that involved his taking the blame for us is that a person's character is defined in part by whether he will risk arrest to protect the people he cares about. Residents of the 6th Street neighborhood tend to downplay how much they put others at risk, and to exaggerate their acts of protection and sacrifice. Men spread the news widely when they testify on behalf of a friend on trial, wanting others to know of their loyalty and good character. On the other hand, people suspected of caving under police pressure vehemently deny having done so, though the strength of the denial is at times taken as a sign of guilt in itself.

The inherent ambiguity and uncertainty of encounters with the police, trial dates, probation hearings, and the like make these events difficult ones on which to base decisions about people's characters, feelings, or motivations. And yet, in part because these events are so uncertain and ambiguous, they leave considerable room for interpretation, sometimes allowing those involved to construct a version of events in which they behaved bravely and honorably.

THE CRIMINAL JUSTICE SYSTEM AS A SOCIAL WORLD FOR YOUNG ADULTS

In the hyper-policed Black neighborhood of 6th Street, the penal system has become a central institution in the lives of young people and their families, coordinating social life and creating a meaningful moral framework through which young people carve out their identities, demonstrate their attachment to one another, and judge one another's character.

The events marking a young man's passage through the system come to serve as collective rituals that confer identity and establish relationships. The sentencing hearing, initial jail visits, and homecomings serve as important social events, indicating how popular he is or how much status he has, as well as where people stand in his life.

By protecting one another from the authorities or risking arrest on one another's behalf, members of the 6th Street community demonstrate their attachment to their family and friends and lay claim to decency and honor. Risking arrest to attend a family function or hiding a wanted relative or partner in one's home becomes an act of love and devotion, binding people together. Such risk-taking can also serve as an apology, healing the wounds of a past wrong. Indeed, how people conduct themselves given their own legal entanglements and those of others becomes a source of distinction, marking them as brave or weak, responsible or reckless, loyal or disloyal, or at least providing the resources for so claiming. In the 6th Street neighborhood and many like it, the criminal justice system now sets the terms for coming of age; it is a key stage on which the drama of young adulthood is played, not only for the young men moving through it but for their parents as well.

To be sure, around 6th Street and other segregated Black neighborhoods like it, the drama of youth continues to play out on the street corner, in class, and on the football field. But it also plays out—and for some it mainly plays out—in bail offices, courtrooms, and jail visiting halls. As boys around 6th Street become young men, many make the transition from home and school to detention centers and jails. The police and the courts increasingly take up their time and dictate their activities; their daily round consists of writing letters to the parole board or waiting in line at the probation office, making phone calls to the house arrest monitor, and meeting with the "back judge" from prior cases.

But to say that the penal system has become a central institutional basis for adolescence and young adulthood is not to say that it is equal to the other institutions which might occupy young people's time and form the basis of their social identities and relationships.

The events marking a man's passage through the penal system may become occasions for his girlfriend to dress up and do her nails, but a trial is not a school dance. These are rituals of diminishment and degradation, not celebration or accomplishment. Even if a young woman can emerge proudly from a sentencing hearing because she sat in the first row with the young man's mother, this doesn't change the fact that she is watching the young man she loves being taken away to prison.

Mothers may express their parental care and support by attending their son's court dates and by visiting him in jail, but these activities don't provide the same gratification they might experience attending a school basketball game, recital, or play. Even a mother who can take some pride in the attention she pays to her son's legal matters must face other, unpleasant emotions: distress for this to be happening, pain for what her son will go through in jail or prison, shame for what the boy has gotten himself into, guilt for having failed to prevent it. While families certainly celebrate a young man's homecoming from jail, dismissed case, or successful completion of a probation or parole term, they rarely do so with a cake and balloons. These happy moments are tinged with the unavoidable fact that even good news from the courts isn't something to be truly proud of. Unlike a graduation or a first day on the job, they aren't moves up so much as a clearing of legal entanglements, a resetting of the young man's life at zero. Now perhaps he might begin to make some progress in the domains that afford him some standing and stability—the domains of school, work, and family, in which he has fallen woefully behind.

The issue of agency also persists. Teenagers everywhere may feel that decisions are being made for them, and that they don't have as much control over their lives as they would like. But school and jobs do afford them some chance to work hard and reap the benefits of their efforts. In contrast, much of a young man's passage through the penal system reminds him every day that he is at the mercy of larger forces that do not wish him well.

The seemingly arbitrary nature of the criminal justice system, from the moment the police stop a man to the moment his parole sentence ends, leaves a young man feeling that he cannot actively determine how his life turns out. At any moment he may be taken into custody, while the man standing next to him is not. Once he catches a case, he begins attending court dates, perhaps one a month for what may turn into more than a year of continuances and postponements. Each time he enters the courthouse, he has little idea whether the authorities will decide he should be taken into custody on the spot and continue his case from jail, or whether he will simply be given a new court date and sent home. Uncertainty persists as to whether this day will mark an ending to his legal woes or his last day as a free man. The difference between a case getting thrown out and moving forward may have very little to do with the young man's conduct—he has only to wait and worry. If he is sitting in jail, he often has no idea how long he'll be there. Even when issued a fixed sentence, he doesn't know when he'll be paroled, and if granted parole, he may wait months for his papers to come through.

Young men cannot control when or where the criminal justice system may take them, nor can they control who attends the events marking their passage through it. Though surely high school offers significant opportunities for humiliation and conflict, a man sitting in jail or prison has less say over who attends the major events in his life than he would in, say, planning his prom date. And so these occasions become times of tension and humiliation, not just for the man in question but for his significant others, creating problems in relationships perhaps more often than do the rituals that we typically associate with coming of age.

The criminal justice system furnishes a good deal of expressive equipment for a man to demonstrate his love, honor, attachment, or open hostility, but upon closer inspection these are also wanting. The uncertainty of encounters with the police makes it hard for these to become the moments when his character is decided on, and the looming threat of prison makes it difficult for him to conduct himself as he might wish.

The act of informing, when done freely and without pressure, can be rightfully taken as an act of aggression, or a payback for some wrong. But people aren't always given the free choice to inform or to keep silent. Rather, informing happens under duress, so people are betraying those they'd rather protect, and their character is becoming established during a situation over which they have little control and certainly haven't freely entered into. Whereas many of us living in other communities are able to construct an identity as a good person without risking much of our safety or security to do so, young people on 6th Street find that their character becomes fixed in moments of fear and desperation, when under the threat of violence and confinement they must choose between their own safety and the security of someone they hold dear.

*   *   *

Thus, the moral world that people weave around the courts, the police, and the threat of prison involves suspicion, betrayal, and disappointment. To repair the damages that so frequently occur to the self and to relationships, young men and women try to cover up the bad things they are made to do, or spin them in a positive light. Relationships between friends, partners, and family members require a good deal of forgiving and forgetting. Still, people create a meaningful social world and moral life from whatever cards they have been dealt, and young people growing up in poor and segregated Black neighborhoods, under heavy policing and the threat of prison, are no exception.

SIX

The Market in Protections and Privileges

Most of this book has concerned young men who are the targets of the vast criminal justice apparatus, and those very close to them. But the movement of large numbers of these young men through the courts, the jails, and the prisons touches many more people beyond those directly involved. In the 6th Street neighborhood, a lively market has emerged to cater to the needs and wants of those living under various legal restrictions. A good number of young people have found economic opportunity by selling their friends and neighbors sought-after goods and services for hiding from the police or circumventing various legal constraints.

Some of these young people got their start by doing a favor for a friend or relative, and later realized they could charge for it. Others found that their legitimate jobs furnished the opportunity to help legally precarious people in a particular kind of way. Meanwhile, some young people working from within the criminal justice system earned additional income under the table by smuggling a number of restricted goods and services to inmates. Taken together, the underground market catering to the needs and wants of those living under various legal restrictions has created substantial economic opportunity for young people living in communities where money and jobs are scarce.

TURNING A PERSONAL CONNECTION INTO A LITTLE INCOME

When I met Jevon, he was a charming eight-year-old who wanted to be a movie star. He'd quote whole sections of *The Godfather* or *Donnie*

Brasco and swear he'd make it big one day. People often said that Jevon sounded like his older relatives. He would entertain himself by pretending to be his cousin Reggie or his uncle when their girlfriends phoned, causing a number of misunderstandings and, in one case, a big argument. Shortly after Jevon turned thirteen, his muscles started to grow, and to his great satisfaction, a thin mustache began to form on his upper lip. Most important, his voice broke. This was the key thing, his voice dropping. Now he could impersonate his relatives and neighbors with astonishing accuracy.

Around this time, Jevon's older cousin Reggie got released from jail and placed on probation at his mother's house. His probation officer would call a few evenings each week to make sure Reggie was in the house for his nine o'clock curfew, a constraint on his freedom he deeply resented, particularly after he met and fell for a girl living a few blocks away. Reggie started paying a neighbor ten dollars per night to sit in Miss Linda's house and answer the phone when his probation officer called, so that he could go out with his new girlfriend. This scheme had been successful once, but on the second phone call the PO had grown suspicious and had asked where Reggie had been sent as a juvenile offender. Reggie's neighbor couldn't answer that question, so the PO told him that the next time Reggie was caught out after curfew, he'd be going back to jail.

Reggie and I were sitting on the stoop facing the alleyway and discussing this while some younger boys played a pickup game with the alley basket. Hearing the tail end of our conversation, Jevon left the game and came over to us. With impressive confidence, he told Reggie that he could take the PO calls for him: not only could he do Reggie's voice better than anyone, but he already knew most of the details of his cousin's life, and could quickly learn the rest.

"What's my date of birth?" Reggie asked.

"February 12, 1987."

"What was the first case I caught?"

"For weed, when you was like ten."

"How many months did I do up Forrest?"

"You never went to Forrest. You was in Mahanoy."

"What's the last birthday I spent home?"

"Shit. Probably when you was like nine."

Reggie grinned. "What's my social?"

"I don't know."

Reggie told Jevon his social security number.

"Okay," Jevon said.

"Repeat it back," Reggie insisted.

Jevon repeated it perfectly.

* * *

Reggie gave Jevon's acting skills a try that night, leaving around seven and returning at two in the morning. Jevon reported that everything had gone according to plan: the PO had phoned, asked what halfway house he'd been sent to, what his first baby-mom's mother's name was, and what part of his body the guard had injured while Reggie was a teenager in county jail. Jevon had answered all these questions correctly.

Jevon launched his enterprise by charging his cousin five dollars a night, but at his mother's urging switched to asking for five dollars an hour. Reggie seemed to resent this rate increase, but admitted that nobody else could come close to his voice, which had the heavy nasal quality of a young Biggie Smalls. When Reggie missed several payments, Jevon offered his services to his uncle and then to a neighbor, both of whom were also on parole, and eager for a stand-in to answer calls from their PO.

Responding to curfew calls required a number of skills beyond the mimicry of voices: punctuality, confidence, a good memory, and the ability to imagine what someone who has recently come home from a long sentence might sound like and say to his PO. Jevon took this all on as any professional actor might, and seemed to delight in his roles. He also took careful notes about the conversations in a little book, so that the next time a man saw his PO he'd know where their relationship stood.

Over time, Jevon developed quite a client base. In his sophomore and junior years of high school, I watched him bring in upwards of one hundred dollars a week. As his graduation neared, though, he seemed to grow tired of sitting in houses all evening and night. After a futile attempt to forward the calls to his cell phone, and another failed attempt to train one of his friends to do the job, he stopped "the phone hustle" and went to work as a mall security guard.

Like Jevon, a number of young people I got to know were making a little money by providing goods and services to friends and to friends of friends who were living under various legal restrictions. One important service was the smuggling of money and drugs to those constrained the most: inmates.

Twenty-four-year-old Shonda got her start by doing a favor for someone close to her.

"You have to wrap the bill around the weed," she explained to me as we sat at her grandmother's round kitchen table. "That way you keep the weed together and you cover the smell."

"Okay."

"And you have to do it a day, two days in advance, because they got the hand machines now."[1]

Shonda first smuggled drugs into jail at the age of eight, when she helped her mom pass a crack-filled balloon to her dad, a heavy user who was on trial for aggravated assault. Her mom's method was to insert the balloon like a tampon, then adjust and pull it out in the visiting room. Shonda's job was to watch the guards and give her mother the green light. Sometimes she handed the balloons from her mother to her father. Her dad would swallow them, and either throw them up or pass them once he got back to the cell block.

After her mom broke things off with her dad, Shonda stopped going to the prison to visit him. There followed a long stretch—about seven years—in which Shonda's life was not punctuated by trips to jails or courthouses. Then during her junior year of high school, her boyfriend caught a gun case. She returned to county jail to visit him. When she was twenty-three, her baby-dad got booked for armed robbery, and she was back again.

Shonda was unemployed when her baby-dad got taken into custody, so her household income evaporated. In addition to taking over the groceries, the diapers, and all the bills, she now had the added expense of sending money to her baby-dad in jail so that he could buy soap, shower shoes, and better food inside. He also asked her to bring in marijuana and tobacco. After a few weeks, she started smuggling small quantities of marijuana into the visiting room along with cash, which he used for buying items like cigarettes from other inmates.

To offset the high costs of visiting him and keeping him in relative comfort while inside, Shonda began taking in packages for other men at the county jail; she either visited them herself or took a girlfriend with her while she visited her baby-dad. We met in this way. Reggie had been on trial for possession of drugs and for fleeing the police, and found out from his cellmate that a woman named Shonda would bring in marijuana for fifty dollars. His mother met up with her one Wednesday afternoon, paid her the money, and gave her a small bag of weed to smuggle in for him. I tagged along.

On one of the first days I spent with Shonda, she put together three packages: one for her baby-dad, one for his cellmate, and one for a man with a bullet lodged in his back who said that marijuana was the only drug that dulled the pain. Her younger sister came with us to the jail and called the cellmate out into the visiting room so that she could pass off the package for him at the same time Shonda was visiting with her baby-dad. After this half-hour visit, Shonda got a new ticket and waited another five hours to visit the third man. On this last visit of the day, she acted as if she were visiting an old family friend, and passed off the small bag of marijuana this man's girlfriend had sent him for the week.

Assembling a package was a four-part process for Shonda. First, she pounded the marijuana down to get the air out, creating a tiny and dense cube. Next, she covered it in one layer of plastic wrap, taping the packet together to form a rectangle of about one inch by three-quarters of an inch. Then she took a dollar bill—though sometimes it was a ten, other times a twenty—and folded it tightly around the packet, making the total package about as thin as a Ritz cracker. Finally, using double-sided tape, she made the package sticky on both sides so that the man could hide it securely between his wrist and his jail ID band.

The sudden appearance of hand-screening machines at CFCF led Shonda to take extra precautions in planning her package deliveries. A few days after the machine appeared, I was visiting Reggie and watched as frightened women passed a bottle of hand sanitizer around the waiting area, scrubbing their hands and arms free of any incriminating specks of contraband. That day, the smell of sweat mixed with that of the ammonia used in cleaning the waiting room. Even women like Mike's mother, who weren't smuggling in packages, worried that they had touched drugs recently and would be denied entry or worse, get arrested.

The heightened risk didn't stop Shonda from bringing in packages for cash: she needed the money. After the screening machines came in, she began placing the packages between the inner and outer lining of her panties, in that rectangular patch of cloth that seems made for small quantities of contraband. In the bus on another trip to jail, she explained to me that the guard on duty that afternoon wouldn't touch your coochie, just the inner thighs. As she explained this, I remembered hearing Reggie and Mike describe how exciting it was, sitting in jail, to hold a tiny square containing a drug that would make you forget where you were, and smelling of woman.

"You have to put the package in before you go," Shonda explained, "because you have to wash your hands enough times so that you pass the drug screen. And always put it in the lining, so it doesn't fall out while you wait."

"Do you get scared?"

"You have to control your fear," she said. "You have to pretend that you don't have anything on you, that you're just a regular visitor. You have to get to the point where it's normal."

Shonda told me that she made enough money to support both her trips to jail and her baby-dad's drug habit. Sometimes she could also afford to put money on his books, but it wasn't really enough extra money to pay, for example, her phone bill.

If the money in smuggling is low, the risk of arrest is substantial, with or without the drug-screening machines. In my years visiting young men from 6th Street in jail and prison, I observed seven women get handcuffed and taken away after a guard found drugs on their person during the pat-down in the search room. Two of these women had come with their children, so Child Protective Services was called. One woman I knew from the neighborhood lost custody of her child and served a year in jail. Reggie seemed fairly unconcerned: "She should have been more careful. That's on her."

Like Jevon, Shonda began her business by doing a favor for someone close to her, and then started to charge a few people for the service. Neither one made a lot of money this way, but Jevon seemed to relish his acting roles, as well as the status it gave him around his older neighbors and kin. Shonda expressed her satisfaction at helping people in great need, like the man who smoked the marijuana she smuggled in to alleviate the pain of his bullet wounds. And they both really needed the money, however little it was.

OPPORTUNITIES AT WORK

Some residents of 6th Street become part of this underground network of support through opportunities provided by their legitimate jobs. They find that the skills in which they were trained or the particular goods or services their jobs make available prove useful to people with legal entanglements, and that they can earn a little or even a lot of extra money by helping these people out under the table.

Rakim, a rotund man in his forties, ran a photo stand in downtown Philadelphia. The stand (or rather, mobile office), sat near the Philadelphia customs office, and a large sign reading Passport Pictures, Cheapest in the City welcomed patrons inside. Rakim's customers entered at the rear of the trailer and saw a row of plastic chairs, a tripod at one end, and a white backdrop hanging from the other. Rakim charged fifteen dollars for three passport-sized photos and took four shots, allowing customers to choose from among them before printing.

On the first afternoon I went to see him, a mother and her teenage son were sitting in the plastic chairs that formed a small waiting area. They came, she told me proudly, because her son was going to London for his junior year abroad. Ahead of her in line was an employee of a large company about to spend two weeks in Canada for training. A lawyer arrived next, needing a passport renewal for a vacation in Argentina.

When these customers left, another customer came in, wearing a torn jean jacket. Seeing me, he made a move to leave. Rakim said, "It's cool, she's cool." The man smiled and said, "I wasn't sure." He handed Rakim a wad of crumpled bills, and Rakim passed him a small plastic bag full of yellow liquid. The man gingerly accepted the bag and walked into the tiny bathroom. He emerged a few minutes later, nodded to Rakim, and walked out.

Rakim had begun working at this photo stand in the mid-1990s, when he took over the business from his father. As he told it, the stand did fairly well until 9/11. "People did not want to cross a border," he explained. "They did not want to get on a plane."

During this slow period, Rakim's cousin would stop by the trailer on his way back from his weekly parole meetings, since the offices of the Probation and Parole Board are located not two blocks away, and they would catch up for an hour or two. Then one week his cousin came in a day early, visibly upset. He asked Rakim if he had smoked weed or used any other drugs recently. When Rakim replied that he hadn't, the cousin confessed that he'd slipped up with drugs, and begged Rakim for the use of his urine for the test the next morning.

"How would I give you my urine?" Rakim asked.

His cousin explained that he would heat it up at home, put it in a Baggie taped to his inner thigh, and release it into the sample cup at the parole office. Rakim agreed, so the next morning, his cousin took Rakim's urine to the parole office meeting and passed the drug test with it. Later, when his cousin asked for the favor again, Rakim told him it would cost him twenty dollars. This arrangement went on for some months, until the police caught the cousin driving a car and the judge returned him to prison for the parole violation.

While inside, Rakim's cousin told a friend about the photo booth, and when this friend came home he stopped by on the way to his parole appointment. News spread, and Rakim's urine business grew.

I met Rakim through Chuck's close friend Steve in 2007. At the time, Steve had been trying to complete a two-year probation sentence while battling a serious addiction to PCP. One afternoon, he came back to the block, favoring his left leg and wincing as he walked. When I asked what was wrong, he said simply, "The piss was too hot." Mike explained that Steve had been buying urine from a guy downtown, and it had burned the skin on his inner thigh, where he had taped the bag.

I asked Rakim about this during our interview, and he knowingly nodded his head.

I had trouble with the temperature at first. Guys were burning their legs, because the coffee warmer was too hot. I had to keep antibiotic ointment and gauze bandages in here because guys were coming back with their skin peeling off on the plastic bag. So I got one with an adjustable temperature, and I keep it at 100 degrees. Problem solved.

A year into this side business, Rakim had three coffee heaters going, and was contracting out to two women to provide supplemental urine. He told me he didn't know of anyone else who sold urine for use at this probation and parole office, noting that you needed a place where people could come inside and safely "put on" the urine. "So if you've got a hotdog stand, a lottery and magazine stand, you can't do this." He explained that most guys on probation or parole get urine from relatives or partners, but that this is an unsatisfactory solution:

> Your girl can always give you her piss, right, but you've got to take it from West Philly, North Philly, all the way downtown. You've got to carry it on the bus, keep it warm, keep the bag from breaking. And then, you never know if the urine is clean. Your girl says she's not using, but you can't watch her every second. Maybe she doesn't want to tell you she's been using, so she gives you the urine and hopes it will come back okay. Then you've got problems with your PO and problems in your relationship. You're back in jail, you're blaming her, now ya'll are on bad terms. . . . If you come to me, you don't have any of that. Hell, I sometimes have women come to me for their boyfriends! Because they don't want him to know what they're doing, you know? So they buy it from me and give it to him like it's theirs.

Another item that people with certain kinds of jobs are able to supply is fake documents. In 2006, a rumor started to circulate that a woman who had recently been transferred to the PennDOT (Pennsylvania Department of Transportation) nearest to 6th Street was accepting one thousand dollars for making driver's licenses for people who didn't actually qualify for them (or who were too concerned about their pending legal issues to try). Mike reasoned that since the tickets on his license amounted to more than three thousand dollars and his parole sentence prevented him from getting a license anyway, it made financial sense to pay this woman the thousand bucks. He never did save enough money to purchase the license, but through his negotiations with her I learned that a number of other men in the neighborhood had obtained one, including Chuck and Reggie's uncle, who had a warrant out for a parole violation dating back to 1983. This woman never agreed to talk with me, but two years later, when she was discovered and arrested, she claimed she'd made over three hundred thousand dollars selling real identities to people who don't otherwise qualify for them. Nobody could figure out who was carrying these phony licenses, or just how many people had them.

More commonly, people help those facing difficulties with obtaining formal identification by providing the goods and services that typically require ID, with no questions asked. That is, rather than supply the ID itself, they instead supply the goods and services otherwise denied to people without proper identification.

Pappi's corner store sits at the corner of 6th and Mankin. A yellow neon sign above the entrance reads Hernandez Grocery, Cigarettes Milk Eggs Hoagies Lottery. A smaller sign below reads We Take Access Card. Mr. Hernandez was known as Pappi, and around 6th Street his store was the go-to place for loosie cigarettes, chips, drinks, and snacks. Since the nearest grocery store was eleven blocks away, neighbors who didn't have a car or bus fare would do most of their grocery shopping at Pappi's.

Bulletproof glass framed the counter, but Pappi kept a one-by-two-foot space open so he could pass customers their cigarettes and lottery tickets by hand.

"A turnstile," he once told me, "would mean that I expect my customers to pull a gun on me. Nobody would ever do that."

Pappi used the bulletproof glass as a giant frame on which to showcase pictures of his grandchildren and other children from the area. Alongside his granddaughter and three grandsons were the faces of his 6th Street customers and friends, in baby pictures, prom pictures, graduation pictures, funeral pictures, and even jail visiting-room pictures. Pappi prided himself that in fifteen years of business in an increasingly violent and impoverished Black section of the city, he had never been robbed.

Across from the main counter and perched above the doorway, a small TV broadcast sports or the news. Customers sometimes stopped to watch for a few minutes, commenting with Pappi on the stories. They also asked Pappi how their friends and relatives were doing. Indeed, the store served as a kind of informational hub for the 6th Street neighborhood. It was often the first place people went when they came home from jail or prison. Though Pappi seldom spoke more than a few words, he quietly kept up with a great many neighborhood residents, and possessed that rare ability to make people feel noticed and genuinely appreciated. He played baseball in high school, and forty years later still cut an impressive figure.

When Mike and Chuck and their friends were home from jail, we'd visit Pappi's four or five times a day to buy a soda, a loosie, or a bag of chips. After a few months, Pappi gave me the nickname Vanilla, which he later shortened to Nil.

Most days, Pappi's college-aged son ran the cash register in the front, taking lottery ticket numbers and selling drinks and snacks. His daughter worked the grill and meat counter in the back, serving up hoagies or grilled cheese. But in addition to common corner grocery store items, Pappi also sold prepaid cell phones under the table. Depending on the day, he might have a hookup for a used car rental with no questions asked, or a "connect" to a local motel where you could check in without showing ID or a credit card.

The goods and services Pappi sold under the table weren't known by the store's normal customers. You had to ask for them, and you had to be the right person asking in order to get them. But they weren't exactly illegal, either. These items ordinarily required the purchasers to provide documentation of both their identity and their creditworthiness—a state-issued identification card, proof of insurance or credit, or a bank account.

Pappi supplied specialty goods and services to his customers, but he also acted as a broker between legally compromised people and individuals providing a range of goods and services they were seeking. One of the people he connected his customers to was Jahim, who worked at a garage a few blocks south. At this garage patrons could ask for Jahim, and get their car serviced or repaired without presenting ID, insurance, or any paperwork on the car whatsoever. Downtown on South Street, a man named Hussein sold stereos and other electronics on payment plans, allowing the customer to give any name whatsoever, and asking for no ID to set up the arrangement. Bobby M on Third Street rented out rooms without any proof of ID or credit. His rates were higher than elsewhere, but he accepted a handshake rather than a lease.

People working in the medical field also find that their jobs enable them to provide under-the-table support to legally compromised people. Indeed, a number of local women who worked in area hospitals and doctor's offices provide medication and expertise to men too scared to seek treatment at a hospital, where their names might be run and warrants or other pending legal matters would come up.

The first time I witnessed this kind of underground health care was the day Steve's fourteen-year-old cousin, Eddie, broke his arm while running from the police. An officer had stopped him on foot just outside Pappi's, and after patting him down found a small amount of crack on his person. Eddie took off when the officer began taking out the handcuffs, and he soon lost him in the alleyways. In his efforts to escape, Eddie had scaled a fence and landed badly. He walked into his grandmother's house panting and clutching his right forearm, the bone exposed.

After an hour on the phone, his grandmother told me triumphantly that a woman was coming over to fix Eddie's arm.

"Is she a doctor?" I naively asked.

"She's a janitor," his grandmother laughed. "But she works at the hospital."

* * *

Two hours later, Eddie's arm was still bleeding, even though we'd wrapped it in dish towels and propped it up on the high back of the couch. Eddie had been taking swigs of Wild Irish Rose, and was now cursing and singing in about equal parts.

The woman finally arrived around midnight, wearing scrubs and carrying a large plastic bag full of medical supplies. She unwrapped Eddie's arm and injected him with some kind of anesthetic. After a few minutes of cleaning the wound and catching up with Eddie's grandmother, she told me to turn up the music. Then she asked his grandmother to hold on to Eddie's torso while she clutched his broken arm between her thighs and pulled the bones back into place with both her hands. Eddie screamed and struggled to get away, then cried for a good ten minutes. The woman dropped two needles into boiling water on the stove and used them to sew up the broken skin. With Eddie quietly crying, she placed a bandage over the stitches, and then began wrapping his arm in white cotton padding, placing rolled gauze in his hand for him to cup in a loose fist. She took some tougher foam material from her bag and cut it to fit his forearm, then wrapped this in an ace bandage. After about an hour, Eddie's arm sat in a sling, and the woman left instructions to change the bandages and check the wounds every day. For her service, Eddie's grandmother paid the woman seventy dollars and a plastic bag filled with three plates of corn bread and chicken she had made that afternoon.

After this memorable event, I began to observe that a number of other local residents who worked in the medical field supplied various forms of off-the-books care to young men who avoided the hospital for fear of encountering the police.

Aisha and Mike's cousin Ronny, sixteen, had been boarding a bus when the gun tucked into his waistband went off, sending a bullet into his thigh. (He had begun carrying the gun when, coming home from a two-year stint in juvenile detention, he found his neighbor and close friend slain and the 6th Street Boys in a series of shootouts with the 4th Street Boys.) Having recently returned from the juvenile detention center on three years of probation, Ronny refused to go to the hospital, convinced that the trip would land him back in juvenile on a violation. He spent the next five days bleeding on his grandmother's couch, his friends and family pleading with him to go to the hospital, but to no avail. Then his grandmother located a woman working as a nurse's aide who agreed to remove the bullet.

She performed this procedure on the kitchen table. Ronny's grandmother shoved a dish towel into his mouth and asked me to turn up the music to cover his screams. When the nurse's aide finished up and Ronny appeared likely to survive, his grandmother paid her $150, and the next day brought her some of her famous spicy fried chicken wings.

OPPORTUNITIES ON THE INSIDE

While some people supplying protections and privileges to legally compromised people launch this enterprise through their personal contacts, or by finding that their job opens up ways to help and profit from these people, others come into contact with people living under legal restrictions directly through their position within the criminal justice system. Certain court clerks, prison guards, case managers, and halfway house supervisors leverage their professional positions to grant special exemptions and privileges to defendants, inmates, and parolees who can come up with the cash. And like those brokers of goods and services who aren't employed by the criminal justice system, these individuals occasionally assist for personal reasons or simply out of a desire to help.

Janine finished high school with great grades and then enrolled in a two-year college to earn a certificate in criminal justice. As she told it, a lifetime of watching her brothers and father deal with the police, the courts, and the prisons had convinced her that she'd be more qualified for this kind of job than for medical work—the other sector of the economy that seemed to be growing at the time. Upon graduation, she tried to get a job as a prison guard, since the benefits were great and the wages good, but instead was hired by the scheduling office at the Criminal Justice Center downtown. The job was pretty straightforward: handle the scheduling of court cases, and manage the calendars of the judges, district attorneys, and public defenders. Since each of the hundreds of cases that came through the criminal courts each month had upwards of twelve court dates before going to trial—or far more likely: settling with the defendant, making a deal—this scheduling provided fulltime work for Janine and two others.

Janine had been going through the cases one day when she came upon a name that looked very familiar to her: Benjamin Greene. Benny—if it was indeed the same person—had been the only guy who was nice to her in middle school, when she was overweight and her mother's boyfriend was touching her at night. Benny would let her sneak into his basement bedroom to sleep without asking anything from her. She looked up his name on the court computer and saw his picture pop up on the screen. It was Benny, sure enough, now fifteen years older.

Janine had heard that Benny had become a major dealer after high school and was even wanted by the feds for a while. But this didn't stop her from remembering his kindness. Benny had a preliminary hearing for a gun and drug case scheduled for the following week, so she waited out in the hallway for him, approaching him shyly as he was leaving the courtroom. "My heart was pounding," she told me a couple of months later while we had coffee across the street from the courthouse. "I didn't know if he was married, or had kids, or if he ever thought about me anymore. But he looked the same, just with more hair [on his face]."

Within minutes of their meeting, Benny asked Janine if she could help to get his case thrown out—if she could perhaps talk to the judge or the district attorney. She refused to do this, but realized she could arrange the judge's schedule so that Benny's court dates would be quite far apart—four months instead of one or one and a half.

I met Janine through Benny; he came through the block one day and told everybody listening that he'd gotten a girl who worked in the courthouse to push his dates back. He acted as if he thought nothing of exploiting her feelings for his own gain and spoke quite dismissively of her. But when I had coffee with Janine, she explained that Benny had offered to pay her handsomely for her efforts to muddle the schedules; in fact, he insisted on paying her each time she was successful.

"How much is he paying you?" I asked.

"Three hundred. Three hundred each time."

"What are you doing with the money?"

"I'm paying off my student loans!"

Seeking additional verification that Janine was really receiving this money, I asked Benny about it in private one afternoon. He admitted he was paying her, and explained that this was in part because he didn't want to be indebted to her for the great favor she was doing him, especially knowing how much she liked him.

A year later, Benny was still on the streets, thrilled to be spending time with his baby-mom and two children. In the end, his court case took three and a half years to process—a good year and a half longer than any other case I'd seen. When Benny was finally sent to state prison, Janine told me that he wrote her that same week, thanking her for giving him the extra time outside with his family.

If court clerks have a bit of leeway to grant certain defendants special privileges such as extra time between trial dates, jail and prison guards have considerably more. And though a number of legal restrictions are imposed on those who are on probation or parole or going through a court case, jail and prison inmates encounter a far greater list of rules and prohibitions, opening up a much larger window of economic opportunity for those working at correctional facilities. While certainly not all or perhaps even most guards participate in the informal penal economy, at least some profit from smuggling in everything from knives to drugs to cell phones.

Twice I accompanied Miss Linda to meet a guard whom she paid to smuggle in marijuana to one of her sons sitting in county jail. Another time I accompanied Mike's girlfriend to a meeting with a prison guard who accepted a blow job and thirty-five dollars in exchange for smuggling in three pills of oxycodone to Mike, which he took to ease the pain from a severe beating received in the yard.

In 2011, I learned that Miss Linda had been paying a guard to smuggle Percocet to her son Reggie in the prison yard. He had been sitting in state prison for six months on a parole violation, this time for driving a car without a license. Shortly after his arrival, a female guard threw a bucketful of ammonia into his face, causing significant injury. My field notes from that visit:

> First time seeing Reggie since the ammonia incident. Wasn't her fault, he says—she was playing. The eyedrops the nurse provided weren't working to dull the pain, so the same guard who ruined his eyes started selling him Percocet under the table for a small fortune. Three days ago, the guard got transferred—apparently unrelated to having injured Reggie or the drug smuggling—so now Reggie's in severe withdrawal. "Like the flu," he says, "but 'way worse." That'll pass, but his blindness likely won't. He's hoping to get another guard to sell him Percocet or oxycontin, but hasn't found one yet.

In addition to drugs, some guards do a good business in cell phones. At CFCF in 2011, these were going for five hundred dollars. The family or girlfriend of an inmate would meet the guard and pay him or her in cash, which I observed on a number of occasions.

Guards also sell something less tangible to inmates and parolees: private time with women.

Mike and I were sitting in the visiting room at Camp Hill state prison, located two hours west of Philadelphia. We were eating microwaved chicken fingers from the turnstile snack machine and catching up on neighborhood gossip. Mike pointed to a small room near the drink machines. "See that?" he said. "There's no camera in there. Niggas was taking they girls in there and smashing [having sex]; this guard was taking, like, a bean [one hundred dollars] for fifteen minutes. He left, like, right after I got here, so I never got to use it."

When Mike finished his three-year prison term, he got paroled to a halfway house in North Philadelphia. There, too, certain guards were willing to extend special privileges, for a fee. This North Philadelphia halfway house held ten beds to a small room, but often twenty men slept there. On the second night, Mike told me that he'd gotten no sleep because one of his roommates had stabbed another, whom the man caught trying to steal his shoes. On my first visit, a dense crowd of young men greeted me as I walked through the doors of the compound, clamoring with one another against the glass for a look at the outside. After years behind bars, Mike found the halfway house untenable: "You get the smell of freedom, but you can't touch it or taste it."

During the few hours he was permitted to leave during the day, Mike began to get reacquainted with the city, learning what kinds of clothes people were wearing nowadays, signing up for Facebook, and acquiring an iPod. On the third day, he was given enough hours to visit his baby-mom, Marie, and their two children. He seemed nervous about it, and I tried to reassure him that after he saw them he'd feel more at ease.

When we spoke after the visit, Mike sounded worse. He learned that his children were staying with their maternal grandmother, who had also taken in her brother, a man in his sixties. Mike believed that this uncle had the habit of asking children to sit on his lap and touching them. Marie was employed by a local hospital as a nurse's assistant and would leave for work at five in the morning; this meant that his seven-year-old daughter and ten-year-old son were alone with their uncle for two and a half hours before their grandmother would return from her night shift and take them to school. What Mike wanted was to stay at his baby-mom's house overnight so that he could be there during those two critical hours when his children were left alone with their uncle. I imagine he also wanted to spend time with his baby-mom, though he didn't voice this reason when we discussed the situation.

The solution came when Mike discovered that a number of the half-way house residents were paying a guard between one hundred and two hundred dollars a night to allow them to leave at midnight and return before the 8:00 a.m. count the next morning. In fact, so many of the men were paying off this guard for the privilege that when I would come to say hello to Mike in the evening, I'd see one after another jump into waiting cars outside the compound. I initially wondered if these men had special evening passes, possibly to work a night shift, or perhaps were choosing to leave the halfway house, violate their parole terms, and go on the run. When Mike explained about the guard, I realized that at least some of these men were paying to leave for the night and sneak back in the next morning.

At first Mike's baby-mom agreed to contribute a significant portion of the payoff, telling me she'd give any amount to know her children were safe. By the second week, however, she refused to contribute any more, saying that she couldn't give over her entire paycheck just to secure a night with Mike.

When Mike's money for nightly payoffs ran out, I asked him if he'd introduce me to the halfway house guard who was taking the cash. Since the guard was single and around my age, Mike invited him to go for a beer with me, introducing me as his godsister, as he often did. He also told the guard that I was writing his biography and might want to talk with him about Mike's experience in the halfway house.[2]

The guard agreed to meet me for drinks at the Five Points, a well-known "grown folks" bar. He wasn't at all what I had expected: a quiet, thoughtful man who showed me pictures of his three children while sipping on an orange soda.

He began our conversation by saying that Mike was one of the guys he worried about the most. If Mike could just get through these first few weeks, he'd be okay.

The guard's phone rang soon after we began talking. He picked up and said, "Yeah, he's a go." I asked what the calls were about, and he told me quite openly that he was helping some of the guys get out of the house at night.

"What do you charge?" I asked.

"It depends," the guard said. "If the guy is going out to sell drugs and, you know, get the gun back that he left with his friend when he got locked up, I charge two hundred dollars. Most of that goes to my supervisor—they think he doesn't pay attention, but he knows what it is; he's taking his cut. If the guy's going to work or looking after his kids—you know, he's a good guy—I charge a lot less, or I let him go for free, and take care of my supervisor from the others."

"Is it risky?"

"Put it this way: this is my third house. The first house got shut down because the toilets were stopped up; for months they weren't working, and men were sleeping in their own shit, getting sick from it. The second got shut down because the guards were selling guns, not just guns—machine guns, M16s. [The guards were] using the men in the house to run guns out of state, okay? You have no idea what goes on."

"So letting men out at night . . ."

"It's against policy. It's a violation of their parole. But show me a house in Philly where that's *not* going on."[3]

* * *

Faced with heavy surveillance and supervisory restrictions, some individuals tangled up with the police, the courts, and the prisons seek a number of specialty goods and services to evade the authorities or live with more comfort and freedom than their legal restrictions allow. A number of young people in the 6th Street neighborhood, as well as people working as court clerks, prison guards, and halfway house operators, are making a few extra dollars by providing an array of underground goods and services to those individuals moving through the criminal justice system. With the exception of prison guards, those working in this market tend not to know one another or form much of a collective body.

Some people sell specialty goods, such as drug-free urine or fake documents, that legally compromised people need to get through police stops or bypass their various restrictions. Others are finding underground ways to supply the basic goods and services that legally compromised people find too dangerous to access through standard channels, or are prevented from accessing because of their legal restrictions: car repair, cell phones, even health care. Moreover, many things that clean people hold as basic rights or free goods become highly sought-after privileges for those under various forms of confinement: fifteen minutes of intimacy with a spouse within the prison walls, an evening away from the home one is obligated through probation or parole restrictions to return to, or a few more months outside jail before a sentencing hearing. These, too, become commodities for which people with a compromised legal status will dearly pay.

What do people participating in this underground market make of what they are doing?

Rakim seemed to take a sympathetic attitude toward his clientele, viewing his urine business as a necessary correction to an unjust system:

> I'm not trying to help people break the law, but the parole regulations are crazy. You fall off the wagon, have a drink, smoke weed, they grab you up; you're in for three years. Even if you start using drugs again, real drugs, should you be sent back to prison for that? That's not helpful at all. So you come to me. For those times when you drink a little too much, or smoke weed, you know, because anything at all in your system will set off the machine.

Jokingly, he noted that this side business encouraged him to stay away from drinking or using drugs: "When your urine is worth something, you can't just put anything in your body. If you sell one dirty bag, you're done."

Rakim also described his efforts to help men on parole in quite political terms, insisting that the men he supplied with clean urine were being wrongfully deprived of full citizenship rights. Indeed, some of the other people helping to supply legally diminished young men regard themselves as resisting police who act as an occupying force in the Black community, and helping to combat a prison system that is a key site for racial injustice. One parole officer I interviewed referred to the Underground Railroad when describing his efforts to smuggle goods to inmates. Others, like Janine who worked at the courthouse, seemed moved by a personal relationship to make an exception for a particular person.

In contrast, some of the prison guards I spoke with expressed considerable hostility toward inmates, and frustration at the inherent tensions in their jobs. One guard reasoned that the risk of physical violence at the hands of prisoners justified the extra money he earned selling cell phones and drugs to them. He and his coworkers viewed the money they earned from inmates under the table as a way of sticking it to their employers and making lemonade out of lemons.

Still others may feel alternately sickened by the money they take from desperate inmates and parolees, justified on personal or political grounds, and guilty about the risks their services pose to people already so vulnerable. During our chat over a drink, the halfway house guard shared his complex and conflicting motives and feelings about taking money to sneak men out at night:

It's a broken system. On a good day, I think I'm doing something for justice, something for the brothers. These men are locked up because they didn't pay their court fees, or they got drunk and failed [their piss test]. They've been locked up since they were kids. Then they come home to this shit [the halfway house], sleeping one on top of the other, no money, no clothes. And the rules they have to follow—nobody could follow those rules. It's a tragedy. It's a crime against God. Sometimes I think, in fifty years we are going to look back on this and, you know, that this was wrong. And everybody who supported this—their judgment will come. So I think, each night I give a man is a night he remembers he's a human being, not an animal. And most of these guys, they've got a few weeks or a few months before they go back in. You can say a night out is a small thing, but it's a big thing, too. And each guy who sleeps out is one less guy in the rooms. We're fifty-three over capacity now.

On a bad day I think I'm taking from men who have nothing; I'm taking from them to pay my kids' tuition, pay the bills. That's not right. And whatever happens [to them when they leave the halfway house], that's on my head. They get rearrested, shot, I did that.

Regardless of the meaning that participants in the underground market apply to these exchanges, or the stated or unstated reasons they undertake them, we must acknowledge that the criminal justice arm of the state extends beyond the persons who are the direct targets of the police, the courts, or the prisons, and even beyond their families. A large number of people provide underground assistance to men running from the police or going through the courts and the jails. Through these illicit exchanges, they, too, become involved in the "dirty" world.

The assistance they provide may give them some sense of contributing to those less fortunate, or even of participating in an underground political movement against the overreach of the police and the prisons. But they also come to rely on legally precarious people for income, and by extension on the criminal justice system that seeks these people and confines them. Through their financial dealings with people with warrants, or who are in jail, or going through a court case, or out on parole, these brokers of under-the-table goods and services also come to be partially swept up into the criminal justice system, to know about it, to interact with it, and to rely on it. And some find that their business with those caught up in the system renders them vulnerable to arrest. We might think of this as a kind of secondary legal jeopardy, a spilling over of the legal precariousness that the young men who are the main focus of this study face.[4]

SEVEN

Clean People

In the neighborhood of 6th Street, many young men become entangled with the police, the courts, the parole board, and the prisons. Their girlfriends and female relatives sustain raids and interrogations, and spend some amount of time managing these men's legal affairs. Still others in the area come to orient themselves around the police and the prisons because they are providing underground support to the legally compromised people around them.

And yet, the neighborhood also contains many who keep relatively free of the courts and the prisons, who go to school or work every day as the police chase their neighbors through the streets. Not only women manage to stay "clean." While 60 percent of Black men who didn't graduate from high school have been to prison by their midthirties,[1] this means that 40 percent have not. Though many of the men who haven't been incarcerated are nevertheless caught up in court cases and probation sentences, the neighborhood also includes a good number of young people who successfully keep their distance from criminal justice institutions that occupy the time and concern of so many others.

This chapter describes four groups of people in the 6th Street community who are carving out a clean life for themselves as their friends and family go in and out of prison and the police helicopters circle overhead. Through these portraits, I describe the variety of relations that clean people come to have with those involved with the police and the courts, how they make sense of their situation, and how they view those on the other side.

INDOOR GUYS

In March of 2004, Mike got sentenced to one to three years in state prison. As I traveled to visit Mike on the weekends, I kept in touch with some of his friends and relatives who wanted to know how he was doing. But having not yet formed independent relationships with his friends and neighbors, I had no reason to hang out on 6th Street in Mike's absence. As I tried to figure out how to return, I met another group of guys who lived in an adjacent neighborhood, roughly fifteen blocks away.

Lamar lived in a three-bedroom row home with an older man who had some cognitive disabilities. Lamar's mother had arranged for her son to live with this man as part of a small caretaking business that she operated from her house a few blocks away. The disability checks the man received from the government were enough to cover the house's mortgage and his food, so in exchange for living there rent free, Lamar made sure the man ate regular meals and didn't burn the house down with his smoldering cigarettes. In her own home, which she shared with Lamar's father, his mother housed three other men with similar disabilities.

Most evenings after work, Lamar's friends came over to his house to drink beer and play video games. His job as a security guard on the University of Pennsylvania campus meant regular hours and working behind a desk, leaving him free after 5:00 p.m. and full of energy for the evening's video game matches. His house was an ideal bachelor pad—warm and roomy but not too well kept, and with no spouse or mother or children hanging about. The older man he watched spent most of the time in his room, listening to records.

Lamar's friends were roughly the same age as Mike and Chuck, and they, too, hung out together as a unit—but they had no dealings with the police or the courts and, from what I could tell, very few connections with others who did. They had legal jobs: security guard, maintenance man, and convenience store clerk; jobs with uniforms and IDs and the formal paychecks large companies print out. When they lost those jobs, they relied on the generosity of friends and family rather than seeking income in the streets.

These young men drank beer instead of smoking pot; many of them had monthly or random piss tests at their jobs. And rather than shoot the shit on the back steps or in the alleyway, they spent their leisure time playing video games indoors. They didn't need thermal wear or heavy boots in the winter, because their houses were well heated and they spent very little time outside.

As Lamar and his friends parked their cars and made their way toward the house every evening, they passed another group of guys in hoodies and black jeans standing on the corner. They didn't talk to these men, exchanging only a slight nod as they passed. I imagined that these young men were much like the ones I had gotten to know around 6th Street: caught up in the police and the courts, and likely selling drugs hand to hand.

Lamar and his friends played just one video game—Halo. The game's premise was modern-day urban warfare: the players hid from the opposing team and tried to kill them with machine guns. Lamar had two small TVs going in the living room; these he connected to four controllers each, so that eight of his friends could play against each other simultaneously. Like many other single men in their twenties and early thirties, the guys amused themselves with this game until the wee hours three or four nights a week.

Much of the evening's conversation concerned the game:

"Nigga, I *told* you he was coming around the corner! That's *it*, you *done*!"

"I ain't fucking with you no more, man. I can't keep taking these hits . . ."

Lamar's two closest friends were Darnell and Curtis. Darnell was a rotund man in his midtwenties who worked as a manager at a health research firm just outside the city. He told me he made about forty thousand dollars a year, which was less than half the salaries of his two sisters, both of whom had advanced degrees and lived in the 'burbs. Darnell's girlfriend had a young son and, as she often reminded Darnell, had put herself through college while raising him. She was now finishing a degree in legal services. Her baby's father, who lived in Virginia, earned almost six figures, a point she frequently raised with Darnell during their heated arguments over his lack of ambition. In contrast to the scene with his sisters and girlfriend, at Lamar's house Darnell was the richest and the best educated—in fact, other members of the group periodically accused him of thinking he was better than they were and sticking his nose in the air.

Lamar's other close friend, Curtis, was in his late twenties and did maintenance for a chemical plant in South Philly. He told me he had been a drug dealer in his youth, but had abruptly quit when his daughter was born. He spoke little; Darnell referred to him as a "deep well."

The only woman who hung out with this group was a heavy and very pretty woman named Keisha who worked as a phlebotomist at a local hospital. After passing the six-month drug screen at her job, she resumed her pot smoking, though Lamar made her take it out on the back porch.

"I love blood!" she'd say after a few puffs. "It does something for me, what can I say."

From what I could gather, Keisha and Lamar had never been intimate, but had been friends since childhood. After Lamar's best friend died in a car crash during their senior year of high school, Keisha had taken his place as Lamar's closest confidant. She didn't play video games but hung out many evenings with the guys.

In addition to these close friends, Lamar's game nights included two of his cousins. One did heating and air-conditioning repair at the University of Pennsylvania and lived with his girlfriend and their new baby in a middle-class Black suburb just inside the city. He was also sleeping with Keisha, this relationship having started long before he met the mother of his child. Keisha had a live-in boyfriend, and saw Lamar's cousin on the weekends at Lamar's house. His cousin explained to me that Keisha could never be his official, full-time girlfriend, because she hung out with men too much, plus she was a cheater. Keisha was also about one hundred pounds heavier than his baby-mom, and he enjoyed her fuller figure in private more than in public. For her part, Keisha seemed happy with her live-in boyfriend, so long as she could still see Lamar's cousin on the weekends.

Lamar's other cousin was a thin young man of eighteen. This cousin had grown up mainly in a group home, and was unemployed for most of the time I knew him. Near the end of my time in the neighborhood, though, he landed a job at a downtown Wawa, a popular convenience and hoagie chain. Lamar and I often visited him there, and sometimes picked him up from his shift, since he had no car.

Bit by bit I came to learn about Lamar's family. His mother, the woman who owned the house in which he lived and who ran the caretaking business, was actually his adopted mother—his birth mother had given him up when he was a small boy, owing to her crack addiction and poverty. Lamar's father was a continuing crack user, and was supported entirely by Lamar's adopted mother, who cared for him as well as three other men with mental disabilities. He'd come to Lamar's house about once a week to drink beer with the guys. He bobbed and weaved and smiled a lot, and Lamar tolerated him with kindness and patience. At one point when discussing with me his cousin's upbringing in the group home, Lamar said, "If not for my mom, that would have been me. That woman's a saint."

One thing that distinguished Lamar and his friends from other groups of guys who played video games together—for example, the young men I'd encountered in the dorms of Penn's campus—was that they lived in a neighborhood in which lots of other young men were getting arrested and locked up. Their indoor life, with its legal pastimes and thrills, meant that they weren't out in the streets. Indeed, when Lamar or his friends would run into someone they hadn't seen in a while, their answer to the question "How you doing?" was often "Staying out of trouble." Perhaps this signified that although they might be unemployed or not advancing in their careers, they weren't out there getting locked up, and this in itself was an accomplishment.

This isn't to say that Lamar and his friends had no dealings with the justice system whatsoever. A few months after we met, Lamar completed the payments on some speeding tickets and recovered his driver's license. Another one of his friends had his license suspended for an unpaid moving violation and was working on getting it back. But this seemed to be the extent of their legal entanglements and civic diminishment. After eight months spending most of my evenings at Lamar's house, I hadn't taken a single field note that contained the word *police*. No officers busted down Lamar's door. I never observed him receiving a phone call that a friend or relative had gotten booked. Once in a while we heard sirens outside, but no one looked up from the video game to investigate, even when they seemed close by. Whomever the cops were looking for, it didn't concern them.

One outdoor activity in the warmer months that did involve a few brushes with the authorities was drag racing. Lamar and his friends liked to refurbish old European cars, especially Volkswagens, and soup them up to be racing cars. They spent hours adding accessories or changing the suspension, and then we'd sometimes go out to the races at the empty strips of road out past the airport. Some of the guys who came to the races were Cambodian and Laotian, others Latino. Once we also drove to a convention in Maryland. Drag racing could have gotten them arrested or injured, but mostly Lamar's friends came to the races as spectators, to admire the other cars and watch the races. We always managed to leave before the cops showed up, and compared to the professional and leisure activities of the 6th Street Boys, the drag racing seemed quite benign.

Nine months into my time with Lamar and his friends, I observed an incident that revealed a great deal about where they stood in relation to the guys I had come to know over on 6th Street. It was the only time I saw any one of them come face to face with a man on the run.

Lamar called me one afternoon and said, "I got some news."

"Oh yeah?"

"Yup. I just found out my mom died."

"What? Oh my god. I'm so sorry."

Turns out it wasn't his *mom* mom who had passed but his birth mother, a woman he barely knew.

Lamar went back and forth about whether to attend the funeral— he'd been recently fired from his security guard job for lateness and didn't have money for a suit, or even black pants. Could he just wear jeans? His friends and I finally persuaded him to go, and to show our support, his cousin, Keisha, and I came along. We all wore jeans.

The funeral was held in a very small church, the coffin made of simple wood. Lamar hardly recognized anyone there, as most of the attendees were from his birth mother's extended family, which he had never gotten to know. Later that day, he admitted to me that his adopted mother had paid for the bulk of the funeral and burial costs, though she hadn't attended the service because she felt she might be unwelcome.

Partway through the sermon, a man a bit younger than Lamar came to sit next to us in the pew. He wore coveralls and smelled of marijuana and clove cigarettes. His hair clumped haphazardly around his face, and he peered around at the other funeral attendees with visible concern. Lamar smiled an embarrassed and knowing smile, and told us that this man was his brother. We introduced ourselves to him and shook his hand.

"How you been doing?" this man asked Lamar.

"You know, staying out of trouble."

"Yeah? That's good, that's good."

"Yup. How you been doing?"

"Hanging in there. I can't stay too long—I got, like, three warrants on me."

"Oh yeah?" Lamar said, with a small chuckle.

"Yeah. I just wanted to, you know . . ."

"Okay. Well, it was good to see you."

"Yup . . ."

When the man left, I asked Lamar how long it had been since he'd seen his brother.

"Maybe six years. No, longer than that, 'cause Dre [his best friend from high school, who had been killed in a car accident] was still alive. Must be like ten years."

"Does he live nearby?"

"I have no idea. All I know is he better stay the hell away from me. I can't get mixed up in any of that. Dipping and dodging the police and all that."

"I know that's right," Keisha said.

Lamar's cousin shook his head, acknowledging the importance of steering clear of such people.

A CLEAN FAMILY IN ISOLATION

When I first met Miss Deena, she managed the basement level of a cafeteria on the western edge of Penn's campus. There, she directed ten or so staff to serve sandwiches and boxed salads along with cookies, fruit, and granola bars. We met in 2001, when she hired me to make sandwiches and ring up orders. At 4'9" and approaching sixty-five, she commanded great respect from her employees, and led with a quiet and dignified reasonableness.

Miss Deena lived with her daughter, Rochelle, and her daughter's son, Ray, in a long-established mixed-income Black neighborhood. Rochelle was in her midforties, and recently laid off from a job as a classroom assistant at an elementary school. Ray was a senior in high school, and hoped to go to college.

Like many people devoted to taxing jobs, Miss Deena seemed lonely and tired at home, uncomfortable even. She would return from her shift looking exhausted and walking gingerly, her energy clearly spent. After exchanging a few pleasantries, she'd change into her slippers, pat her small dog Dutchess, make herself a bowl of leftovers, and retreat upstairs to her bedroom, which her daughter and grandson dubbed "the fortress." Sometimes she'd contemplate visiting the retirement community two blocks away to socialize; maybe she'd meet some nice man at their bingo night. On Saturday afternoons, she'd often iron her clothes for church, only to rehang them the next morning, not having the energy to go.

Though Miss Deena was the financial provider in her household, little of the respect she commanded at work seemed to extend to the home she shared with her daughter and grandson. Rochelle and Ray seemed to dominate the social life of the home, using the kitchen and dining room to cook, go online, or watch TV. Occasionally, Miss Deena would come down and try to chat with them, but she often dozed off where she sat. Other times, she'd begin a story about the ceiling leak at work or her troubles with diabetes, but her daughter or grandson would interrupt her before she could finish, or simply walk out of the room. With shame, I also found myself guilty of this behavior; something about her way of telling stories made it difficult to stay focused.

From September to December of 2002, I spent two to three evenings a week at Miss Deena's house, first as a tutor for her two grandchildren, then gradually also as a guest. With her grandson Ray, it was SAT prep, college essays, and financial aid forms, to which his mother was tirelessly devoted. And in my sessions with her granddaughter Aisha, who stopped by Miss Deena's after school, we concentrated on homework and strategies for staying away from the girls with whom she was getting into fights.

The first encounter that I observed the family to have with a person caught up in the criminal justice system occurred one Tuesday afternoon in early November. The doorbell rang, and Ray got up to answer it. He didn't invite the man in but spoke to him outside, with the door half-shut behind him. As he spoke to the man, Rochelle leaned toward the door with what looked to me like trepidation.

"I just want to see if it's who I think it is," she said.

When Ray came back, she looked at his face and said, "I knew it."

Ray told us that the man had asked for Tyrell, though he didn't explain to me who Tyrell was. Before Ray could tell us what else the man had said, Rochelle launched into a series of stories about him: how he and his wife would come over empty handed and eat up the whole house; how his wife was "country" but street smart and eventually left him; how he'd come by the house even then, just by himself; how he had given a bath to his fourteen-year-old daughter when he said her armpits smelled. From what I could gather, this man was a friend of Tyrell's, though it was still unclear who Tyrell was.

Apparently, this man who hadn't been allowed inside had just returned from jail, or perhaps a halfway house. Rochelle explained to me how he had held a great job at the electrical plant, but lost the position when he was charged with sexual harassment for picking up a female coworker and moving her out of the way to get to the Coke machine. Rochelle also didn't like that he had once come to the house and insulted Ray, telling him he should mind his manners and behave. How dare he insult her son in his own house, in front of everyone! Rochelle described the man as "sort of bipolar." Miss Deena said simply, "We still pray for him, but he can't be trusted."

Talk of the visit passed; the family resumed their previous conversations. It wasn't until a month later that I learned that the Tyrell this man had asked for was Miss Deena's son and Aisha's father, currently sitting in prison upstate. His crime, Rochelle told me, was dressing up as her, his own sister, walking into her bank, and attempting to empty her twelve-hundred-dollar savings account. "He had stockings on and everything," she laughed half-heartedly. "Even a wig!"

For this attempted robbery, Tyrell had been in prison for five years.

It's very likely that Miss Deena's family had been making a special effort to conceal the fact of their imprisoned family member from me and spoke about him more frequently when I wasn't around. But that any knowledge of Miss Deena's imprisoned son could be kept from someone spending twenty hours a week in their living room, tutoring this man's daughter, is important information—a testament to their success in carving out a life apart. In the families on 6th Street that I would later come to know, it would have been impossible to conceal such a thing, because daily life is flooded with court dates, prison visits, phone calls from probation or parole officers, parole regulations, and police raids.

Also significant was the deep embarrassment Miss Deena's family appeared to feel about Tyrell's imprisonment. For many of the neighborhood families jail and prison were simply the places where many relatives were located.

Once the topic of Miss Deena's imprisoned son had been broached, he occasionally came up in conversation. On these days Rochelle would shake her head about him, as if to say, "Yeah, he's my worthless brother. What can you do?"

For Miss Deena and Rochelle, Tyrell's imprisonment seemed a quiet sadness lurking in the background, a reminder of an earlier era in which their lives had been more chaotic and troubled. Sometimes Miss Deena expressed fears about the havoc he might wreak on their calm and stable household if he returned to Philadelphia upon his release. At other times, she expressed shame at how her son had turned out and what he had done. Perhaps she also felt guilty that she could not to steer him in the right direction. But Tyrell seemed more of an offstage emptiness than a daily problem. Nobody went to visit him, and mostly nobody wrote to him, though they did accept his phone calls every so often and read his occasional letter.

One afternoon in December 2002, Aisha drafted a response to her father:

5:30–8:00 pm Miss Deena's House
Aisha lets me in, and I say hi to Dutchess. Miss Deena and her daughter are downstairs in the kitchen when I get there. They are talking about

someone in the hospital. Aisha is working on a letter to send to her father. The letter explained that she was going to be a computer technician when she grew up. Her father had requested this info, and she had been worrying about her reply for some time. The letter also mentioned that she wanted to bake pies and cakes and cookies as good as grandma's. Then it said she wanted to be just like her dad. At the very end, it said, "You told me when you come home you want to start youre won business [*sic*]." That was the last sentence. She signed it and I explained what a P.S. was, which she said she'd like to do, and later we got an envelope from her aunt.

Aisha didn't spend much time talking to her father or writing to him, nor did she ever visit him during the years he was away on the sentence discussed here. But she did occasionally talk about how angry she was at him, or reflect on the things he had said, giving me the sense that her father and his absence were never far from her thoughts.

For Miss Deena, her daughter, Rochelle, and Rochelle's son, Ray, their imprisoned family member seemed rarely to intrude into everyday life. This isn't to say that they didn't think about him, worry about him, or feel ashamed about him—just that on a day-to-day basis, they led their lives separately from his and from the involvement in the courts and the prisons that he required.

A GRANDFATHER LIVING APART

When his three grandsons were sitting in jail, the house quieted down and Mr. George would come outside, sit on the porch, and drink a beer. Sometimes he talked about the neighborhood's better days or about his childhood.

George Taylor, known as Mr. George to his grandsons' friends, had come up from Georgia when he was five. His mother and father worked the cotton fields south of Atlanta; like many sharecroppers, they often came up short at the yearly settle, since the cost of the basic necessities they had bought on credit from the plantation store was more than what they cleared in the fields. Mr. George remembers his father cursing the owner of the small plantation for manipulating the numbers, which his father could not read, and the family leaving late at night for the next farm, his mother hopeful that this one would be better.[2]

The Second World War meant opportunity up North, so with hundreds of thousands of fellow field hands, Mr. George's father boarded a train to Philadelphia. He sent for his wife and three children later that year, once he found work. This was 1943.

For most of Mr. George's childhood, the family lived in a two-room flat in South Philadelphia. His father shoveled coal down at the docks; like many a stevedore, he showed up for work not knowing if he'd get any and faced long hours of backbreaking labor if he did. Mr. George's mother cooked and cleaned house for two white families in downtown Philadelphia. To his father's shame, it was this money that really supported the family. Neither job paid as much as had been promised when the family made the move North during the war.

Mr. George's parents fought a lot in their cramped apartment, but the couple stayed together and had two more children. Mr. George graduated from high school with strong grades and entered the US Army in 1959. Anything to get out of the house, he explained.

Mr. George did well in his newly integrated unit and left the military with a bad knee and an honorable discharge before the Vietnam War began. It was a piece of luck that he never forgot. He applied for a job with the postal service, and worked as a clerk at a branch in Southwest Philadelphia from the age of twenty-one until he retired at sixty-five.

A few years after taking this job, Mr. George bought a three-bedroom row home on a quiet, tree-lined block in the neighborhood of 6th Street, right at the edge of the city limits. At the time, he was raising his young daughter, Linda, alone. His wife had taken off with another man.

Mr. George and his daughter were among the first Black families to move to the neighborhood, and after them came physicians, bank tellers, government workers, and shop owners. Like Mr. George, these middle-class families hoped to escape the crowded and run-down ghetto by moving just past its outer edges.

The move to 6th Street represented the culmination of years of effort for Mr. George and his family, but in many ways his military career, his job at the post office, and now this spacious house in a good neighborhood also exemplified the triumphs of the Civil Rights Movement. Gone were the days of separate drinking fountains, perpetual debt, and police harassment. In one generation, the Taylors had moved from second-class tenant farmers in the Jim Crow South to white-collar respectability in the North.

Not that their new neighbors had exactly welcomed them with open arms. One of the families that moved in shortly after Mr. George and Linda got a brick thrown through their living room window, and Linda refused to sleep in her own bedroom after that.

Mr. George hoped his daughter would grow up in an integrated community, but by the 1980s every white family in the 6th Street neighborhood had packed up and moved. Legal segregation had ended, but not a single white student attended his daughter's school. Even so, 6th Street remained a middle-class area, less violent than other Black neighborhoods nearby, with cleaner sidewalks and better-kept lawns.

In the mid-1980s this, too, began to change. Developers started placing low-income housing in the area, initiatives that the older residents didn't have the political power to resist. It was this second wave of less refined residents, George felt, that set his daughter, Linda, down the wrong path.

By her own account, Miss Linda's father had spoiled her hopelessly as a child, especially after her mother left. She came of age at the height of the crack boom and dropped out of high school during her junior year. The men she dated worked at the bottom of the crack business, which at the time offered decent wages and even the promise of wealth to unemployed young men growing up around 6th Street. Many of her boyfriends also shared her addiction. During a decade of hard living, Linda gave birth to three sons: Chuck in 1984, Reggie in 1987, and Tim in 1991. By this time, the ghetto Mr. George had worked so hard to escape seemed to have grown up around them.

By the late 1980s, the neighborhood of 6th Street and others like it had a heavy police presence. At first Mr. George and his neighbors viewed this as a welcome sign of change: the neighborhood had been neglected by law enforcement for far too long. But as more and more young men disappeared into jail and prison, Mr. George and his neighbors started to question the motivation behind this ramped-up policing. Some suspected that under the cloak of tough-on-crime rhetoric was white discomfort about Black civic and economic incorporation. To put it more bluntly, they figured that white people were not going to accept Black people as full citizens without a fight.[3]

When I met Mr. George's family, the house he shared with his daughter Linda and her three sons had deteriorated well past the point of basic decency. Small roaches and ants crawled incessantly across the countertops and floors, over the couch and TV, and frequently onto the house's inhabitants. The house itself reeked of cigarette smoke, urine, vomit, and alcohol. In the kitchen, cabinets were sticky with grease and dirt; cat urine and feces covered a corner of the floor. Ashtrays in the kitchen, dining room, and living room collected mountains of old cigarette butts and would frequently topple to the floor, dumping their contents into the carpet. Linda refused to throw the butts away, insisting that they were her reserves when she had no money for cigarettes. The upholstered couches, the living room carpet, and the walls were stained a monochromatic brown—the aftermath of years of smoke and dirt. A gaping hole in the floor between the toilet and the tub in the upstairs bathroom made washing up or relieving oneself quite perilous. The floor and wall tile had also crumbled away.

Yet the state of the house's interior was hardly as disconcerting or worrisome as the daily lives of its inhabitants. By my count, the police came to the house thirty-two times over the six years I knew the Taylors. After the police on one of these calls broke the lock on the front door, Miss Linda started sleeping in the living room with a shotgun by her side, in case someone should push the door open and try to rob the family. Also during my time on 6th Street, each of her three sons got into shootouts with other young men in the neighborhood, and for a while afterward Miss Linda did not feel it was safe to walk outside alone.

Amid this chaos, filth, legal drama, and violence, Mr. George somehow succeeded in living a life apart. He would leave in the midmorning and return in the early evening, often bringing his longtime companion home with him. The couple lived in a separate apartment on the second floor, complete with a kitchenette and bathroom Mr. George had built himself during the 1980s. During the day, the heavy door to this apartment stayed firmly shut with the help of a deadbolt. In case his daughter or grandsons should find their way in through the windows, Mr.

George had padlocked his refrigerator. This way, the rest of the family and whoever else they had running through the house couldn't eat up the groceries that his companion brought over on Sunday afternoons.

I had seen Mr. George's apartment only once, when I came up the stairs and knocked on the door to tell him that Brianna, Chuck's girlfriend, was giving birth. As he opened the door, I glimpsed shiny white linoleum floors and a spotless countertop. I'm not sure if he was able to keep the roaches out—they had so deeply infested the rest of the house—but I saw none on the walls or the floor, and the room itself smelled fresh, like clean laundry.

How did these two households coexist under the same roof? After a few years of knowing the Taylors, I noted a number of tacit house rules, which Linda and her boys more or less stuck to—or at least acknowledged when breaking them. One rule was that no friends or partners could live in the house. Mr. George wasn't running a shelter or a hotel for everybody in the neighborhood, he said. An exception was made for Chuck's two daughters, who frequently came to stay for weeks at a time since shortly after their birth. Another rule was that Mr. George would not tolerate loud noise inside the house or outside his window after about 11:00 p.m. Often when we were sitting outside, Chuck or Reggie would tell their friends to pipe down around this time. A third house rule was that if the police ever came looking for one of the boys or a friend of theirs, Mr. George would immediately pick up the phone and alert the police the next time he saw the young man in question. He refused to shield his grandsons from the law.

In supporting the family, Mr. George contributed a great deal: he paid the mortgage, the heating, water, and phone bills. He would not, he said, pay for collect calls from jail or prison and did not allow this service on the landline, which he limited to local calls. He also gave Linda money to buy food and other household items. And he allowed his daughter and grandsons to live in his house rent free, though Miss Linda sometimes persuaded her sons to pay rent directly to her without relaying any to her father.

In the day-to-day activities of his daughter and grandsons, Mr. George didn't appear to intervene much. Miss Linda had free reign of the house, which she considered hers to do with as she deemed fit. Her father didn't tell her to clean the house, nor did he tell her boys what

to do or when to come in at night. So long as his daughter and grandsons weren't bringing the police to his door, what they did was their
business.

In their early teens, Chuck and his younger brother Reggie began selling crack in the neighborhood. Their ready access to the drug seemed
to help control the chaos that their mother's addiction had brought
into their lives. By supplying their mother, they could reduce the number of food stamps she sold to get drugs, and keep her from trading or
selling off their possessions for crack. They could also reduce the number of men she would have sex with in exchange for drugs. Sometimes
these men beat her, and Chuck would come home and get into fights in
an effort to defend her. Through much of this, I gathered, Mr. George
remained up in his apartment.

Mr. George and I had only a few lengthy conversations, but during
those he'd speak about the neighborhood's early years and once in a
while about his childhood. He did not talk about the troubles with his
daughter and grandsons, and he dodged my questions about them the
few times I asked. I wanted to know about the period when his teenage
daughter became addicted to crack and gave birth to his three grandsons. I also wanted to know when and how the house had deteriorated
to its present condition, and how he'd come to allow his daughter and
her sons to live there without having much to do with them.

I was able to piece together some of this family history through the
stories that Chuck and Reggie would occasionally offer. The excerpt
below is taken from field notes in the late summer of 2006, when Chuck
was twenty-two and Reggie was eighteen.

Chuck and I are on our way to visit Reggie at CFCF [Curran-Fromhold Correctional Facility], the county jail on State Road. As we drive through West
Philly, we pass a park with a couple of swing sets and a basketball court.

"I used to play in this park," Chuck comments.

"Did you used to live around here?"

"Yeah, for a little bit."

I'm surprised by this. In four years of knowing the family, I had never
heard Chuck or his two younger brothers mention living anywhere but
their grandfather's house on 6th Street. I say as much, and Chuck replies:

"We were staying here with Reggie's dad. My grandpop kicked us out and shit, and we went to this homeless shelter for a minute [a little while] and I guess my mom wanted to get out of there, so she called Reggie's dad and he came and got us. He used to live right there in that building."

I look at the dilapidated gray and brown high-rise building and nod my head.

"That was the first time I ever saw somebody get shot."

Chuck pauses after this, and I wait to see if he will go on. He doesn't.

"Who got shot?"

"Reggie's dad."

"Who shot him?"

"My grandpop."

Another pause.

I ask, "Over what?"

"I remember I was happy as shit to leave the shelter, but then he used to beat her, like, not just slap her, but really fuck her up, and I used to be mad, like, and try to jump on him and pull him off of her."

"So you used to protect her."

"Not really. I couldn't do no real damage, 'cause I was only like seven. Yeah, seven, 'cause Tim was just born. One night, he was beating her and he just kept going and then he started choking her and I called Pop-Pop [Mr. George]. Pop-Pop came over there, shot him three times in the stomach. Then he said get your stuff."

"Then you went back to live with him on 6th Street."

"Yep."

"When you saw him get shot, were you scared?"

"No, I was happy. I was relieved."

"Did Pop-Pop [Mr. George] catch a case?"

"No. Reggie's pop never reported him. He never did no time or nothing."[4]

From stories like these, I came to understand that while Mr. George's general policy was to live alongside his daughter and grandsons without much interference, he would occasionally step in—sometimes for their benefit, such as the time he rescued the family from an abusive man and agreed to house them once again, and sometimes for his own, such as in late 2006 when, after repeated raids on the house, he cleared out his daughter's belongings and told her she could not return if she continued to hide Reggie from the police.

After these raids, Chuck and Reggie were sitting in county jail and state prison, respectively. A month later, their younger brother Tim got booked outside the Chinese takeout store for resisting arrest and possession of a small amount of crack. In the absence of his three grandsons, the house became strangely quiet, and Mr. George began sitting outside on the second-floor porch. One evening the following fall, after I'd come back from visiting Chuck in county jail, we sat down and had a beer and a cigarette:

I'll tell you. [*shakes his head*] I feel sorry for the man with sons. What's the use of raising a boy today? You feed him and clothe him and teach him how to ride a bike and you done checked his tests, then at fifteen they shipping him off to juvie. You don't know when you going to see him again. Maybe he makes it to 18 before they take him away. And once they grab him, that's it! Your son locked in a cage, just sitting. And the worst part about it is, you still supporting him! Even though you can't see him, you can't watch him go to school, go to work, have kids of his own, he can't do nothing but just sit, and you still supporting him. You put money on his books, visitation, he come home for a few months, go back in. You worry about him, what's happening in there. You hope he come home and do what he's supposed to be doing. You hope and pray he don't tear your life apart, put *you* in jail. That's the most you can hope for. Or you say I can't do it, I'm not getting involved. I wash my hands. They say it's changed now with Obama, it's a new era. But can't nobody protect our sons, not even the president. I'm telling you, if I was thirty years younger, I'd be praying for girls. If I had a son I'd be done lost my mind by now. I'd start mourning and praying the day he was born.[5]

*   *   *

Each of the people described in the chapter thus far manage to insulate themselves from the police, the courts, and the prisons as well as from their legally entangled neighbors and family members. Some, like Miss Deena and Lamar, accomplish this by cutting off ties to sons and brothers who are either sitting in prison or living on the run. Others, like Mr. George, continue to provide support from a distance, even if that distance is only the space of a thick door and a deadbolt. The next section concerns a young man who remained deeply connected to his neighborhood friends, yet managed to go to college and secure a well-paying job while they dodged the police and cycled in and out of jail.

A CLEAN MAN WITH DIRTY FRIENDS

Directly across the shared alleyway from Mr. George, his daughter, and his grandsons on 6th Street lived a mother and her three children, the youngest of whom was a young man named Josh. Josh was three years older than Miss Linda's oldest son, Chuck; the two had played together as children and remained close all through high school. Josh's mother, who worked in administration at the Hospital of the University of Pennsylvania, had two daughters with her first husband before marrying a second time and giving birth to Josh. Neither marriage lasted longer than a few years, so she raised the family on her Penn salary and intermittent child support payments. When Chuck's mother went out searching for drugs, he would often walk across the shared alleyway and eat at Josh's. When Miss Linda didn't come home for a few days, he'd take his younger brother Tim with him, and spend a few nights there.

When I started hanging out on the block, Josh was twenty years old, and getting his degree in business administration from a historically Black college in Upstate New York. When he returned home for the holidays, he'd spend evenings with Chuck and his other neighbors. A tall man who spoke quietly and laughed easily, Josh seemed eager to reunite with his boys from back home, and quickly fell into their routine of late-night drinking and marijuana smoking. For their part, these young men seemed happy that one of their own had made it. They didn't expect him to partake in the drama of the streets. When they were in shootouts, for example, nobody looked to Josh to strap up.

Right out of college, Josh moved back home and began working for a doctor who was conducting trials for a pharmaceutical company. His college girlfriend had moved back to Virginia and given birth to their son, so he traveled back and forth a few times a year to visit them, and his son came up for Halloween and most of the summer. Josh seemed to always be talking about the boy, and to look forward to their visits. They'd speak on the phone a few times a week.

Josh worked long hours, so we didn't see him much. Then the cops stopped him while he was driving with two friends from 6th Street. The officers searched the car and found a small amount of cocaine behind the front seat, and all three men were arrested. Josh made bail quickly enough to keep his job with the doctor, and the case went to trial a year later. The doctor let him take off work to attend the almost monthly court dates, and at the sentencing persuaded the judge to give Josh three years of parole instead of time in prison. Later that year, this doctor also got the judge to expunge Josh's record—the only time I had heard of a judge doing this. Later, Josh described these events as a turning point: if it were not for this man, he would have done time and come home a convict.

In the summer of 2007, Chuck was shot and killed outside the Chinese takeout store, where he had gone to buy dinner for himself and his younger brother Tim.[6] Tim had been standing just a few feet away and watched his brother fall. The 4th Street Boy who shot Chuck had apparently become fearful that Chuck, though unarmed, was going to shoot him first. Actually, for the past two months Chuck had been working hard to squash the ongoing conflict between the 4th Street Boys and the 6th Street Boys that had begun a few years earlier, when Tino killed Jay-Jay at a dice game.

It could be that Chuck's peacekeeping efforts in this and other conflicts made his death more of a blow for his family and friends and for the neighborhood as a whole than the deaths of other young men whose funerals we attended every few months. For Tim, Chuck's death meant the loss of the only father figure he had known.

There was little time for Tim to grieve. With many of the core members of the 6th Street Boys locked up that summer, the expectation to avenge Chuck's death landed squarely on his fifteen-year-old shoulders. In anticipation of his retaliation, Tim received near daily calls and texts from the 4th Street Boys that they were going to kill him, and by the end of July he had been in three shootouts. It was a chilling way to come of age, and one that those of us watching events unfold seemed unable to stop.

At the time of Chuck's death, Josh had already moved out of his mother's house on 6th Street and was living with a roommate in the suburbs. He had landed a job doing administrative work for the medical research branch of a pharmaceutical company, and was earning a sixty-thousand-dollar salary. He began getting calls at work from Tim, who said that 4th Street was shooting at him and he needed a place to stay. A couple of times, Josh took a long lunch break to pick Tim up on 6th Street and take him to his apartment for safekeeping. Meanwhile, some of Josh's coworkers found out about his expunged record for cocaine possession. To make matters worse, they overheard several of his conversations with Tim about flying bullets. Josh soon lost his job and went on unemployment for a number of months, and then for a bit longer when President Obama extended it. Didn't help, he said later, that he was the only Black man working on the floor.

Josh could no longer afford his apartment outside the city and moved back in with his mother on 6th Street. In the first few months, he'd frequently talk about the wrong moves he'd made, or how things might have gone differently. He seemed to feel that he was largely responsible for losing the job and had been insufficiently appreciative when he had it.

A few weeks after Josh moved back to the neighborhood, we were walking to the corner store to buy beer when a young man of maybe fourteen approached him in the checkout line.

"Heard you was back on the block. Welcome home."

"Yeah, I just moved back not too long ago."

"That's what's up. You back to take what's yours, Old Head?"

Josh's face crumbled, clearly humiliated at the suggestion that he might go back to selling crack, as he'd done as a teenager.

"No, I'm not back back. I'm just job-hunting right now . . ."

"Okay, okay," the young man replied, unconvinced.

When we got back to the block, Josh laughed it off, but in that moment all the confidence and pride of being the neighborhood success seemed to flood out of him. Years later, he would bring up this incident as one of the most humiliating of his adult life.

During two years of unemployment, Josh occupied himself by looking after the guys on 6th Street as well as their struggling family members. He visited his friends in jail and prison; he wrote them letters and accepted phone calls; he sent them some of his unemployment money for their commissary.

After Chuck's death, Josh tried to keep Tim from getting killed, which was more than a fulltime job. He also tried to persuade Miss Linda to allow Tim to go to Virginia and stay with relatives, at least until the drama died down. But she refused to let Tim leave, and accused Josh of trying to take her last remaining son away from her.

Finally, Josh got Miss Linda to take Tim down South, away from the dangers of 6th Street. On the morning of their departure, we sent them off on a Greyhound bus with a cooler filled with sandwiches, chips, and fruit. But Miss Linda and Tim ran out of money two weeks later, and came back home. Apparently Miss Linda could find no relative willing to keep Tim, including his father, who had promised to do so before they made the trip.

"He a fuckin' nut," Tim said, hiding his hurt.

Josh and I started traveling back and forth together to visit Reggie and other incarcerated friends, pooling gas money and sharing the driving. Together, we tried to keep Tim safe from the guys who killed his brother. We hadn't been close in the years before this, but with Chuck dead, and many more of our mutual friends in jail, we were united by our bond to the men no longer with us. We also commiserated and joked about the difficult relatives these friends had left behind, with Chuck's heavily crack-addicted mother, Miss Linda, being first on that list.

As we drove together to jails and prisons, I soon realized that Josh faced a series of dilemmas in dealing with men on the block as well as with their relatives. These weren't the same dilemmas that young men dipping and dodging the authorities faced—they were particular to a clean person with dirty friends, not unlike some of the dilemmas I myself had experienced in the neighborhood over the years.

First was the dilemma of balancing his job and his middle-class life with the chaos and emergencies of his poor and legally entangled friends and neighbors. This he'd failed at when his efforts to help Tim after Chuck's death cost him his corporate job.

But Josh's clean identity also meant that people asked him to do things that they couldn't ask of dirty people. After Chuck died, his paternal grandmother gave a speech at his midnight vigil, urging his friends and neighbors not to retaliate. She seemed to mean it at the time, but in private the next day she asked Josh to buy the guns that the remaining 6th Street Boys would need to support the coming war with the guys who had shot her grandson. As the only member of the 6th Street Boys with no felony convictions, pending criminal charges, or parole supervision, it fell on him, she said, to gear up. Josh was torn. Should he buy these guns? Guns that would avenge his best friend? These guns wouldn't be just for vengeance, either. By this point the friends of the man who had shot Chuck were driving by 6th Street, shooting at innocent bystanders and leaving neighborhood residents terrified to come outside. The 6th Street Boys needed something to fire back with. In the end, however, Josh didn't buy the guns—or if he did, I never found out about it.

Another time, a guy on the block came to Josh and asked to borrow three hundred dollars because the cops had taken the money he needed to pay back his "connect" (supplier) when they stopped and searched him. He said that the man he'd gotten the crack from would probably kill him if he couldn't pay him back. Should Josh give this man the money and help him avoid a beating or even death? But then he'd have access to more crack on commission, which could get him locked up, or shot later on. In this case Josh didn't loan the man the money, but he did let him hide in his apartment for a week.

Bail was another tough decision Josh faced. These payments require the payer to show ID at the bail counter, so the person who takes the money to the basement of the Criminal Justice Center in downtown Philadelphia needs to have a real ID, and one that isn't going to return holds or warrants when it's run through the system. Not surprisingly, then, when a young man on 6th Street got arrested, his family often would gather the money and ask Josh to go to the office and pay it. Should Josh help bail out his neighbors and their family members? What if they were shot, or rearrested for an even worse crime, while home? On the other hand, he also expressed his concern that if he didn't help the family get the young man out, whatever happened to the young man in jail would be his doing, like the time a neighbor was stabbed in the stomach in the jail cafeteria the week after Josh refused to help his family make bail and get him home.

In July of 2011, Josh's bad luck broke. After two full years of unemployment at the height of the recession, he landed a job with another medical company. Within six months he was promoted to assistant director. He again became too busy to look after the 6th Street Boys or spend his days arguing with their difficult and addicted relatives. He got full custody of his son, who came to live with him in his mother's house.

*   *   *

Josh's ties to dirty people clearly played a role in his losing a well-paying management job in the suburbs. Being on intimate terms with legally compromised young men also presented him with a series of ethical dilemmas that those with their own legal entanglements didn't face, and which at times caused him considerable distress. On the other hand, Josh's devotion to the guys he had grown up with made the years of his unemployment more meaningful and fulfilling than they otherwise might have been. And this community welcomed him back whenever, in the subsequent years, he was spit out of the formal labor market.

THE FANTASY (AND REALITY) OF BEING CLEAN

Those walking around with a warrant or a pending court case often blame life's disappointments on their legal entanglements. That is, dirty people often imagine that if they could just get past these difficulties, many of their other problems would go away: life would be easier, or better, or not so disappointing. Just as people in prison plan the good times they will have when they get out, or the straight line they will walk upon release, so those on the outside often talk about all the great things they will do once their warrant is lifted, their case dismissed, or their probation term ended. As a corollary, they sometimes assume that clean people have every opportunity for success open to them. In Mike's words, clean people attend more weddings than funerals. If clean people aren't leading the good life, it's no one's fault but their own.

These beliefs aren't entirely untrue: research has shown that those who have gone to prison do suffer from the experience, socially, civically, and economically, as do their families. And because those who avoid incarceration tend to be better educated, better employed, and better paid, the perception that clean people are better off is also accurate. But the rosy image that dirty people hold of clean people's lives is not always matched by their lived experience.

For Miss Deena's family, life was filled with disappointments. But they were the older, more hidden injuries of class, race, and gender, not the more visible and readily blamable ones that accompany a compromised legal status. A few of these disappointments are worth mentioning here, as they have stayed with me despite the more traumatic events I later encountered on 6th Street with the kinds of people Miss Deena and her family were careful to avoid.

The first misfortune I witnessed at Miss Deena's concerned her grandson Ray. When we met, he was in his senior year of high school, and studying hard in the hope of going to college. His best friend, Cory, lived a few blocks away and spent a lot of time at Ray's house, though he was quite shy around Ray's family. Ray's mom once mentioned that she was happy to feed Cory, because his family had a lot of kids and really didn't have the money for a growing boy.

Like many teenagers, Ray and Cory were looking forward to the events and occasions that mark the coming of age: getting a driver's license, moving out of the house, going to college, and, of course, attending the prom. What set Ray apart from Cory, and from many of the teenagers I had come to know, was that at seventeen he seemed convinced of his own bright future. Perhaps his mother truly had succeeded in insulating him from the violence and poverty of neighborhood life, or in carving out a path for him that would lead out of it. Ray looked forward to graduation and to college with confidence, as if both were well within his reach.

Months before prom season, Ray began talking about the dance—who he'd take and what he'd wear. He wanted matching outfits for him and his date, which he planned to design himself and get made by a local tailor. When I'd come over for SAT prep tutoring, he would show me his sketches of the different outfits, and I'd weigh in on the length and fabric. The one he finally settled on looked a bit like a Batman costume to me, but he seemed very enthusiastic about it.

Ray was eyeing two girls to be his date: Charlene, his on-again, off-again girlfriend, and Desiree, the girl who cut and braided his hair. He had a big crush on Desiree, and was hoping to get up the courage to ask her out in the coming months.

Every detail of the event was of great importance. One afternoon, we had a lengthy conversation about corsages, in which Ray lamented that girls change their hair so often nowadays that it would be very hard to plan the correct corsage in advance. His mother overheard our conversation and joked that Ray inherited a love of nice clothes and fancy occasions from her. She used to live for this kind of thing.

As the prom drew nearer, problems began cropping up in the plans. I had taken Ray and Cory to the Department of Motor Vehicles a number of times to work through the costly and lengthy process of obtaining a driver's license, but after we obtained the necessary doctor's form and assembled all the other required documentation, Ray failed the computer permit test despite months of studying. A month later he failed it a second time, dashing all hope of driving his date to the prom himself. Cory had a learner's permit, but it kept expiring because he couldn't afford the thirty dollars to take the driver's test. I took him twice to get the permit renewed, but he finally had to let it lapse when his doctor's form became invalid after one year. At that point, he couldn't afford a new doctor's form or the fee to take the driving test.

Around this time, Desiree's boyfriend got shot in the hip, and according to Ray, she entered a period of prolonged depression. She refused to go to the prom with Ray or with anyone, preferring to "practically live" at the hospital.

As if this weren't enough, a week later Ray had to abandon his plans for a custom-made suit when he discovered that the tailor wanted three hundred dollars to make it. In fact, he couldn't afford to buy a regular suit and shoes, or even to rent them. Finally, he admitted to me that even if he somehow came up with the money to rent a suit, he wouldn't be able to find a date who could afford her own sixty-dollar ticket. He couldn't pay for another person's in addition to his own.

Ray and Cory began saying that they didn't want to go to the prom after all. The weekend before the event, Ray told me they were planning on going to an "anti-prom" party at a friend's house, which was infinitely preferable to the corniness of a prom being held in "a warehouse in South Philly."

"I never wanted to go," Cory informed me. "I'm not into the school thing, that's Ray." Later he said, "There ain't nobody to go with! All the pretty girls graduated last year."

When I asked Ray's mom about the prom, she mentioned nothing about the high cost, saying only, "Yeah, I guess he doesn't want to go anymore, he thought it would be stupid. I kept telling him he'd regret it."

On the night of prom, Ray called me around 9:30.

"Are you busy?" he said.

"No."

"Can you give us a ride to South Philly?"

"For what?"

"For the prom."

"I thought you were going to that other party."

"He's not having it. His mom came home, I think."

"Oh."

"So will you take us? It's just on 16th and Passyunk."

"How are you going to get in?"

"We're not going in the prom. This girl I know is having an after-party down the shore, so I'm gonna meet everybody there."

"Okay, what time?"

"Now? If you aren't doing anything . . ." Ray said, rather sheepishly.

I picked up Ray and Cory, who was wearing a pretty threadbare sweatshirt. Ray carried a duffel bag, which I assumed contained their change of clothes and maybe some alcohol. They gave no explanation for their change of heart, nor did I ask for any. We drove to the prom location, which did indeed seem to be a warehouse, and parked in the large lot, full of cars and even a few limos.

"Can you pull up closer?" Ray said.

"To what?"

"To the door!"

"Okay."

We waited pretty quietly for about ten minutes as Ray and Cory watched the two large metal doors on a dimly lit side of the concrete building. Then the doors opened and a young woman in a sheer purple dress came out, walking carefully and adjusting her hair. Cory and Ray leaped out of the car and then stopped short, hesitating to approach the door, and finally leaned against the car. I realized then that Cory was clutching a disposable camera. Young women in dresses and heels began to emerge with their dates into the night, and Cory and Ray talked in whispers about who looked good, and who had come with whom.

They saw a couple they knew, and walked over shyly to say hi. Ray shook the guy's hand, and Cory told the girl how nice she looked.

This continued for about forty minutes, and halfway through Cory used up his roll of film. He seemed happy to be posing with the girls in all their finery.

Then Ray saw a girl he liked, and he turned to us with an embarrassed smile. Cory whispered, "Go up to her!" which he finally did. The girl give him a hug, keeping a fair distance between them so as not to smudge her makeup or dislodge her hair, and he came back smiling. Then he spotted the group who were having the party down the shore, and asked me to pop the trunk. As Ray got his bag, Cory opened the passenger side of my car.

"What are you doing?"

"Getting in the car."

"Wait, you're not going to the after-party?"

Cory shook his head.

"So why did you come with Ray, then?"

"For the Let Out," Cory said.

I looked confused.

"To see everybody come out," he tried to explain.

It was an uncomfortable ride home. Cory looked bleakly out the window most of the way, and I couldn't think of a single topic to lift the mood. All I could think was how adamantly he had argued that he wanted no part of the prom, and then how he had come anyway, to watch from the parking lot as his wealthier classmates made their grand exit. I wished I hadn't conveyed my expectation that he'd be going to the after-party, because now he had that added shame. At one point in the thirty-minute drive home, though, his face lit up a bit and he said, "I got pictures with, like, eight different girls."

Both Ray and Cory graduated from high school that spring, and Ray enrolled in a historically Black college down South. His mother and grandmother proudly drove him down there in early September and got his dorm room all set up. Then after six months, Ray dropped out— the family could no longer afford the tuition, and his student loans weren't nearly enough. Now he works as a security guard at the mall, and as of this writing has paid off about half his college debt.

The second disappointment that has stuck with me through the years concerns Ray's grandmother, Miss Deena.

One afternoon in late April of 2002, Miss Deena and I were in the kitchen when she began to talk about how hard it was working at the cafeteria. I asked her what she was doing that summer, hoping that she'd be getting some time off. She confirmed that she would be taking some vacation days. I asked where she might spend them, and she said she was thinking of visiting her sister in California, who said she would pay for her ticket.

"California's nice," I say.

"Or I might go to Florida, to see my friend."

"Oh yeah?"

"He asked me to marry him. We were going to get married, but then we didn't, and he moved to Florida."

I had never heard anything about Miss Deena's love life before. I am embarrassed to say that at twenty years old, the idea that Aisha's grandmother might have a love life hadn't occurred to me.

"When did he move?"

"About a few years ago, when he retired."

"Oh."

"He just got strange, so I didn't go with him."

The discussion turned to the summer cutbacks, and her concerns about what would happen to her staff members if management laid them off. She told me how in the summertime it's really hard, because the Penn students have gone home, and the area high school kids, who are part of college prep programs, come in. And they are bad, really bad. They get into fights in the dining room, all kinds of trouble. Then Miss Deena circled back to her called-off engagement and the man who moved away.

"He was a really nice man. I met him at the cafeteria. He collected Westerns, loved Western movies—new ones, classic ones, those really hard-to-find ones. But he didn't watch them, he just collected them. He was going to watch them when he retired. That's what he got them for. He had, like, must have been over two hundred. And I used to ask to watch them, but after a while I just gave up because he really didn't want to watch them yet, he was saving them."

I nodded for her to go on.

"So he retired and we were planning to go to Florida. And then one night, someone broke into his house and stole all his movies."

"My god."

"I asked him what he was going do if he found him, and he says, 'Deena, I won't tell you what I'ma do with him, but I will make it so's he don't do that to nobody else.'"

"Wow."

"And that scared me, 'cause I thought: what is he going to do to me if I do something to upset him or make him mad?"

"Right."

"And then he bought some barbed wire, you know that wire that you get all caught up in that they use for fences and everything, and he bought that new kind, the kind that really gets you so's you can't get out, and do you know, Alice, he put it all over his living room and his house, he lined the walls all up and down, so he could only use the kitchen and the bathroom and the upstairs, and you couldn't hardly get around down there at all."

"He didn't hurt himself?"

"Well, he knew where they was laid, I guess. So after that I said I can't marry you. You being really strange. I can't trust you, so I'm not going to go with you."

"What did he say?"

"He says, 'I'ma wait and see if you change your mind. I'ma give you three weeks; if you don't change your mind, I'ma go to Florida.'"

"Wow."

"But I couldn't change my mind, 'cause after all that, I didn't know what would happen, I didn't know what he was going to do. So he came to me after three weeks and says, 'Deena, did you change your mind?' and I says, 'Nope, my mind's the same.' And he says, 'Well, they'll be other prospects in Florida, anyway.'"

"Huh."

"But I guess he didn't find no other prospects yet, 'cause he wants me to come visit this summer."[7]

Miss Deena didn't make it to Florida that summer to see her former fiancé, or to see her sister in California. Instead, she got laid off from the cafeteria—seven months before her retirement would have kicked in. To this day, she receives no pension from the University, though she worked there full time for twenty-two years. Her daughter, Rochelle, and I were horrified, and made a number of futile attempts to right the wrong. Miss Deena took it with stoic optimism. "At least I get to sleep in now, and rest my feet."

Those walking around with warrants and court cases and probation sentences sometimes viewed people like Miss Deena and her grandson Ray as the privileged and free: clean people who could go to school, work legal jobs, and build a family, all without looking over their shoulder or getting the rug pulled out from under them. The disappointments that Miss Deena and Ray sustained over the time that I knew them remind us that the constraints the criminal justice system imposes are only additional to the poverty, poor schools, and unjust and racist institutions that have long dampened the hopes and happiness of Black families living in segregated Northern cities.

* * *

As the police chase neighbors and family members through the streets, some residents in the 6th Street community are successfully living a life apart from prisons, court dates, and probation regulations. They negotiate relationships with their legally entangled friends, neighbors, and relatives in ways that limit the risks they bring and the damage they cause. Some clean residents go to school or work every day with a relatively easy lack of awareness of the young men locked up or running from the police; others manage a more concerted and sometimes painful avoidance; and still others negotiate a complicated interweaving of the dirty and clean worlds.

Miss Deena's family steered clear of the dirty world by remaining indoors, cutting themselves off from neighborhood life, sending their son to a charter school outside the neighborhood, and cutting ties with a son who had gone to prison. Lamar and his friends steadfastly avoided young men who sold drugs or had warrants over their heads, drawing a firm line between their indoor lives and legal jobs and pastimes and the guys out there on the corner who were dipping and dodging the police. Mr. George didn't cut himself off from his legally entangled grandsons—in fact, he lived with them and supported them financially. Yet he kept relatively free from their drama by building himself a separate apartment in the house, and keeping out of their affairs so long as they abided by basic house rules. Josh succeeded in going to college and securing a job as a project manager in the pharmaceutical industry, all while remaining connected to his old friends from the neighborhood as they went in and out of jail or lived on the run. These relationships sometimes became highly problematic, but they also offered him support and a rewarding way to help others.

The question of why some young men wind up in prison and others do not is an age-old one, and I can't pretend to fully speak to it, let alone answer it, here. Certainly, it is poorer young men around 6th Street who tend to find themselves arrested and sentenced to jail and prison, though the crimes that start them off in the penal system are often crimes of which richer young men, both Black and white, are also guilty: fighting, drug possession, and the like.

In a community where only few young men end up in prison, we might speak of bad apples or of people who have fallen through the cracks. Given the unprecedented levels of policing and imprisonment in poor Black communities today, these individual explanations make less sense. We begin to see a more deliberate social policy at work. In that context, simply bearing witness to the people who *are* avoiding the authorities and the penal system seems worth a few pages. The people featured here are all, in a variety of ways, leading clean lives in a dirty world. In so doing, they demonstrate that the criminal justice system has not entirely taken over poor and segregated Black neighborhoods like 6th Street, only parts of them.

CONCLUSION

A Fugitive Community

In the last third of the twentieth century, the Civil Rights Movement helped forge a new Black middle class with considerable political and economic power. At the same time, the United States embarked on a new and highly punitive era in regard to poor communities of color—a profound change in how American society governs segregated urban areas and those living within them.

Around 6th Street, police helicopters circle overhead, police cameras monitor passersby, and police routinely stop, search, and arrest people in the streets. Many young men are going in and out of jail or attending court dates; many others are living under probation or parole supervision, under house arrest, or with open warrants out for their arrest. When these young men are home, they live as suspects and fugitives, afraid that any encounter with the authorities will send them back to jail or prison.

In the popular imagination, to be on the run is a condition reserved for those exceptional criminals who make the FBI's Most Wanted lists. Fugitives are the stuff of action movies and legends. Yet today, the United States' tough-on-crime policies have turned its poor and segregated Black neighborhoods into heavily policed places where many young men are using fake names, looking over their shoulder, and living with the genuine fear that those closest to them may bring them into the hands of the police.

Most of these men are out of work and spend some portion of their time trying and failing to secure the lowest-paying part-time jobs. Some are intermittently involved in the risky but ready drug trade, selling small and sometimes larger amounts of marijuana, crack, or pills hand to hand. Periodically they go hungry, and sleep in abandoned cars or their neighbors' unfinished basements.

Around 6th Street, young men's compromised legal status transforms the basic institutions of work, friendship, and family into a net of entrapment. Hospitals become dangerous places to visit, as do jobs. Their mother's home becomes a last-known address: the first place the police will look. As the police track these men through their known addresses, bill payments, and cell phone activity and round them up at the hospital, at work, and at family gatherings, they learn to cultivate a lifestyle of secrecy and evasion, and to see those closest to them as potential informants. As long as a man is at risk of confinement, staying out of prison and routine participation in family, work, and friendships become contradictory goals—doing one reduces his chance of achieving the other.

To be on the run is a strange phrase for legally compromised people, because to be on the run is also to be at a standstill. Indeed, many on 6th Street use the terms *caught up* and *on the run* interchangeably. On the one hand, young men are quite literally running from the police, who chase them on foot or in cars, through houses, and over fences. They are also running from the information in the police database that designates them as arrestable on sight. At the same time, their legal entanglements leave them stuck or caught in place. The policing technology now in use to track people with legal entanglements means that leaving the city or the state will not enable them to escape their legal woes. Possessing few resources or skills they can take with them to succeed elsewhere, they remain in the neighborhood, dependent on the generosity of family and neighbors to hide them and help them survive.

These young men are also at a standstill in the sense that their warrants and court cases and probation and parole sentences loom over them as barriers to advancement. They sense that they cannot proceed with school or work until their legal issues are cleared up—until their warrant is lifted or their court cases end. While employers hesitate to hire a man on parole, they are perhaps even less inclined to take on a man with an arrest warrant or pending court cases, often advising him to come back after these are dealt with. The likelihood of a man with pending legal entanglements being sent back to jail or prison also makes it difficult for partners and family members to build him into their future. Even if he doesn't get sent back to jail, the number of meetings, court dates, and other appointments he must keep up with to continue in good standing with the legal system can feel like a full-time job, or at least a part-time job with unpredictable hours that undermine regular attendance at school or work. In this sense, living on the run is akin to treading water—continual motion without getting anywhere.

The authorities' efforts to hunt, capture, try, and confine large numbers of young men in poor and segregated Black neighborhoods are not only changing the way these men see themselves and orient to the world around them. The heavy police presence and the looming threat of incarceration are spilling out past their targets and tearing at the fabric of everyday life, sowing fear and suspicion into the networks of family and friends that have long sustained poor Black communities. Under the threat of prison, a new and more paranoid social fabric is emerging—one built on the expectation that loved ones may become wanted by the police or may inform on one another to save their own skin. It is woven in subterfuge and trickery; in moves and countermoves; in the paranoiac practices of secrecy, elusion, misinformation, and unpredictability. If there is solidarity, it is an occasional solidarity against the police.

The pressure the police put on young men's partners and relatives to provide information about their whereabouts places women under considerable duress. As officers raid women's houses, threaten to arrest them or get them evicted, and take their children away, they must decide between their own safety and the freedom of the men they hold dear. Women's pledges to protect the men in their lives dissolve under sustained police pressure, and some find they become the unwilling accomplices of the authorities. This descent from trusted partner to snitch or abandoner causes considerable personal anguish as well as public humiliation.

In ghettoized communities there has long been distrust between men and women, and also between people living respectably and those living on the edge. The divide between members of respectable society and those oriented toward the fast life or criminal activity has long been noted. But generosity and trust, and bonds of family and friendship, also have endured through great duress. Around 6th Street, intensive policing and the looming threat of prison are tearing at these bonds, shutting people up in their homes, sowing suspicion and distrust into friendship and family life. In this community, there is simply not enough safety from the authorities to go around. Staying out of jail may mean giving up a son or brother or right-hand man. A central tension in the relationships of men and women on 6th Street involves having to depend heavily on those whom they cannot trust, and wanting to be trusted by people they may put at risk or deceive.

The long-standing divide between the respectable and the shady members of the Black community has been at least partially supplanted by a new line between *clean* and *dirty* people: those able to make it safely through a police stop, and those likely to be seized. An underground market has emerged to supply those seeking protection from the authorities or a bit more freedom than their legal restrictions allow. The buyers and sellers of these protections and privileges forge new bonds together, though these transactional relationships also become complicated by the threat of discovery and arrest.

Men and women also turn the heavy presence of police, the courts, and the prisons to their advantage in ways the authorities never intended. For young men, jail sometimes serves as a safe haven when the streets get too dangerous. The bail office becomes a de facto bank, and warrants become a ready excuse for failure. In times of anger and desperation, women harness the threat of the police to control the men in their lives; during calmer months, they build meaningful routines around their son's or partner's bail payments, court dates, visiting hours, and parole meetings.

The threat of prison and the heavy presence of the police and the courts come to permeate the social fabric of the community in more subtle ways, shifting the currency of love and commitment and creating a new moral framework through which residents carve out their identities and relationships. People express their devotion by refusing to tell the police which way a friend went, or by offering a nephew wanted by the law a few nights' safety on the couch. The events marking a man's passage through the criminal justice system—his first jail visits, his bail posting, his sentencing—become de facto rites of passage and collective events: the weddings, graduations, and school dances of the fugitive community. The threat of prison also creates opportunities for acts of bravery and loyalty: by protecting one another from arrest, people make claims for themselves as honorable and decent, and demonstrate the strength of their commitment to others.

And yet, it is important to remember that the world the criminal justice system creates—of stops and searches, of stints in jail, of warrants and court dates and parole meetings—is not total. While many young people spend their days running from the police, making court dates, and visiting their parole officers, some residents continue to go to school or work every day. Those with a close personal connection to someone on the run or sitting in jail can still build distance from this association, and carve out a life with little connection to the world of cops, court dates, and jail time. Still, these people often work very hard to avoid contact with the dirty world, and come to think of themselves in relation to those enmeshed in it.

THE PROBLEM WITH INTENSIVE POLICING IN POOR URBAN NEIGHBORHOODS

Crime and violence are undeniable problems in poor urban communities. Levels of homicide and gun-related violence in particular set poor minority communities apart, creating pressure for some kind of government action. Around 6th Street, the problems of drugs and violence are real ones, and the young men described here are intimately connected to them.

Some might say that in neighborhoods plagued by drugs and violence, the police have little choice but to arrest large numbers of young men and zealously run down outstanding warrants, particularly when those on the run may carry guns, become involved in serious violence, and/or deal drugs in the neighborhood. But around 6th Street the street trade in drugs, neighborhood rivalries, and their potential for violence are all deeply woven into community life. Under these conditions, the role of law enforcement changes from keeping communities safe from a few offenders to bringing an entire neighborhood under suspicion and surveillance.

In this context, the highly punitive approach to crime control winds up being counterproductive, creating entirely new domains of criminality. The level of social control that tough-on-crime policy envisions—particularly in a liberal state—is so extreme and difficult to implement that it has led to a flourishing black market to ease the pains of supervision. A new realm of criminal activity is produced as young people supply the goods and services that legally compromised people seek to evade the authorities or live with more freedom and comfort than their legal restrictions permit. This black market runs second to the fugitive status as a kind of corollary illegality. Moreover, mothers and girlfriends find themselves committing a seemingly endless series of crimes as they attempt to hide, protect, and provide for their legally entangled sons and partners. Thus, the great paradox of a highly punitive approach to crime control is that it winds up criminalizing so much of daily life as to foster widespread illegality as people work to circumvent it. Intensive policing and the crime it intends to control become mutually reinforcing. The extent to which crime elicits harsh policing, or policing itself contributes to a climate of violence and illegality, becomes impossible to sort out.

Another irony of tough-on-crime policies is that they are so disruptive to the bonds of family, friendship, and community that they have united drug dealers and working people around what all can agree is the unjust overreach of the police, the courts, and the prisons. This is not to say that law-abiding residents of the 6th Street neighborhood are untroubled by the violence and drug selling in which many young men in the neighborhood become engaged. They *are* troubled, and they wish these young men would either leave or change their ways. Some residents insist that their sons and nephews could get legitimate jobs if they simply tried hard enough to find them. But police officers' public violence and efforts to pit neighbors and family members against one another have caused working residents to regard them as an additional problem, not a solution, and in this they find considerable common ground with dirty members of the community.

From the perspective of 6th Street residents, distrust and anger at the police are understandable. The police (along with courts, the jails, and the prisons) are not solving the significant problems of crime and violence but instead are piling on additional problems to the ones residents already face.

This justifiable anger does not mean that we should view the po-

lice as bad people, or their actions as driven by racist or otherwise ma-
levolent motives. The police are in an impossible position: they are
essentially the only governmental body charged with addressing the
significant social problems of able-bodied young men in the jobless
ghetto, and with only the powers of intimidation and arrest to do so.
Many in law enforcement recognize that poverty, unemployment, and
the drugs and violence that accompany them are social problems that
cannot be solved by arresting people. But the police and the courts are
not equipped with social solutions. They are equipped with handcuffs
and jail time.

THE POLICE AND THE COMMUNITY

Here it might be worthwhile to comment on just how complex the relationship actually is between members of the 6th Street community
and the criminal justice personnel who operate in that neighborhood
(or remove people from it). On some level the police are seen as a white,
anonymous occupying force that swoops into the area to round up
whichever young men are unlucky enough to cross their path. Fear and
hatred of the police are palpable, and it's not uncommon for people's
anger and resentment to boil over during police stops. But many residents also count a few police officers as neighbors and relatives. These
personal connections to the police force make it harder to see all officers as outside invaders, though some cops who live in the community
are reviled just as much as the ones who do not, if not more so.

Another contradiction lies in the fact that young men getting
chased by the police may at the same time be romantically involved
with female members of the force. Women in the Black community
are significantly better educated and better employed than their male
counterparts, and a good share of them work in criminal justice. This
means that a number of romantic partnerships cross the line between
police and criminals. Such ties are only multiplied by the intimate association in which young men like Mike and Chuck so often find themselves with female halfway house operators, prison guards, and probation workers. Another surprising fact here is that young men sitting in
jail or prison urge the women coming to visit them to apply for jobs in

law enforcement. Mike and Chuck and their friends understood better than most that criminal justice is one of the few robust branches of the economy, and a field in which those who do not have legal issues of their own would be smart to enter.

Similarly, the moral view of snitching is quite fluid. A generalized norm against informing certainly exists, but people call the police on one another every day. What is even more interesting is that many people who blatantly call police on others in the neighborhood are not judged for it; this action is expected of them, and understood as part of their character as upstanding, clean people.

THE FUGITIVE GHETTO IN HISTORICAL AND COMPARATIVE PERSPECTIVE

What sense might we make of the heavily policed community of 6th Street, and of the millions of Black young men going in and out of jails and prisons today? Sociologist Loïc Wacquant and Civil Rights advocate Michelle Alexander have drawn strong parallels between the current levels of targeted imprisonment and earlier systems of racial oppression such as slavery and Jim Crow, both of which denied Black people basic rights such as voting, running for office, and free movement.[1]

Accompanying slavery and Jim Crow were policies that granted a fugitive status to large numbers of Black men and women—during slavery through the fugitive slave laws, and during the Jim Crow era through the vagrancy statutes that suppressed large numbers of Black people moving to the North during the first and second Great Migrations.[2] The vagrancy statutes held that men could be arrested for being unemployed and unhoused, as well as for drinking, loitering, disorderly conduct, or associating with known criminals.

Though vagrancy statutes had existed in the United States since the colonial era, widespread efforts to round up men on vagrancy charges occurred after the fugitive slave laws were struck down, as Black people migrated to Northern cities after emancipation. In turn, these statutes were stricken from the books in the 1960s and 1970s, just as the laws and practices of the tough-on-crime era began to take effect.[3]

From this history it would seem that large numbers of Black people in the United States have been assigned not only a diminished form of citizenship but a fugitive status through slavery, sharecropping, the Northern migration, and now through the systems of policing and penal supervision accompanying the War on Crime. In this sense, what I have described here represents only the latest chapter in a long history of Black exclusion and civic diminishment in the United States.

Yet it would be incorrect to conclude that the history of US race relations has been one of unrelenting domination. Instead, there have been gains and reversals, and the quality of African American citizenship has expanded significantly in recent decades. An important difference between current levels of policing and imprisonment and earlier periods of racial oppression is that heavy policing and high levels of imprisonment are restricted largely to *poor* Black men and their communities, as well as to many poor white and Latino men. Educated Black men and their families are not enveloped in intensive penal supervision: they may on occasion be subject to public police harassment and mistreatment, but they are not spending their twenties sitting in jail, or living on parole or with warrants out for their arrest.

* * *

If the current treatment of poor Black people in US cities bears at least some similarity to earlier periods of racial oppression in the United States, it might also remind readers of the experience of other groups whose ethnicity, religion, caste, or sexual orientation has in various moments placed them on the social and economic margins. Tools of state oppression may vary, but the experience of persecuted groups throughout history—from the Jews in Europe to undocumented immigrants in the United States to people anywhere living under a repressive, authoritarian, or totalitarian regime—shows astonishing threads of commonality across time and space.

At the level of lived experience, these cases all involve the denial of basic rights to large groups, and the risk of some extreme sanction—confinement, expulsion, deportation, torture, or death—becoming a real possibility facing many people. The combination of restricted rights and threatened extreme sanction criminalizes everyday life as people work to circumvent their restrictions and avoid the authorities. We frequently see curfews as well as identity checks and searches being established, and the practices of evasion, hiding, and secrecy becoming techniques for daily living. A black market in false documents and prohibited goods flourishes. We also see the pernicious issue of informants, both through the police's efforts to cultivate them and through people turning each other in for their own gain. The authorities not only cultivate professional informants but routinely pit close friends, neighbors, and family members against each other, asking people to choose between their own freedom and the security of those they hold dear. Residents experience frequent acts of state violence in the streets—people getting beaten, strangled, kicked, or even shot in public view, for example—and see that the authorities are fairly useless for protection or mediation, despite their omnipresence. Diminished rights and the looming threat of extreme sanction are felt at the level of the community's social fabric—for example, the taking on of legal risk is understood as a gesture of sacrifice and personal attachment—and legal restrictions and diminishments become key social distinctions, particularly the divides between those more or less safe from the authorities.

To be sure, these cases involve as many differences as similarities. In many instances, those seized by the authorities didn't circulate back into the general population; once they were gone, they didn't return. The fear of torture and death isn't the same as the fear of prison or deportation. But these cases share enough so that a deep knowledge of one may teach us something about the experience of people living in others. Certainly, the contemporary US ghetto can take its place among them.

Taken in these terms, we might understand the US ghetto as one of the last repressive regimes of the age: one that operates within our liberal democracy, yet unbeknownst to many living only a few blocks away. In a nation that has officially rid itself of a racial caste system, and has elected and reelected a Black president, we are simultaneously deploying a large number of criminal justice personnel at great taxpayer cost to visit an intensely punitive regime upon poor Black men and women living in our cities' segregated neighborhoods.

EPILOGUE
Leaving 6th Street

Some say you should stop a research project when you stop learning new things. I'm not sure it usually goes that way. At any rate, I never got to a point of "saturation"; never felt that I'd understood enough and it was time to leave and write up my findings.

In the end, I left when my funding ran out, and I had to write a dissertation and get a job. By then it didn't feel like I was leaving the 6th Street Boys as much as the 6th Street Boys had left me—or rather, that the group as we had known it had ceased to exist. By 2008 Chuck was gone, along with two other members we'd also lost to shootings. Steve committed suicide the following year, a tragedy that some attributed to his growing addiction to PCP, and others to his inability to keep going without Chuck. Mike went to federal prison, and when he came home in 2011, he moved to another neighborhood and got a job washing cars. Chuck's middle brother, Reggie, and his youngest brother, Tim, were in prison upstate on long bids. Anthony served a three- to five-year sentence in state prison and was shot to death by the police shortly after his return to 6th Street in 2013. According to neighbors, the police had been working undercover, and when they ran up on Anthony in the alleyway he shot at them, thinking they were 4th Street Boys. Alex has long since moved off the block and out of the area.

I continue to see Aisha and some of her family when I return to Philadelphia, and also visit Alex and Mike, who now hold regular jobs and live with their children and partners. I stay in touch with Reggie and Tim by letter and through phone calls, as well as by the occasional trip upstate when I'm in the area. Reggie and Tim have been bored enough by their incarceration to ask how the book was coming along, so sometimes we talk about that. But more than that, I believe we remain tied to one another by times past, and by the memory of the men who are no longer with us.

ACKNOWLEDGMENTS

For a decade of generosity and friendship, I thank Miss Deena and her grandchildren, Aisha and Ray; Miss Regina and her son Mike; and Ronny, Anthony, Steve, Josh, and the Taylor family: Mr. George, Miss Linda, and her sons, Chuck, Reggie, and Tim. Over many years, Mike, Chuck, and Reggie provided substantial research assistance and feedback on the writing; Reggie gave his from a prison cell.

My parents, William Labov and Gillian Sankoff, provided crucial comments on drafts of the work, every step of the way to the final manuscript. Their unwavering support, as well as that of my sister, Rebecca Labov, and the entire DelGuercio family, made the book possible.

At Penn, Elijah Anderson supervised the undergraduate thesis I wrote about the struggles of the 6th Street Boys. I hope these pages make evident just how much his ideas continue to inspire me. David Grazian, Charles Bosk, Randall Collins, and Michael Katz also gave freely of their time and assistance, joining with Elijah to provide a vibrant intellectual community for a young person to conduct urban ethnography. Many of these early mentors continued to lend their advice and support long after I left Penn, and I am in their debt.

At Princeton, Mitch Duneier devoted himself to my sociological education with more care and attention than any graduate student deserves. Ethnography is a tradition passed down from teacher to student in a set of sensibilities and practices conveyed in off moments and parenthetical conversations. Over many years, Mitch instilled these ethnographic ways of being, transmitting the ideas of his teachers as well as his own. One lesson he stressed above the others: the importance of investigating the social world while treating people with respect. His contributions to the research and writing of this book are more than I can express here; he is a teacher in the highest sense of the word.

Viviana Zelizer, Paul DiMaggio, Devah Pager, and Cornel West joined Mitch to form a dissertation committee second to none. Marvin Bressler, Bruce Western, Martin Ruef, Patricia Fernandez-Kelly, and Sara McClanahan also gave generously of their time and advice. The doors of these Princeton faculty members were always open to me, and to them I owe this book's core arguments.

Part of this work had its origins in a paper published in the *American Sociological Review*. Editor Vincent Roscigno, coeditor Randy Hodson, and reviewers Steven Lopez, Philip Kasinitz, Jack Katz, and Patricia Adler gave me crucial feedback (and graciously disclosed their names to me after the article was accepted).

The Robert Wood Johnson Foundation's Scholars in Health Policy Program and the University of Michigan provided the time and resources I needed to revise the dissertation. In Ann Arbor, a terrific group of fellow postdocs pored over chapter drafts: Trevon Logan, Edward Walker, Greggor Mattson, Sarah Quinn, Brendan Nyhan, Graeme Boushey, Seth Freedman, Jamila Michner, and Christopher Bail.

At UCLA, a community of scholars dedicated to the study of social interaction and urban life lent office space and encouragement to a part-time visitor. For their support and advice, I am particularly indebted to Jack Katz, Robert Emerson, Stefan Timmermans, and Brandon Berry.

At the University of Wisconsin, Erik Olin Wright, Mara Loveman, Joan Fujimura, Doug Maynard, John Delamater, Pamela Oliver, Monica White, and Mustafa Emirbayer offered generous comments. I am deeply in their debt. Students in the undergraduate seminar "The Ghetto" gave sound advice on early drafts. I thank Mitch Duneier for inviting me to co-teach the course with him while I was a graduate student, as well as our students in Princeton, Rome, and Krakow, and then in Madison. I also thank the students in the ethnography seminar at Madison, the participants in the CUNY Graduate Center Methods Workshop, the Harvard Justice and Inequality Working Group, and the UCLA Ethnography Working Group for their close readings and helpful advice on chapter drafts.

Over the course of this research and writing, a number of people hosted conferences, read portions of the book, or took the time to mention things about the project that significantly shaped my thinking. Others extended friendship when I felt myself losing the struggle to inhabit university classrooms and the 6th Street community simultaneously. Among these generous friends and colleagues are Eva Harris, Rebecca Sherman, Sara Goldrick-Rab, Hilary Levey, Alexandra Murphy, Mafalda Cardim, Theo Strinopoulos, Kathleen Nolan, Forrest Stuart, Colin Jerolmack, Joseph Ewoodzie, Jooyoung Lee, Jacob Avery, Mariah Wren, Susanna Greenberg, Nikki Jones, Laura Clawson, Corey Fields, Matthew Desmond, Anna Haskins, John Sutton, Mario Small, Loïc Wacquant, Paul Willis, William Kornblum, Terry Williams, Megan Comfort, Iddo Tavory, Fredrick Wherry, Brian Kelly, Cristobal Young, Glenn Loury, Javier Auyero, Monica White, Marion Fourcade, and Diane Vaughan.

Carol Stack, Howard Becker, and Herbert Gans have been invaluable correspondents—I am grateful for all they taught me from afar. Howard Becker, Robert Emerson, Jack Katz, David Garland, Bruce Western, and Susanna Greenberg read the final manuscript with great care, each providing comments that improved it considerably. Doug Mitchell deserves his reputation as the heart of the editorial group at the University of Chicago Press. Working with him, and with his colleagues Tim McGovern and Levi Stahl, has been a great gift.

In the final stages of writing, I relied on the superb research and editorial assistance of Morgen Miller, Martina Kunovic, Esther HsuBorger, Heather Gordon, Katrina Quisumbing King, Sarah Ugoretz, Matthew Kearney, and Garrett Grainger. Sandra Hazel at the University of Chicago Press lent her considerable wisdom and editorial assistance to the final manuscript.

This book is dedicated to Reggie and Tim's older brother Chuck, whose ready laugh and moral strength live on in our memories.

APPENDIX
A Methodological Note

To evaluate any work of social science, it helps to learn how the researcher found out what he or she claims to know. For the study that became this book, this means explaining how a white young woman came to spend her twenties with Black young men dipping and dodging the police in a lower-income Black neighborhood in Philadelphia. In what follows, I describe how the study came about, how the research was approached and conducted, what difficulties arose and how I tried to overcome them, how the project developed, and how it ended. The reader may also learn something about how my identity shaped what I came to learn, what those inside and outside the group made of my presence in the neighborhood, and how the years on 6th Street affected me.

STARTING OUT

During my freshman year at the University of Pennsylvania, David Grazian offered an urban ethnography class to undergraduates. Dave was a new hire from Chicago, steeped in a tradition of studying urban life through firsthand observation. Early in the course, he instructed us to pick a field site where we would be able to observe social life and take notes. My first choice was to work at TLA, an independent movie rental store in downtown Philadelphia. I believe I was interested in the relationship between the rather snooty staff, who carried on a near-constant internal conversation about obscure and artsy films, and the far less knowledgeable and ambitious customers, who glanced through the offbeat movies but usually chose from among the newest Hollywood releases. This idea was an utter failure: the manager wouldn't give me a job, the stated reason being that I didn't know enough about film.

The next place I tried was a large cafeteria building on the western edge of Penn's campus, where I ate with fellow students a few times a week. There, too, I noticed an interesting tension between staff and customers: the mostly white and fairly privileged Penn undergrads spent a lot of time complaining about the older Black women who served their lunch and dinner, though to me the staff seemed perfectly pleasant and highly competent. I wanted to get a job there and understand what the staff made of the students.

Success! I got the job the week after I applied.

I was hired by Miss Deena, a short and reserved Black woman in her sixties who managed a largely Black staff on the basement level. Miss Deena was entering her third decade of service at the university's cafeteria, and her fifteenth year in management. That fall I worked under her twice a week, mostly making sandwiches and taking food orders.

In the first week I learned that the cafeteria staff didn't spend any time worrying about their interactions with students. Instead, they were embroiled in internal disputes over de-unionization. Penn had stopped hiring student workers, and had begun changing over its almost entirely Black cafeteria staff from a unionized labor force to part-time employees working for a private food services company. As the union workers retired or went on medical leave, the University replaced them with women and men in their twenties who worked under twenty-five hours a week and were being paid through this outside company. I watched Miss Deena patiently train these new employees who were taking the place of her lifelong friends, and the conflicts between the older unionized women and the younger part-time staff became the focus of my field notes.

After a few months, it dawned on me that many of Miss Deena's employees—both union and nonunion—couldn't read very well. I began to notice the things she did to accommodate them, like offering job applicants the option of taking the employment forms home and returning them the next day instead of filling them out on the spot. The sandwich-making job required affixing a small white label to the plastic wrap covering each sandwich to indicate whether it was turkey and Swiss, ham and cheddar, peanut butter and jelly, and so on. The salad-making job didn't require labeling, as there were only two kinds of salads, and they were easily distinguishable from each other. Miss Deena separated the salad making and the sandwich making into two rooms so that her staff could choose which room they wanted to work in. Her staff gave lots of reasons for wanting to work in the room she had designated for salads: because the chairs were more comfortable there, or the music more to their liking. Alongside these perfectly legitimate reasons were hidden ones: the salad room allowed a person to work an entire shift without coming across any printed words.

When workers called in sick or had to care for their children, Miss Deena was occasionally obliged to move someone from the salad room over to the sandwich room. To deal with this eventuality, she organized a system by which the sandwich labels went in manila folders marked with drawings, so workers could memorize that turkey and Swiss went with the star, and ham and cheddar with the smiley face. Those not attuned to this system would sometimes return the labels to the wrong folders, so Miss Deena checked the folders and re-sorted them at the end of each day. One week, when she was out with kidney stones, I came to work to find that forty peanut butter and jelly sandwiches had been labeled turkey and Swiss.

Another problem for staff with lower levels of reading were the time cards they had to use for clocking in and out; these sat in towering rows in metal holders on the wall near management's office on the first floor. With over seventy name cards lined up on the wall, and the names written in a small cursive hand, it often took me more than a minute to locate my own card. It wasn't possible to memorize a card's position on the wall, because the upper-level managers removed the cards each day to count the hours.

Staff members had different ways of dealing with this problem. A few of the older women would stand under the clock, telling anyone who asked that the clock on the wall was fast, and that they were waiting for their final hour to clear so they would get their full pay. While they waited, someone who was "taller" would offer to take down their card for them, for which they got thanked politely.

The younger men who began arriving as members of the part-time staff had a different strategy for dealing with the time-card problem: they would tell a friend on another floor that they were leaving early and ask him or her to punch them out at a later time. At first I thought they were stealing time, but soon came to realize that more often than not, they left when their shift ended, giving only the appearance of logging more hours than they had worked. Stealing time was a way to cover up the fact that they could not locate their name on the wall.

Not only did Miss Deena look the other way, she actively embraced these strategies as a management technique. She personally clocked out some of her employees, offering to do this on her way to get extra napkins or place food orders. As I continued to observe, I realized she was also helping some of the staff on the first and second floors to clock in and out.

To the two white men sitting in the supervisor's office on the first floor, the almost entirely Black staff appeared lazy, difficult, or patently dishonest. They saw the women refusing to work in the sandwich room for all kinds of silly reasons, the young men stealing time, the older women standing around the clock; and once after Miss Deena had gone home, I heard them rail against her for putting up with such insubordination. They also accused her of hiring her relatives and friends, though I never observed her to do this. Despite the tension with the management, Miss Deena seemed to take great pride and pleasure in her work. As far as I could tell, most of her staff respected and trusted her.

* * *

I wrote up my final paper for David Grazian's class and quit the cafeteria job when the term ended.

The following fall, I asked Miss Deena if she knew anyone who needed tutoring. She immediately volunteered her two grandchildren: her daughter's son, Ray, a senior in high school who lived with her along with his mother, and her son's daughter, Aisha, a freshman in high school who lived with her mother and siblings a few blocks away. Miss Deena said Ray was a good boy who was applying to college. Aisha, on the other hand, was having considerable difficulty staying out of trouble. We agreed that I would tutor Ray and Aisha in English, history, and SAT preparation.

What I can remember of my motivation for tutoring was that I wanted to understand the lives of my fellow workers at home and in the neighborhood, outside the mainly white campus where they came for their jobs. After working alongside a number of people with quite poor reading skills, I was also preoccupied with the problem of literacy. In any event, tutoring seemed a decent reason for a young, middle-class white woman to be spending time in a working-class-to-poor Black section of the city.

The first time I drove to Miss Deena's, I couldn't find the right address. As I walked around peering at the two-story brick row homes, a young man stopped and asked me if I was a cop or a caseworker, there apparently being no other reason that a person like me would be in the area. I had grown accustomed to being the only white person working at the cafeteria, but there the students and the surrounding area were majority white. When I began coming to Miss Deena's house for evening tutoring, I entered a world in which white people were a tiny minority.[1]

To my relief, Miss Deena's family was warm and welcoming. Her daughter, Rochelle, was a talkative and vivacious woman in her forties who had worked as a teacher's assistant at a day care downtown before getting laid off. She and her son, Ray, both seemed to be acquainted with the wealthy white section of the city in which I'd been raised, and attuned to my gaps in cultural knowledge.

Miss Deena's granddaughter, Aisha, was also very welcoming, but seemed to have experienced little outside Black Philadelphia. Like many who grow up in segregated northern cities, she spoke in what linguists refer to as African American Vernacular English.[2] Added to this, she had the rapid and muffled speech of a teenager. At the beginning of this tutoring, I frequently couldn't understand what she said, and would awkwardly ask her to repeat it. Or I'd pretend to follow, and she'd realize well into the conversation that I hadn't understood her at all.

For the school year, I tutored Aisha and Ray at Miss Deena's house two and then three evenings a week. After a few months, I could follow Aisha's stories much better, and even our phone conversations had become largely intelligible to me.

AISHA'S FAMILY

After about four months, Aisha's mother stopped by Miss Deena's house to meet me. A somewhat overweight woman in her late thirties with a light complexion and cornrows in her short and thinning hair, she looked as if she had seen it all before, or simply was exhausted by her diabetes and caring for her three children. Our meeting was fairly awkward on both sides, but at the end of it she told me I was welcome to stop by the apartment a few blocks away. After spending months in Miss Deena's pristine home with its museum-like quiet and plastic-covered furniture, this was a big breakthrough. A whole world of extended family and neighbors was opening up to me.

I began spending time at Aisha's place, and got to know her mother and older sister as well as a number of her relatives, friends, and neighbors. We would sit on the steps of her apartment building, cook food, do laundry at the corner Laundromat, or walk to the Chinese takeout store. As we went around the neighborhood, Aisha introduced me to a cousin working as a deli clerk, an uncle selling DVDs from a stand on the street, and another uncle who managed the corner seafood joint. Her family had been in Philadelphia for many generations; she counted what seemed to be a vast number of neighbors as close relations.

Slowly, I began to perceive the social distance between Aisha's and Miss Deena's households. At Miss Deena's the fridge was often full, the family had no problems keeping the lights and gas on, and Ray spent his evenings on SAT prep and college applications. I never observed any member of the household to sit outside on the stoop, and relations with neighbors were polite but brief. In my two years of spending most weekday afternoons at their place, I observed them entertaining guests only twice, and one of these was a relative from out of town. In contrast, Aisha lived with her mother and sister in a four-story, Section 8–subsidized housing unit on a poorer block. A steady stream of family and neighbors came into and out of the apartment, and Aisha's family also spent a lot of time at their neighbor's, whose three kids they considered part of the family.

Aisha's mother admitted to me that she had sold drugs for a while before going on welfare. While she had been out doing her thing during Aisha's childhood, Aisha's maternal grandmother had taken over her care. She was a thin woman in her sixties with shockingly bright dyed-red hair and a love of cognac. In middle school, Aisha would join her at the corner bar, spending the evening laughing with fellow customers and walking home with her grandmother late into the night. By the time I met Aisha, she regarded this bar as a second home, coming and going as she pleased, borrowing a dollar or grabbing a bite.

In those early months, Aisha seemed often on the cusp of expulsion or dropping out; the week that we met, she had been suspended for punching her teacher in the mouth. Later I would learn that she was Miss Deena's granddaughter through her errant middle son, who was in prison upstate. The following year, in Elijah Anderson's urban ethnography class, I would learn about the tension between *decent* and *street*, and the divides between Miss Deena's and Aisha's households began to make a lot more sense.

MOVING TO THE NEIGHBORHOOD

In the middle of my sophomore year of college my lease was up, and with encouragement from Aisha and her family, I started searching for a place nearby. This proved difficult: I could not find a real-estate agent willing to rent to me in the Black section of the city of which Aisha's neighborhood was a part. Some agents never returned my call, while others said I wouldn't want the apartment that was listed or told me it had been taken. Finally, Aisha's older sister made some calls on my behalf and came with me to the appointments.[3]

Once I'd moved into a one-bedroom a few blocks from Miss Deena's, I began to spend most days and evenings with Aisha's extended family and friends or at Miss Deena's house, commuting to Penn for classes. At this point I had become interested in the experience of mothers and daughters, aunts and grandmothers—the domestic world of women in Aisha's community. My time on Penn's campus was limited mostly to the Sociology Department, where I tried to take classes in which I could turn in a final paper based on the fieldwork I was doing. Though I continued to tutor Aisha for three and a half more years until she graduated from high school, my role was gradually changing from tutor to friend and resident.

MEETING THE 6TH STREET BOYS

In December of 2002, Aisha's fourteen-year-old cousin Ronny came home from a juvenile detention center. He was short for his age, and the worn ends of his pants dragged and frayed in long trails behind him when he walked. He had light skin and curly hair, a soft voice, and a big grin when he saw Aisha. I hadn't heard much about Ronny in his absence, but on the day he returned, Aisha ran up the street to greet him, hugging him and hanging on him the whole afternoon. It was the first time I had heard her really laugh.

Ronny and Aisha were cousins because her aunt had taken him in when his own mother had proved unable to care for him, due largely to her crack addiction, Aisha told me. This aunt had died the year before Aisha and I met, leaving Ronny to move in with his grandmother, who didn't seem to understand the first thing about him. The trips to detention centers started shortly afterward.

When Ronny came home this time, he was a freshman in high school, though he spent most weekdays outside the classroom, running from truant officers or serving suspensions. He was living with his grandmother about fifteen blocks away from Aisha, in a neighborhood called 6th Street. Ronny was a self-proclaimed troublemaker raised, as he put it, by the streets. An impressive dancer, he'd sometimes jump out of a car at the light to put on a quick show for whoever happened to be walking by.

Upon hearing that Aisha was single, Ronny decided to set her up with his friend Tommy, a quiet and dark-skinned young man of fourteen who lived on 6th Street a few houses down. Tommy was tall, shy, and very handsome—a perfect counterpoint to Ronny's mischievous exuberance. Aisha was smitten. She began taking the bus over to 6th Street one or two afternoons a week. I came along, with Aisha introducing me sometimes as her tutor, and sometimes as her godsister or simply her sister.

The Date
One afternoon as we were hanging out on 6th Street with Ronny and Tommy, Ronny told me that his old head Mike wanted to meet me.

According to Aisha, who had heard it from Ronny, Mike had grown up next door to Ronny's grandmother, and he looked *good*.

Until that point, I'd resisted Aisha's attempts to set me up with various boys she knew, though I'd always declined politely, taking her offer as a genuine gift of teenage friendship. But in the weeks leading up to this discussion about Mike, I'd attended a birthday party for Aisha's younger brother, where I overheard a disturbing conversation between her mother and another relative. After the cake, the woman quietly asked Aisha's mother what I was doing spending so much time with Aisha and her girlfriends. Aisha's mother answered firmly that I was her daughter's tutor and also her nephew's tutor, and that I lived down the street. The woman asked what I was getting for all this tutoring, and Aisha's mother said she thought it was for school. Where does she take her? the woman wanted to know. Aisha's mom stated that I took her to the library, the bookstore, and sometimes out for food. Does she go with anybody? No, Aisha's mother replied, I think she's single. The woman nodded, as if my lack of a boyfriend confirmed some suspicion. Aisha's mother then said that I was "like a big sister" and "part of the family."

I left the party humiliated and distressed. Without coming out and saying it, I imagined that the woman was implying that because I had no boyfriend to speak of, I might have some interest in high school girls. At least, it was strange that I was unattached, and spending so much time with Aisha and her friends. Aisha's mother's behavior toward me didn't seem to change, but the idea that a rumor could circulate that my motives toward Aisha and her teenage girlfriends were questionable left me horrified. The next time someone offered to set me up with a guy, I instantly agreed. This someone was Ronny's old head Mike.

When Ronny introduced us in January of 2003, Mike was a thin young man of twenty-two—a year older than I was. We had a few short phone conversations, followed by one excruciatingly awkward date to the movies on 69th Street. It was a group outing: I brought Aisha along, and one of her girlfriends; for his part, Mike brought his two young boys Ronny and Tommy. We piled into Mike's ten-year-old Bonneville—more like a boat than a car—with the kids squished into the back and me riding shotgun next to Mike. Aisha seemed thrilled to be on this date with Tommy, and the friend she brought along tried her best to flirt with Ronny, though she was a good ten inches taller than he.

One of the first things Mike told me about himself as we drove to the movies was that he had recently finished a long course of physical therapy after a gunshot wound to the upper thigh. Did I want to see the scar? With some apologies that he wasn't trying to be ignorant by exposing himself, he pulled down his jeans to show me where the bullet had entered just below his hip bone. Later, I heard that he'd been shot by a man who was trying to rob him after a dice game.[4]

We bought popcorn and Swedish Fish candy and played video games while we waited for the movie to start. I was the only white person in the theater but I was prepared for that, and nobody stared too much or said anything particularly unsettling. Things started to go downhill soon after the movie started, though. I'd suggested *The Recruit*, with Al Pacino and Colin Farrell, thinking it would be a good action movie. It turned out to contain not enough action or comedy, tons of boring dialogue, and no Black characters whatsoever. Mike and Ronny fell asleep within fifteen minutes. Aisha's girlfriend got sick midway through—perhaps from Twizzler and slushie overload—and so I spent a large part of the movie in the bathroom with her. On the way home, I realized that the showtime had been quite late, which had likely contributed to our party's younger members nodding off, so then I felt irresponsible as well as lame. I said something about the movie on the drive home—I didn't write down what it was and can't remember now—that caused Ronny and Tommy to burst out laughing and Aisha to attempt a repair on my behalf, saying, "She didn't grow up around our way."

After we dropped off the girls at home, I made a joke to Mike about Ronny's ill-conceived matchmaking.

"You ain't ugly," Mike said frankly. "And you got a nice lil' body."

"Thanks."

"You just . . . you don't know how to act."

Mike then explained precisely what it would take for me to become attractive to the men in his neighborhood—not just to an in-the-way (no-account) guy but to a worthwhile suitor. First off, my clothes were all wrong—they didn't even match. My toenails were bare and uneven, and what was I doing wearing flip-flops in January anyway? Maybe I could answer this question for him: why did white people wear shorts and sandals in the dead of winter? I needed sneaks—white Air Force Ones would work, he mused. The way that I spoke was strange, and I could stand to get a little more husky. Plus, I didn't know how to walk or hold my body right. I had a bad habit of staring at people, which was rude, especially since I was a white girl. And I was trying way too hard to be liked. I should stick up for myself when someone insulted me, not stand there speechless and take it. And I should be a lot less generous. Why was I offering to pay so often? Finally, my hair looked like I'd slept on it and left the house without even combing it through. For this critique I at least had a counterargument:

"Well, yeah, I don't comb it because it's kind of curly . . ."

Mike shook his head in exasperation.

At this point I said something like, "Okay. Thanks for making me feel even more strange and unappealing than I already did."

The date was humiliating, but it gave me something to talk about with Aisha and her family for a good two weeks. And it helped me get over the deep anxiety the suspicious woman at the party had prompted about how people might be perceiving my motives toward Aisha and her friends.

Mike Takes Me under His Wing

The date had gone so badly that I assumed I wouldn't be hearing from Mike again. To my great surprise, he occasionally called me in the weeks that followed. He'd ask how I was doing, and what the girls and I were up to. Or he'd say he was on his way to work, which apparently was a warehouse in Northeast Philadelphia. Once he told me he'd gotten into a fight, and his hand was sore. Sometimes he'd promise to stop by Aisha's block and say hi, perhaps with one of his young boys in tow, though he never did. These fleeting exchanges fueled a great many conversations with Aisha and her family: Would he call again? Did I truly like him, or only feel interested because he was so hard to pin down?

I'm not sure if people's behavior toward me changed, but I imagined that this date with Mike helped something click for Aisha's neighbors and relatives. If I had been something of a puzzle before, now my presence in the neighborhood made sense: I was one of those white girls who liked Black guys.

Shortly after our group outing to the movies, Ronny got into a fist-fight with his sister's boyfriend and got shipped back to a juvenile detention facility on charges of aggravated assault. Aisha was crushed. Mike bemoaned Ronny's parting also, especially since his other close friend and neighbor, Chuck, had gotten locked up recently. He was sitting in county jail on charges of assault and fleeing the police, also for a fight in the schoolyard.

Perhaps it was partly because of this temporary gap in his social circle that Mike began phoning me and telling me to stop by 6th Street. Or maybe it had nothing to do with the absence of Ronny and Chuck; maybe he simply liked having a white girl—however awkward and poorly dressed—sitting on the alley stoops with him. Whatever his motivations, I began hanging out with him at his uncle's house, in his absent friend Chuck's house, and other homes around the neighborhood. Bit by bit, Mike introduced me to other young men who were part of his circle.

One night, he called me around ten to ask if I had a state ID. I said I did. He then said, "Take this ride with me." We drove down to the local police station, where Mike indicated that I should sign for Chuck's younger brother Reggie to be released. He was being held for making a terroristic threat and fighting with a boy from school (the terroristic threat purportedly had been "I'ma hurt you"). On the form, I wrote that I was his mother, though it was plain to the women working behind the counter that we weren't related. When he emerged from the side door, a heavy and dark-skinned fifteen-year-old towering over my five-foot-two-inch frame, he grinned and greeted me with "Yo, Mommy! Thanks for coming to get me."

At this point I was still tutoring Aisha and her cousin Ray twice a week. I believed that the study I was conducting concerned the world of women: Miss Deena and her daughter, Aisha and her mother and sister, the other teenage girls she hung out with, their neighbor across the way, her three children, and so on. But more and more, my notes began to concern Mike and his friends over on 6th Street—people who sometimes overlapped with Aisha's group of friends and family, and sometimes didn't.

There were probably a number of reasons why I began spending more of my time with Mike and his friends, beyond the need to demonstrate that I wasn't molesting teenage girls. For one, I had been reading *All Our Kin*,[5] *Making Ends Meet*,[6] and *No Shame in My Game*,[7] and had learned a lot about the lives of working poor people and women struggling on welfare. I wasn't sure how much my notes about Aisha and her family and friends could add to what these books had already said. Mike and his friends, on the other hand, were a mystery. They sort of had jobs, but they also seemed to have income that they didn't speak about. They were getting arrested and coming home on bail and visiting their pro-bation officers. They got into fights; their cars were stolen or seized by the police. It was all confusion and chaos—I couldn't follow what was happening from minute to minute.

In late March of 2003, I asked Mike what he thought of my writing about his life for my undergraduate thesis at Penn, due the following spring. We agreed that I'd conceal his name and the neighborhood lo-cation, and that I wouldn't include any events he wanted me to leave out. Over the next weeks, I broached the topic with Chuck, Steve, Alex, Anthony, and some of the other young men who hung out together on 6th Street. Over time, I discussed it with their mothers, girlfriends, and other relatives.

Mike Catches a Case

A few months into hanging out with Mike, he phoned me in a panic at four in the morning to say that the police had just raided his uncle's house looking for him. He was at his baby-mom's house, and his uncle had just called to warn him that the law would probably be there next. The police had issued a warrant for Mike's arrest on a shooting charge. He told me he hadn't been involved in any shooting, and for the next week he hid out in friends' apartments, including mine, while he fig-ured out what to do.

Since this was a "body warrant" for a new and significant crime, rather than a bench warrant for, say, failure to appear in court, failure to pay court fees, or technical probation and parole violations, a number of police divisions started actively searching for Mike, raiding his fam-ily and friends' houses and interrogating and intimidating his uncle, his mom, and the mother of his two children. After a few weeks of dip-ping and dodging the police, he secured a lawyer and turned himself in. From county jail he'd phone me for the ten minutes he was allotted in the morning and then again for ten minutes at night, and I'd three-way his other friends or the girl he was dating, or we'd catch up on what was happening back on the block.

Mike was being held at the Curran-Fromhold Correctional Facility (CFCF, locally known as the F), which is the largest county jail in Philadelphia. It's a pink and gray building that sits on State Road in Northeast Philly. As this was my first time visiting someone in jail or prison, I was quite intimidated by the other women in the waiting room. A visitor to CFCF can easily spend five hours waiting to be called, so there's a lot of time for women to talk and size one another up. Some of these women knew each other, and sometimes they'd openly insult me or ask who I was going to see and how we were related and was he Black.

My first attempts to visit Mike were unsuccessful: once I got turned away because my clothing hadn't conformed to jail visitor policy (no white T-shirts, no flip-flops, no hoodies, no tops exceeding hip length) another time because Mike's visit period had already been used up a few hours before, and the third time because the warden had canceled all visits when the evening count of prisoners didn't clear. I got the hang of it after about a week.

A few weeks later, Mike got into a fight with another inmate and got sent to solitary confinement. After he spent three days of solitude in the dark, his mother, Miss Regina, and his grandmother raised the fifteen-hundred-dollar bail to bring him home. Miss Regina and I went to the bail office in the basement of the courthouse to pay it, and then I waited for six long hours down at the county jail on State Road for him to be released.

The night Mike came home, we drove back to the block around 2:30 a.m. With almost everyone asleep and the neighborhood quiet, he couldn't get anybody to wake up and celebrate his homecoming. We drove around for a while, and then Mike told me to pull up next to a dark truck. He knocked on the passenger door, and soon a man rose from the seat cushions and opened it for us.

This was Anthony, a thin man of twenty-three with outgrown hair who smelled of sweat and cigarettes. Apparently, he'd been living at his aunt's house on 6th Street, but she had kicked him out when she caught him stealing money from her purse (accusations he vehemently denied). We shared a celebratory cigarette, and then Mike said goodbye and Anthony went back to sleep. Mike shrugged. "He's homeless, but that's our man, though." When I asked later, he told me that Ant had been living in various abandoned cars around 6th Street for over a year.

When Mike had first gotten the news that he was wanted on this shooting charge, I was quite shaken, and thought the case was a unique and significant experience in his life. When he came home on bail, his first court date was scheduled for the next month, and as the date neared I urged him strongly to buy a suit. When he refused, I attempted to persuade him to at least locate some khakis and a tie. Instead, Mike came to court wearing jeans, sneakers, and a well-pressed white T-shirt.

His initial hearing was at the small courthouse within the district police station that served his neighborhood and many adjacent ones, located about a mile from 6th Street. As we approached the cement building, he recognized a man he knew and smoked a cigarette with him while they exchanged some details about their respective cases. As we walked into the building, he shook hands with more young men he knew by name; by the time we were sitting in the benches on the defendant's side of the large wood-paneled courtroom, he'd greeted over a dozen more young men awaiting trial. While we waited, he whispered the back story on three of the cops who were standing against the wall waiting to testify. He recognized two of the public defenders, and told me which guys from the block had been assigned to them for various cases they'd caught.

Another shock: compared with many of these young men, Mike's jeans and T-shirt looked like formal attire. Or at least, they were new and clean and pressed. Some defendants had visible holes in their clothing; others had matted-down hair or worn and dirty shoes without laces. I began to understand that this case for attempted murder, though not insignificant for Mike, was nothing new—not to him or the other guys he hung out with. In fact, this was the third criminal case Mike had caught in the past two years. He had just finished going to trial dates for one of them and had recently completed probation from the other. Gradually, I realized that a great many young men in the neighborhood were getting arrested regularly, living with warrants, going to court date after court date, and dipping and dodging the police. And judging by the clothing and shoes they could assemble for their day in court, these men were poor—far poorer than Mike, whose economic circumstances had seemed quite desperate to me previously.

NEGOTIATING A PLACE ON 6TH STREET

When I first began spending time with Ronny and Mike on 6th Street, their neighbors and relatives often remarked on my whiteness and asked me to account for my presence. I don't think they wondered what I was doing there as much as Aisha's friends and neighbors had when I met them, because I'd come in via Aisha and so was already connected to Ronny and Mike through a series of family ties. Even before they met me, their friends and relatives had "seen me around" with Ronny's cousin and aunts and grandmother for half a year. Then after Mike came home on bail, he began referring to me as his godsister or simply as his sister. Sometimes I also mentioned that I lived nearby.

Because Mike held some sway among the young men in the neighborhood, being his adopted sister gave me a good deal of legitimacy. It also seemed to establish that I wasn't available for sex or romance, as Mike simply wouldn't put up with his sis "messing with a no-job-having, in-and-out-of-jail-going, weed-smokin' motherfucker."

I'm not sure how to account for Mike's adopting this protective older-brother relationship with me. Sometimes he mentioned that as an only child he'd often wanted a sister. At the time we met, Mike had a great many women pursuing him: Marie, the mother of his two children, other ex-girlfriends, and a number of neighborhood women he was seeing casually. Like many other young men in the neighborhood, he'd sometimes sleep with these women when he was broke, receiving room and board or a small amount of cash, and often talked about sex with them as something of a chore. So maybe he liked having a female friend who wasn't asking for sex. Or maybe on the whole he didn't enjoy sleeping with women very much. Whatever his reasons, getting adopted by Mike as a kind of sister was a major stroke of luck.

As an adopted sis, cousin, and chronicler, my role with Chuck and Mike and their friends might be similar to that of a female buddy at a fraternity. Fraternity brothers distinguish between two types of women who are attached to their group: buddies and slutties. Slutties are women who sleep with fraternity members and are viewed as sex objects to be shared around. Buddies are women who don't sleep with any of the members and serve as largely desexualized, gender-neutral sidekicks.[8]

Often I was the only woman present in the group from 6th Street.

For his twenty-third birthday, Mike threw a party at a local motel. He paid for the room and bought two hundred dollars' worth of hard liquor and another fifty dollars' worth of marijuana for his guests. Steve and Alex split the cost of a large birthday cake covered in green icing. Nobody remembered to bring plates or forks, though, so the cake sat uneaten until Reggie took a fistful, grinning and saying, "I'm fuckin' *hungry*, man." With Chuck locked up at the time, fifteen-year-old Reggie was relishing the time with his brother's friends.

Mike hadn't invited any women to the party, so the event consisted of fifteen of his friends crammed into the small room, drinking and watching music videos on the television. As the night went on and Mike got drunker, guys he barely knew started coming in and out of the room, taking the half-full bottles of booze he'd spread out on the windowsill. By 1:00 a.m., he was sitting below the windowsill with his gun out in his lap, threatening to pistol-whip the next guy who came in that tried to touch the booze he bought for his guests. He railed for a while about how nobody had contributed any money to the room or to the alcohol, only to a twelve-dollar fucking cake, and then he fell asleep.

I thought Mike had passed out completely, but then he began screaming, "Where the fuck is my money at?" Apparently, someone had taken the roll of bills he'd wedged into the side pocket of his jeans while he slept drunkenly on the floor.

Steve drew his gun and started pointing it at the party guests, demanding that they return Mike's money. I had never seen anybody pull a gun before and took the opportunity to promptly leave the party. As I made my way down the corridor to the elevator, Steve bounded up behind me, apologizing profusely.

"My bad, Alice. I ain't mean no disrespect. You understand, like, I can't just let niggas take advantage of my man. They think it's sweet [an easy target] 'cause he drunk, but it's *not* sweet! I'm on they *ass*, A."

"Yeah, I know. You're a good friend, Steve. I was getting tired anyway."

Fifteen minutes later, Mike phoned triumphantly to say that the money had "magically" reappeared on the bedside table, and all had been forgiven. Did I want to come back to the party?

* * *

My role of sidekick and adopted sister to Mike didn't mean that sex or romance never came up. Occasionally when men were incarcerated, they wrote me letters explaining that their confinement had made them realize that they were in fact romantically interested in me. In the language of the community, I chalked this up as jail talk: in all but one case, this interest, or at least its overt expression, ended when the man came home and had access to a wider range of women.

Outside our circle, people had different stories about what I was doing on the block and what my relationships to Mike and Chuck and the other young men were. The owner of the apartment I rented, a retired Black man in his sixties, referred to Mike as my friend, indicating he assumed we were romantic partners. Some of the 6th Street residents also thought I was sleeping with one or even many of the 6th Street crew, and some young men's girlfriends remained perpetually suspicious about this. While we were out in public or in court or in jail visiting rooms, we sometimes let people assume that we were romantic partners. Though they mostly ignored me during stops, interrogations, and raids, the cops sometimes indicated that they believed I was looking for drugs, or for sex with a Black man (in their words, "Black dick"). In contrast, some people in the neighborhood assumed I was a lesbian, which helped to explain why I liked to hang out with the guys. Miss Regina would often say I was her son Mike's right hand, and should have been born a man. Some just seemed to think I was a bit of a loser, unable to make friends with people like myself in the neighborhood I had come from. Even when Mike and I began talking about the possibility of my writing a book, and I discussed this with Chuck and others, these interpretations and suspicions didn't go away.

* * *

People have asked how I "negotiated my privilege" while conducting fieldwork. Given that I am a white woman who comes from an educated and well-off family, this is a good question. In fact, I had more privi-

lege than whiteness, education, and wealth: my father was a promi-
nent sociologist and fieldworker. Though he died when I was an infant,
his ideas hung in the air of my childhood household, and I had read
some of his books by the time I entered college. My mother and adopted father were also professors and devoted fieldworkers: my mother
an anthropologist turned sociolinguist who had conducted studies in
Papua New Guinea and Montreal, and my second father a well-known
linguist who had done studies in Harlem and other parts of Manhattan
as well as Martha's Vineyard and Philadelphia. Not only did my parents
give substantial financial support, they understood what I was trying
to do and brought their own experience to bear on the project I was
undertaking.

This peculiar background may have given me the confidence and the
resources to embark on this research as an undergraduate, and consequently the years to get established and take it in various directions.
The shadow of my late father may have pushed me to go further than
was safe or expected. Perhaps my background, and the extra knowledge
and confidence it gave me, also contributed to professors encouraging
the work and devoting their time so freely to my education. It may
have also grounded me and kept me going in the face of the profound
discomfort that accompanies a new social milieu.

None of these advantages seemed to translate into what sociologist
Randall Collins refers to as situational dominance, or at least not very
often.[9] On 6th Street I often felt like an idiot, an outsider, and at times a
powerless young woman. The act of doing fieldwork is a humbling one,
particularly when you're trying to understand a community or a job or
a life that's far away from who you are and what you know.[10] In many
situations, my lack of knowledge put me at the bottom of the social
hierarchy. I hung out on 6th Street at the pleasure of Mike and Chuck,
along with their friends and neighbors and family. They knew exactly
what I was doing and what I had on the line; whether I got to stay or go
was entirely up to them.

Gaining a Basic Working Knowledge

My initial efforts to describe what was happening for Mike and his
friends were at first greatly hampered by a lack of knowledge about the
neighborhood, the police and the courts, the local drug trade, and rela-

tions between men and women. My confusion in these early months cannot be overstated; I couldn't seem to follow events and conversations, and people were often too busy or frustrated to explain things to me when I asked. My sense of stupidity wasn't just internal—people would openly express their frustration and bafflement at how slow I was to grasp the meaning of what was going on.

In part, I was struggling to overcome a language barrier. Mike and Chuck used what linguists have called African American Vernacular English, and unlike Aisha's mother and aunt, they didn't shift their speech much for my benefit. They also employed more slang than Aisha and her girlfriends did. I had to work hard to learn the grammar and vocabulary they were using.

From a late night on Chuck's back porch in the summer of 2005:

There are a few cars that drive by, and when they do, Chuck and Steve discuss the clandestine doings of these neighbors. Chuck says to Steve, "You see Lamar creeping? He probably came home, came right back out." They both laugh.

"Yo, you know who your young-boy, you know who your young-boy?" Chuck says. "The boy Lamar your young-boy."

"No he not!" Steve says, laughing and protesting. "I put all these niggas on, A," he tells me.

Steve leaves to see his girlfriend, saying, "I'm out, A. I'm 'bout to go get me some cock." I ask Anthony about this, and he confirms that the word *cock* can mean sex with a woman as well as male genitalia. In the discussions about the neighbors' late-night activities, I also learn four new words for orgasm: to bust (buss), to yam, to chuck, and to nut.

The confusion ran deeper than this language barrier: I didn't understand the significance of events as they occurred, misinterpreting people's gestures and actions.

Once I saw Ronny in a fistfight with some other boys, and along with two young men standing nearby, I went over and tried to break up the fight. Only I was pulling Ronny away from another young man who was also trying to break up the fight, thinking he was the one Ronny was fighting. One of the other guys started shouting, "Not him! Not him!"

What a fucking idiot, I thought. I can't even tell which person is fighting and which person is pulling the fighters away from each other. The looks I got that afternoon humiliated me further.

Dealing with Difference

Some ethnographers maintain that their difference is an asset to the research: their distinct background, gender, or race allows them to see what the locals or natives cannot; their foreign identity gives them some special status or opens certain doors; their situation as an outsider prompts people to explain things that would otherwise go unsaid; their novice mistakes and blunders reveal the social fabric that would otherwise remain obscured.[11]

I didn't take this approach. Or rather, I didn't have this experience. In some ways my identity was an encumbrance, and one I had to invest significant time and effort to overcome. Particularly in the early months on 6th Street, the presence of a white young woman seemed to make people uneasy if not outright angry or visibly threatened. My lack of familiarity with what sociologists St. Clair Drake and Horace R. Cayton referred to as the lower shadies of the Black community, my lack of familiarity with the neighborhood, and my wholly different family background meant that I didn't understand what was going on much of the time, and so had to work hard just to keep up. My concern about how my strange presence was changing the scene and my efforts to reduce its impact became preoccupations in their own right, distracting me from understanding what daily life was like for Mike and his friends and neighbors. If it is indeed true that an ethnographer's mistakes are revealing, I could not afford to make them. Here an extra word during a police stop could cost a man his freedom.

Like many outsiders have done, I learned to defuse tension by making a joke out of my difference. Though in practice I was steadily adopting more and more of Mike and Chuck's attitudes and ways of doing things, I learned to give verbal credence to expectations about my white, college-educated preferences, like whiny rock music and sushi and cut-up vegetables with no dressing. With those young men around 6th Street who seemed interested in flirting with me, I learned how to negotiate a joking sexual banter, to strike a delicate balance of them wanting me around without feeling like they could approach me directly about a romantic relationship.

In his study of street vendors in Greenwich Village, Mitch Duneier notes that his status as a white and middle-class Jewish man wasn't fixed but became more or less salient depending on the circumstance.[12] Likewise, my gender seemed to come into and out of focus depending on what was going on. Sometimes my status as a woman seemed in the forefront of people's consciousness, like when the police had to call a female cop to the scene in order to search me. But there were many other times when it seemed I was taken almost as an honorary man, permitted to hang around when men spoke about shootouts and drug deals and robberies, or about romantic escapades with women other than their main partner.

That I was Jewish, or rather, half-Jewish on my father's side, didn't seem to register very much, perhaps because last names were so little used. Reggie complained to me once about another guy who wouldn't share his profits after a gambling win, saying that the guy was "acting like a Jew."

"Do you know any Jews?" I asked.

"No. It's a fucking expression."

"You know I'm Jewish, right?"

"You ain't a Jew. You white."

"I'm half-Jewish, Reggie, swear to god."

"Where's your beard?" he laughed.

If my Jewish identity wasn't readily recognized, certainly my whiteness was. Though I have little way of proving it, I am fairly confident that Mike and his friends and family spoke more about race, and about the racial politics of policing and imprisonment, when I wasn't around. Sometimes they discussed these topics when I was with them, but not, I believe, as freely or as frequently as they did in my absence.

If my being white was a permanent fact that nobody ever forgot, it, too, seemed to come into and out of focus, as if my whiteness were a property of the situation or interaction in play, not merely a trait I possessed.

One winter, a pair of white female police officers began appearing around 6th Street, chasing young men in cars, stopping people on the street and running their names, and searching houses. In a week they'd taken eleven young neighborhood men into custody on new arrests or old warrants. Mike, Chuck, and their friends began referring to them as The White Bitches, with a small apology to me after they did so.

ALEX: Just seen the White Bitches come through—no offense, A.
ALICE: None taken. Where'd they go?

After a while the apologies stopped, and my being the same color and gender as these most hated officers seemed to move further down in people's consciousness.

Though I never exactly blended in on 6th Street, by showing up every day, month after month, I became an expected part of the scene. The Puerto Rican family who ran the corner grocery store began affectionately calling me Vanilla, which they eventually shortened to Nil. After about a year, young men in the group began referring to me as their sister, cousin, or "our homie" who "goes way back." As Howard Becker has pointed out, it's virtually impossible for people to continue to take special notice of something or someone they see day in and day out.[13]

Yet even after people had gotten used to me, my whiteness became problematic during certain occasions, at certain locations, and among certain groups of people.

Prison and jail visiting rooms were among the easiest public places for me, once I'd gotten the hang of them. The guards have seen it all and don't bat an eye when a white woman comes to visit a Black man. In fact, many women coming to visit Black men in state prison are white; even in county jail, my sense is that there are more interracial couples than what would be found in public in Black or white neighborhoods. I often figured this was because a community's interracial couples have learned how to hide in public—for example, by going to the grocery store late at night—but in a visiting room this is impossible. Or perhaps inmates have more interracial relationships than their communities do as a whole.

Courtrooms, bail offices, and probation offices were other public spaces in which Mike and I tended to feel more at ease, at least those located in downtown Philadelphia and in the district. Perhaps the shared legal woes and the collective fear of jail time helped forge some bond between the white and Black people on the defendants' side of the courtroom. The easy conversations across racial lines might even qualify these courtroom seating areas as what Elijah Anderson has referred to as a Cosmopolitan Canopy—a place where many kinds of people come together and keep their ethnocentric opinions in check, treating one another decently.[14]

Venturing out together into white neighborhoods or into various other buildings in Center City besides the courthouse could be difficult. As any interracial couple knows, the simple act of appearing together in public can create a level of tension that is difficult to bear. Often, people would be so thrown off when Mike and I showed up together that we learned to walk some distance apart from each other on the sidewalk, so that passersby wouldn't necessarily know we were together. We'd often enter a store or bar or restaurant separately, so that clerks and hostesses and security guards wouldn't have to address us simultaneously.

When Chuck, Mike, or Reggie and I went into the city's white neighborhoods, those which Anderson refers to as more ethnocentric,[15] sometimes people were openly rude, or would tell us that the kitchen was closed or that we couldn't enter. Sometimes we got the impression that we were catching people on a very bad day. Beyond our skin color, our ages and apparent class differences helped make these interactions highly charged, though it was hard to know if these reactions stemmed from the sight of Black young men with a white young woman, a middle-class white woman with Black men who appeared decidedly "ghetto," or Black men in white spaces, period.

In addition to public spaces and white ethnic neighborhoods, large social gatherings on 6th Street remained tense for me. In seven years I attended nineteen funerals for young neighborhood men who'd been killed by gunfire, as well as three funerals for older people. I learned to dread these occasions, along with the far rarer event: weddings. Inevitably, these occasions brought in strangers and relatives I'd never met before, who demanded to know who I was and how exactly I was connected to the deceased or the bridal couple. Large gatherings also involved special activities or behaviors I hadn't learned, and the chance to screw them up before a large audience. And they involved the mixing of many audiences; the public display of private relationships.

Methodologically, my task was not to let my comfort level guide the inquiry. That is, I tried to be careful not to give greater weight to the places and situations where I was most at ease, or to the people or places that gave an easier time to the biracial group that the 6th Street Boys and I became whenever I was present.

While my race came into and out of focus depending on the context, my behavior and appearance were gradually changing as well. Scholars in the social constructionist tradition have written about race as a performance versus race as cognition.[16] In a similar approach, Reggie sometimes took it as his mission to instruct me on matters of language, dress, and movement, proudly proclaiming to others that he was turning me "into a Black chick." Of course he didn't mean this literally; I think he was referring to a set of behaviors, attitudes, and orientations toward the world that a person can acquire.

I wasn't always as dedicated a student as Reggie wished. When I came back to the neighborhood after attending a family wedding out of state, he accused me of sounding and acting like a white girl again, as if those three days had undone all his careful teachings. The next summer, I spent two weeks out of town with my parents, and Mike insisted that this hiatus had "taken all the Black" out of me.

Becoming a Fly on the Wall

The most consistent technique I adopted to reduce the impact of my difference was social shrinkage—to become as small a presence as possible. If the goal was to find out what life for the residents of 6th Street was like when my strange presence wasn't screwing things up, then I'd try to take up as little social space as I could.

Blending into the background became an obsession. When sitting on a stoop, I'd sit behind a bigger person or I'd sit halfway inside the house, so that people walking by wouldn't necessarily see me. This is something like how people learn to hide a deformed or scarred limb, only I learned to do it with my whole body. I also learned to become a quiet person, someone who doesn't say or do much, who isn't known to have strong opinions.

I came up with tests for how well I was doing. If someone told a story about a past event and couldn't remember whether I had present for it, then I knew I was doing fairly well. If Mike or Chuck began a distinctly different kind of conversation or used another tone of voice once I'd gone to bed or left the room, I inferred that my presence was in the forefront of their awareness, and I had work to do.

Receding into the background became a technique to reduce my influence on the scene but also to limit any risk I might be placing people under. This was particularly concerning given that the older policing literature says that the police start paying attention when they see something out of the ordinary. Was I increasing Mike's or Chuck's dealings with the police simply by hanging around? After a while I decided that this wasn't the case: the tough-on-crime policing approach currently at work in Black neighborhoods like 6th Street doesn't wait for something out of the ordinary—police routinely swooped into the neighborhood to make stops, conduct raids, and search men who were walking around whether I was present or not. Still, it couldn't hurt to be as small a presence as possible.[17]

At a practical level, my goal of not altering the scene could be difficult to work out. In order to understand whether one's words or actions are creating something strange and foreign, one must first learn what is normal. In a scene so different from any I'd known, it took months and sometimes years for me to work this out.

Take violence. Young men on the block often made promises to beat up or shoot someone who'd injured or insulted them or someone they held dear. For instance, one afternoon Steve, Chuck and I were sitting on a porch. Steve was rolling marijuana into a hollowed-out Phillies cigar when Reggie came walking up the block.

REGGIE: I'm about to fuck this nigga up, man.
CHUCK: Who, Devon?
REGGIE: Yeah! I ain't like that shit, man.

At first when Reggie or Mike would make these threats, I sat quietly by, like a good fly on the wall, waiting to see what would happen. Later, I learned that people within earshot of these threats often take it on themselves to talk the person down or even to physically restrain him. In fact, young men and sometimes women typically make it a point to make these promises to fight or to shoot when someone else was around whom they can count on to hold them back; in this way a person can preserve his honor without risking his life. Of course, this isn't all show—often people promising to go and shoot genuinely want to, at least for a time. At any rate, months later I realized that as a friend or sis or cousin, men were expecting me to hold them back; to fail to do this would put them in danger of having to make good on their promises. So after a time I learned that taking someone's car keys or hiding a gun wasn't changing the outcome of events as much as sitting idly by would be. Blocking the door was the way to blend into the walls.

Roommates

When I met Mike, he'd been working nights at a warehouse in Northeast Philadelphia—a great job paying $7.50 an hour that his mother had found for him. He was supplementing this income with sporadic work in the crack business, which also intermittently employed his friends Chuck and Steve along with many other guys from the neighborhood. Shortly after we met, Mike's second child was born, and after complications with the birth, he didn't show up for two weeks of work. He lost the warehouse job and moved to selling crack full time.

Later that year, Chuck returned from county jail. He had spent nine months there awaiting trial for a school yard fight in which he had pushed a fellow student's face into the snow. Unlike his younger brother Reggie, Chuck had attended school regularly before he was taken into custody; during the months he spent in jail awaiting trial, he lost a full year of school. When he returned to his high school the following fall, after the case was dismissed, he tried to register again as a senior. He was then nineteen, and the secretary said he was too old to enroll.

In the weeks after Chuck came home, he and Mike drove around looking for work. They applied online or in person at Target, Walmart, McDonald's, Wendy's, Kmart, PetSmart, and Taco Bell. They listed the landline at my apartment or my cell as their contact, since their cell phones got shut off too often to be reliable conduits for job leads. They'd come in and play the machine every evening, or ask me if anyone had called when we met up in the afternoons. No employer ever did.

After weeks without a single job lead, Chuck, Mike, and their close friend Steve pooled their money and bought some crack to sell. Some days they'd begin cutting and bagging the drug around midday, and then spend the afternoon and evening selling it hand to hand to people in the neighborhood. Mostly these customers were frail and thin members of their parents' generation, who I gathered had started smoking crack when it was cool and popular in the '80s. But many days Mike and Chuck had no crack to sell: their supplier had gotten arrested or was simply unavailable, or the money they owed this "connect" had been seized from their pockets by the police during a stop and search, and so they'd been unable to pay the man back and hence obtain any more drugs. Sometimes they'd made enough money the previous week to get by without selling any. Though they sometimes spoke of ambitions to become major dealers, Mike and Chuck approached selling as a part-time and undesirable income-generating activity. They picked up the work when they had no other income or had exhausted the women or family members who'd give them small bits of money to live on.[18] Chuck in particular frequently articulated his distaste for crack and for selling it to people who, like his own mother, had been ruined by the drug and couldn't help themselves.

In the spring of 2003, Mike lost the lease to his apartment on 6th Street, which his mother had left to him when she moved across town. We packed up the apartment and he moved back in with his mom. During this time Mike, Chuck, and Steve would stop by my place to hang out or do their laundry. They'd often fall asleep watching movies on the couch. Getting back to his mother's at the end of the night was a major inconvenience, so Mike began keeping more and more of his possessions at my place. After a while I said that if he was going to be crashing so much, he should contribute to the bills and groceries. Gradually we became roommates, with Mike taking the pull-out couch in the large living room and Chuck taking the smaller couch next to it. Steve alternated sleeping at his grandmother's house on 6th Street, his girlfriend's house a few blocks over, and our living room floor.

Becoming a roommate was a gradual and unplanned thing, but it greatly enhanced the depth of the study. I could now compare what happened on the block with what happened at home, and for days on end. I was also able to take notes as events and conversations took place, often transcribing them on my laptop in real time as they were going on around me. This meant, too, that Chuck, Mike, and other young men could read over my shoulder as I was typing these field notes, correcting something I'd written or commenting on what I was writing about. A few times, Mike and Chuck read some of the notes as they watched

TV and remarked, "Yo. She gets every fucking thing!!" Very occasionally someone would say, "Don't write this down" or "I'm going to say some shit right now, and I don't want it to go in the book." In these cases, I took careful heed and did as people requested.

* * *

During these months, I was learning a lot about work at the lowest levels of the local drug trade. I was also learning about relations between men and women in the neighborhood. I was spending so much time on 6th Street that few people there hadn't met me, and things were starting to become much less awkward.

One problem I still encountered during this period was that Mike, Chuck, their neighbors, and their relatives didn't think I had any female friends. When you get older and have a job and a family to attend to, friends may not be such a big deal—but when you're twenty-one and friendless, especially in a community of dense social networks and extensive family ties, being friendless can be a major point of shame. Though I gradually developed close friendships with Reggie's girlfriend, Aisha's older sister, and other women my own age, people wanted to know where my friends were from my own community, friends who looked like me. They'd ask whether I had any and who and where they were, wondering out loud if in my community I was somewhat of a lame, as I was here.

From time to time I'd mention various friends from high school and even a few from college, but then Reggie or Alex would ask me to set them up. As Mike's sis I was off limits, but that didn't go for my girlfriends. Where were my girlfriends? And what about my younger sister? Where was she? Did she like Black guys? Sometimes I was stricken with the thought that I was keeping these social worlds apart in a way that concretized the unequal status of Mike and Chuck and Alex, as if I were saying that Black men from 6th Street weren't good enough for my white sister and friends. Other times I attempted mixed outings or events with disastrous results.

At my twenty-second birthday party that year, white friends from high school and grade school came to the apartment to throw a dinner party. When Aisha and a number of her friends walked in, my best friend from eighth grade immediately offered them some brie and crackers. Aisha assumed that the round of cheese was cake, and spit it out on the floor when she tasted the sour rind. Then a high school friend got so afraid when Mike and Chuck and Steve came in that she left only a few minutes after their arrival, claiming to have a sudden migraine. I was outraged and humiliated, and apologized profusely.

Walking in the Shoes

Beyond being a fly on the wall, I wanted to be a participant observer. I wanted to live and work alongside Mike and his friends and neighbors so that I could understand their everyday worries and small triumphs from the inside. The method of participant observation involves cutting yourself off from your prior life and subjecting yourself as much as possible to the crap that people you want to know about are being subjected to.[19] How do you do this when nobody treats you the same way? When you are a different color, and class, and gender?

At a practical level, the divides between us made participant observation a confusing endeavor. Should I try to take on the attitudes and behaviors and routines of Mike and Chuck and their friends, though I was clearly not a man? Or should I instead try to take on the role of a woman associated with them? This made more sense, except that the world of women was a separate sphere from the life of the street. Certainly, the experience of a girlfriend or mother of a man on the run is different from the experience of this man, who is actually dodging the authorities. Over time, I tried to take on some of both.

In her ethnography of police, Jennifer Hunt describes how the officers she studied assigned one of three roles to the women in their lives: good woman, slut, and dyke. Yet for her study she successfully operated outside these categories, negotiating a new role "betwixt and between" that was something like "street woman researcher."[20]

Though I came to 6th Street as a young blond woman, my body, speech, clothing, and general personality marked me as somewhat strange and unappealing. After spending a few months with Mike and his friends, I moved even further away from their ideals of beauty or femininity, in part as a strategy to conduct the fieldwork, and in part because I was, as a participant observer, adopting their male attitudes, dress, habits, and even language.

What about relations with the police? That the police consistently ignored me when they approached Mike and Chuck and their friends was in many ways very lucky. It certainly helped to reassure me that I wasn't placing anyone in greater danger just by hanging around. But it also made it difficult for me to experience searches, arrests, or jail time—all fundamental experiences for these young men. Should I try to get arrested on purpose? Even if I did, I'd go to a woman's jail as a white female, a first-time inmate, knowing nobody from my own community. This seemed significantly different from the experience that Mike and Chuck and Reggie had when they got locked up. And given that the police largely disregarded me, I might have to go to great lengths to get taken into custody. This would seem like madness to the guys on 6th Street, who devoted so much energy to avoiding the authorities. It might even cause them to question whether having me on the block was a safe or reasonable thing.

Should I instead learn their techniques of evasion and do my best not to get arrested? This would be comparatively easy, given the police's lack of interest in me, but at least here I would be taking on something of how they saw the world and oriented themselves toward it. In the end I went with this second approach, of learning how to spot undercovers, anticipate raids, conceal incriminating objects or activities. "Approach" may imply too much concerted effort—I believe I simply picked up this orientation by spending time with Mike and Chuck and their friends. Still, given that the young men I was attempting to understand got arrested with great frequency, often had multiple criminal cases going at once, and spent half their young adult lives in jail, in prison, or under court supervision, I missed a lot by not moving through the criminal justice system alongside them.

Selling drugs was another conundrum. I'd surely learn a lot by selling crack alongside Chuck and Mike and Steve, but hustling was considered largely men's work, not the purview of women. It required skills I didn't have, like tough negotiating techniques and violence. On some level, Chuck and Mike and their friends considered this work the work of desperation, second only to robbing dealers at gunpoint. It was morally polluted, not to mention legally and physically risky. They looked askance at young men in the neighborhood who came from good families but nevertheless wanted to try their hand at the game. This all led me to think that as a woman and a person from a comparatively well-off family, selling crack would appear to be a strange thing to do. On the other hand, how else would I learn what it felt like to work in the drug trade, especially in this Tough on Crime era in which arrests and jail time are so routine? In the end, my participation was more like what girlfriends and mothers who lived with men selling drugs were exposed to.

Some aspects of life on 6th Street were easier to adopt, and involved fewer moral dilemmas. After a couple of years, I abandoned my vegetarian diet and started drinking wine coolers and liquors like Courvoisier and Hennessy. I lived on very little money and unpredictable amounts of it—not the same as being truly poor, but I certainly felt firsthand the strain of having bills to pay and no money to pay them with. One thing I did not adopt was smoking marijuana—it inhibited my memory and dulled my reflexes. Also, it hampered writing the field notes. I wrote these most evenings and often throughout the morning and early afternoon as well. They formed the main record available to me to make sense of a complex world I was struggling to understand; I couldn't afford for them to suffer.

I restricted my media to what Chuck and his friends watched, read, and listened to. This meant mainstream hip-hop and R&B, and gangster movies. Aside from coursework, I read what Mike and his friends read: "'hood" novels while they were in jail, and the paper when someone we knew had been killed.

I cut myself off from most of my previous friends in Philadelphia, restricting my social life as much as possible to the world of 6th Street. Of course, as I came to spend more and more time in that neighborhood, my old friends cut me off, too—some of these relationships ended with harsh words about the strange and risky life I was leading.

I learned how to sleep on cue and in short intervals, and amid the clamor of others; to distinguish between gunshots and other loud bangs; to run and hide when the police were coming; to identify the car models, haircuts, and body language of undercover cops in plain clothes. I learned how to get through a stop without placing myself or anyone else at greater risk, and how to remain silent during an interrogation so as not to give up any information. I learned how to be a woman closely linked to a man on the run, to go through his hunt and capture and court dates and confinement and release. Some of the ways in which I gradually became more like Mike and Aisha and their friends and family were deliberate and planned. Others, like my appreciation for hip-hop and my fear of the police, developed organically over time.

It is virtually impossible for ethnographers to become full members of a community not their own.[21] It scarcely bears mentioning, then, that this was also the case for me. Beyond the situations and events I never experienced, my background and identity were so different from those of the people I was observing that I couldn't always trust my reactions to events and situations that I did experience firsthand. That is, I had to be cautious in generalizing from my reactions to the feelings or experiences of others.

With all these frustrating barriers, a lot can be said for sustained observation and involvement. If I didn't understand exactly what Mike and Chuck or their girlfriends and mothers were going through, I approximated it in various ways. Certainly, I came closer to understanding than when I started out.

THINGS TAKE A TURN FOR THE WORSE

In the last semester of my junior year of college in 2004, Mike's case for attempted murder was finally coming to a close after a year and a half of monthly court dates. Because he'd made bail before the detainer on another case could come through, he was in a state of legal limbo—not technically wanted but with a detainer out, and liable to get taken into custody if the police stopped him or if he showed up in court. On his court dates, his mother and I would wait nervously down at the courthouse for his lawyer to appear. Mike would hover a few blocks away, waiting to hear if the case was proceeding and he needed to come in. If the lawyer didn't show, Mike would get a warrant for failure to appear, and then the cops would be really looking for him. Since the lawyer Mike had paid dearly for was typically over forty-five minutes late, this was harrowing.

At the same time this was happening, Mike and I started notic-
ing that unmarked cars were following us around 6th Street and to
the apartment. Mike's parole officer confirmed that the feds were indeed considering a case against him. To make matters worse, Reggie
had come home from county and reignited the conflict with the 4th
Street Boys, which his older brother, Chuck, had largely managed to
squash in his absence. Mike returned to the apartment one night with
seven bullet holes in the side of his car. We hid it in a shed so the cops
wouldn't see. As he looked ahead to a long stay in state prison, and
negotiated this precarious holding pattern of making his court dates
without actually showing up, he took to wearing a bulletproof vest and
watching for any unknown cars on our block. Steve, Chuck, and Reggie
seemed increasingly concerned about getting shot as well. If we were
away from one another, we'd check in every half hour or so via text
message.

You good?

Yeah.

Okay.

At school, things were deteriorating at a rapid pace. I'd been taking
extra courses each semester and attending classes during the summer
so I could graduate a year early and get to grad school. But I started to
think that I wouldn't make it through this final semester. It was becoming hard for me to do anything but focus on the drama and emergencies
on 6th Street.

The first real sign I was slipping away from academic life was the
missed meetings. I had made an appointment with historian Michael
Katz, and then failed to either show up or cancel it. I remembered the
meeting only days later, and in the vague way you remember a dream,
or perhaps a movie you had seen years before while intoxicated or very
tired. Michael graciously agreed to another meeting, which I also forgot about. I showed up a week later, hoping he might happen to be in
his office, which he wasn't. What concerned me was not so much that
I'd missed these meetings with a professor I greatly admired, but that I
couldn't find it in myself to feel bad about it. Amid the swiftly changing fortunes and limited resources of Mike and Chuck and their friends
on 6th Street, a promise to be somewhere in the future is understood

as a wish in the moment more than a concrete eventuality or binding contract, and I was starting to absorb that same orientation.

It happened again with Elijah Anderson, who had agreed to supervise my senior thesis, a paper based on the field notes I'd been collecting while living with Mike, Chuck, and Steve. I got an e-mail from Eli asking what had happened—apparently we had agreed to meet at the Down Home Diner in the Reading Terminal. This missed meeting was even more troubling than the one with Michael Katz, because I couldn't recall even having made the appointment. It became clear that my memory itself was changing, not just my orientation to time and obligations. The consummate fieldworker, Eli later wrote up the experience in his book *The Cosmopolitan Canopy*.[22]

That spring, I had to take a number of required courses I'd been putting off, such as science and statistics. These were courses that had no link to the fieldwork, no way to write it up and have it count toward the grade. I registered for these dreaded requirements, but didn't attend the classes or even remember to drop them. This lapse scared me, too, especially as Fs began appearing on my transcript.

The prospect of graduate school became my lifeline. I had applied to UCLA and to Princeton with my fall grades, hoping they'd accept me though I was only a junior, since I could show I had most of the needed credits. I figured that if I didn't get in to either place, I would likely drop out of Penn. There was no way I could complete another year of school and continue in the 6th Street neighborhood, that was for sure. At this point I was still taking daily field notes, but in most other ways I was leaving the academic world behind. Its rules and obligations were ceasing to matter. With the cops circling the apartment and the feds looking into Mike's case, the threats they had been making to arrest me—for harboring fugitives, or interfering with an arrest, or holding drugs in the apartment—were becoming more and more real. The likelihood that I'd soon go to prison seemed about equal to the chance I would make it to graduate school. After looking over my shoulder for so long, the prospect of prison came almost as a relief.

In the spring of that year Mike's attempted murder case closed after more than a year of monthly court dates. On the advice of his lawyer, he pleaded guilty for gun possession and took a deal for a one- to three-year term in state prison, shipping off to Graterford that night. In a silent apartment filled with Timberland boots, empty cartridges, and a sizable gangster movie collection, I found out I had been accepted to graduate school at Princeton.

REGROUPING

When Mike got taken into custody, I lost all three roommates, since Chuck and Steve had been staying at the apartment at Mike's invitation. More than my roommates, though, I lost the right to hang out on the block. I was still spending a lot of time in Aisha's neighborhood with her family and friends, and after Mike went upstate, I kept in touch with a number of the guys from 6th Street who wanted to know how he was doing. But I was, at the time, only Mike's person—there was no reason for me to hang out on 6th Street with him sitting in state prison. I was cut off from the block before I had fully worked out what was happening there.

To bide my time in the last months of junior year, I started hanging out with a group of guys I'd met through a man who worked security for a building on Penn's campus. These young men lived in the same Black section of Philadelphia, about fifteen blocks from 6th Street. But some of them had legitimate jobs, and even proper addresses. They also had driver's licenses. Their routine of working a legal job during the day and drinking beer and playing video games in the evening provided a nice counterpoint to the insecurity and unpredictability of Mike's group of friends, and I welcomed the calm and safety of men whose only connection to guns, drugs, or the police came in the form of video games.

CULTURE SHOCK

In September, classes at Princeton began, and I decided to continue with my research in Philadelphia rather than relocate to New Jersey. I began commuting from the 6th Street neighborhood to class a few times a week. These day trips to the tree-lined campus, nestled in the wealthy and white suburban town of Princeton, were not an easy adjustment. The first day, I caught myself casing the classrooms in the Sociology Department, making a mental note of the TVs and computers I could steal if I ever needed cash in a hurry. I got pulled over for making a U-turn, and then got another ticket for parking a few inches outside some designated dotted line on the street that I hadn't even noticed.

The students and the even wealthier townies spoke strangely; their bodies moved in ways that I didn't recognize. They smelled funny and laughed at jokes I didn't understand. It's one thing to feel uncomfortable in a community that is not your own. It's another to feel that way among people who recognize you as one of them.

I also began to realize how much I had missed by not living in the dorms or hanging out with other undergrads during college. The Princeton students discussed indie rock bands—white-people music, to me—and drank wine and imported beers I'd never heard of. They had witty chitchat and e-mail banter. They listened to iPods, and checked Facebook. I'd also apparently missed finding a spouse in college—many of the students had brought one along to graduate school. And since I'd been restricting my media only to what Mike and his friends read and watched and heard, I couldn't follow conversations about current events, and learned to be silent during any political discussions lest I embarrass myself. Moreover, I had missed cultural changes, such as no-carb diets and hipsters. Who were these white men in tight pants who spoke about their anxieties and feelings? They seemed so feminine, yet they dated women.

More than discomfort and awkwardness, I feared the hordes of white people. They crowded around me and moved in groups. I skipped the graduate college's orientation to avoid what I expected would be large numbers of white people gathered together in a small space. In cafeterias and libraries and bus and train stations, I'd search for the few Black people present and sit near them, feeling my heart slow down and my shoulders relax after I did.

Above everything, I feared white men. Not all white men: white American men who were relatively fit, under the age of fifty, with short hair. I avoided the younger white male faculty at all costs. On some level, I knew they weren't cops, they probably wouldn't beat me or insult me, but I could not escape the sweat or the pounding in my chest when they approached. Office hours were out—I couldn't be in a room alone with them. When I had to pass them in the hallways, I could feel my heart racing, like I was getting ready to run. Very few professors of color were in the Sociology Department at the time, so for advising I stuck to women, non-American men, and men who had accents or who were otherwise far outside the cop mold. Retired professors were good. I took an independent study course with Marvin Bressler, a retired Jewish professor in his seventies.

I also discovered that sudden noises, like a balloon popping or a pan falling from the counter, left me panicked. So did quick and close movements. I had been heading out of Princeton with another grad student in a heavy downpour. At a traffic light, a fellow motorist walked over to our car and knocked loudly on the driver's-side window. I threw up my arms to shield my face when she rapped on the glass, protecting myself from whatever she meant to aim at us. When I realized why she'd come up to us—simply to alert me that my headlights weren't on—I began to cry right in front of my passenger, who said kindly that at first she hadn't realized what the noise was, either. Later, Mitch Duneier and I were entering a restaurant in New York when a flock of birds flew out of the rafter, passing quite near us. I walked out of the restaurant and stayed out for a number of minutes, my hand on my chest. Mitch came out and gently remarked, "I'm sorry, that must have really scared you. Do you want to eat somewhere else?" Around that time a friend of Chuck's had been shot and killed while exiting my car outside a bar; one of the bullets pierced my windshield, and the man's blood spattered my shoes and pants as we ran away. I had been staying at Mitch's spare apartment in Princeton for a few days until things calmed down.

These visits to Princeton also made it clear that I'd developed substantial confusion about my sexual and gender identities. After spending six years in a Black neighborhood, hanging out with young men, I'd come to feel almost asexual. During college, I dated no one; I'd sometimes feel surprise when a mirror returned the image of a young woman. Putting my gender and sexual identity aside seemed like an easier path, given that I couldn't live up to the 6th Street community's ideals of femininity: I wasn't "thick" enough, I didn't dress the right way, I couldn't dance. I was not Black. It was a shock when I began to spend time again with middle-class white academics that some of them found me young and at least somewhat attractive. More than this, they were fixated on what sexual relationship I may or may not be having with the guys on 6th Street, as if it were the first thing that popped into their minds when they saw me and heard about the project.

There was also the confusion of thinking and seeing like Mike and his friends.

Upon meeting my fellow grad students during the sociology orientation, I quickly sized up the women in the cohort, and as one walked away I turned to admire her. This is how we passed a lot of time around 6th Street: standing or sitting on the stoop, watching women walk by and talking about their various attributes. This woman turned around just as I was looking, and actually caught me staring. There was very little else I could have been doing, and I'm fairly certain my face registered open appreciation. I never did become friends with her, though who knows if she even remembers this incident.

Social awkwardness and identity confusion aside, driving to New Jersey a few times a week was in many ways a good thing. The hour-long ride gave me some distance from the chaos and emergencies of 6th Street, and a chance to think about what I was seeing.

I was also learning for the first time about mass incarceration. With Devah Pager and Bruce Western both in the Sociology Department at the time, the corridors of Wallace Hall were a hotbed of activity on the causes and consequences of the prison boom. After muddling through a slew of topics and themes, I came to see, through Devah and Bruce's influence and Mitch Duneier's guidance, that my project could be framed as an on-the-ground look at mass incarceration and its accompanying systems of policing and surveillance. I was documenting the massive expansion of criminal justice intervention into the lives of poor Black families in the United States.

By the spring of my first year of graduate school, I was visiting Mike in state prison on the weekends and spending my evenings in Philadelphia with the group of guys I'd met shortly before I left Penn—the ones who were working regular jobs. I'd learned a lot about how they differed from Mike and his friends—for example, when one of them lost his job, he didn't move to selling crack but instead relied on the support of friends and relatives. This group had virtually no legal entanglements and didn't run when the police approached. Some of them had brothers or cousins whose lives more closely resembled those of Mike and his friends, but they made a considerable effort to avoid these men and the risks that any association would pose.

*   *   *

One night, Chuck's younger brother Reggie, now nearly eighteen, phoned to tell me that a man who was loosely associated with the 6th Street Boys had killed a man from 4th Street during a botched robbery at a dice game. He insisted that I come immediately to his uncle's basement, where the guys were assembling to work out what to do next.

I sat on top of the washing machine for four hours and listened while five men berated the shooter for his thoughtless actions, discussed what the fallout would be from this death, and whether and when to shoot at the guys who they knew without question were now coming for them. In those four hours I learned more about gun violence than I had in my previous three years in the neighborhood.

In the end, nobody strapped up. The plans fizzled, and we parted ways around 3:00 a.m.[23]

Through this emergency, it seemed I'd somehow been asked to come back to 6th Street—not as someone connected to Mike, but on my own steam. Reggie seemed to feel that as at least a resident guest of 6th Street and the group's main chronicler, I shouldn't miss these important events.

Over the following weeks, young men from 4th Street drove through the 6th Street neighborhood and shot up the block. Chuck took a partial bullet in the neck, and Steve took a bullet in his right thigh. Neighbors stopped going outside and instructed children to play indoors. From prison, Mike sent heated letters home to Chuck and Reggie, voicing his outrage that they'd allow me to be on the block during these dangerous times. I was pretty pissed off about how Mike reacted, though looking back I can understand how, sitting in prison, he may have felt that the younger men no longer listened, or that the world was moving on without him.

By that summer Mike and I had reconciled, and Chuck, Steve, and Reggie were sitting in jail and prison. For four years of graduate school, I continued to live near 6th Street, coming into the university two or three times a week and spending much of the rest of my time hanging out with whichever members of the group were home, as well as with

Aisha and her family and friends. On the weekends, I visited incarcerated members of the group in jails and prisons across the state. Chuck's and Mike's families already knew me well, but I came to know the families of other young men better as we dealt with the police together, attended court dates, and made long drives upstate for visiting hours.

After serving his full sentence in state prison, Mike returned to 6th Street in 2007. As often happens when a man comes home, he spent the first couple of weeks admonishing his boys on the block for failing to do enough for him while he was away—for not visiting enough, for not writing back to his letters, for not sending money when they had promised, and for sleeping with various girls he had dated and then lying about it. As time went on, he seemed to forgive and forget; it appeared things were back to normal.

That summer, Chuck gave me the nickname A-Boogie. It remains the way many members of the group refer to me, like when addressing letters from prison. Now when I go back to the block, people often say I am from 6th Street, though that's not literally true, as I never actually lived on the street.

THE SHOOTING AND ITS AFTERMATH

In the summer of 2007, a tragedy rocked the 6th Street community and altered the lives of the 6th Street Boys, as well as my own. For many it represented a pivotal event, an event around which other events, relationships, or habits came either before or after. For some, it even signaled a final ending to a young adulthood spent in the streets, trying to make it by selling drugs and dipping and dodging the police.

Around ten o'clock on a Wednesday night, Mike phoned me with the news that Chuck had been shot in the head outside the Chinese takeout store. As Mike had heard it, he'd been walking there to buy dinner for himself and his youngest brother, Tim, who was with him and saw him fall. I asked Mike how serious it was, remembering the time a bullet had merely grazed the skin above Mike's ear a few years before.

"He got shot in the *head*," Mike said. "What the fuck do you think?"

I debated whether to go right to the hospital or drive for an hour to pick up Mike from the suburb where he'd been staying. Finally, Mike persuaded me to get him, and I headed out. We drove back into Philly in silence. The idea that Chuck might not make it was incomprehensible to me, so I thought about his long recovery, with physical therapy and pain and depression. I made a mental list of what I would do to lift his spirits. I thought about the day before, when Chuck and I had shared a quick meal of cheese fries and a cigarette, and made plans to visit his middle brother, Reggie, in county jail. Chuck hadn't seemed to feel that tensions with 4th Street were particularly high that day; things had been calmer for the past few weeks. Did they catch him off guard? I thought about the times Chuck and I had driven to visit Mike in state prison before Mike came home last month, and about how silly Chuck would get in the visiting room, trying to make Mike laugh. And about a few years ago, when the three of us had first become roommates.

As we approached the hospital, Mike told me that apart from Chuck's mom and girlfriend and baby-mom, females really shouldn't be around right now; it would be a whole bunch of niggas in there, since the shit was fresh, talking about shit that females didn't need to hear about.

He was right: as we pulled up, we saw a crowd of men on the corner outside the ER. There were, by my count, twenty-seven young men standing across the street from the hospital. And just as if 6th Street had been fully transported downtown, two white cops stood across the street, watching them and talking to each other. I recognized a number of the guys and realized that some had open warrants or pending cases and were risking a great deal to stand here, in plain view, obviously linked to a man who had just been shot. An act of respect and love and sacrifice. A midnight vigil for Chuck.

Mike went over to stand with them, giving me another look to indicate that I was in no way welcome to join. I parked and walked into the ER instead. No one in the crowd of men said anything to me as I passed, or even nodded.

The waiting room was full of cops and patients waiting to be called—Chuck's was one of three shootings that had come in that evening. I gave his name to the woman behind the counter, and she told me he was in the intensive care unit, and that only immediate family could go in. Not wanting to walk again past the men outside, who had become strangers now in downtown Philadelphia, and not wanting to leave Chuck in this strange place, I got lost in the wings of the hospital, finally walking out another way. On the drive home, I pondered whether Steve and the other guys had ignored me because they thought I shouldn't be there, or simply because in white Philadelphia we aren't supposed to know each other or stand together. Perhaps they'd just been preoccupied with their grief, and with figuring out who had shot Chuck: the conversations men hold when no women are present.

I'd been home for a while when Mike called to say that the cops had cleared them off the sidewalk and told Chuck's uncle and girlfriend, who were waiting inside, that they had to go home. He said they'd all gone back to Chuck's mother's house, where they would be sitting with her until there was any news. Then he asked me if I had an update on Chuck's condition.

"I'm at home."

"You left?"

"You told me not to be there."

Mike made a noise to indicate that I didn't understand anything, and hung up. His surprise and annoyance that I'd left was enough encouragement; I drove back to the hospital immediately.

Chuck's family and friends and neighbors had gone. When I asked at the desk, I was told that Chuck was no longer in the ICU; he was in the NICU, the neuro intensive care unit. Seeing his description in the computer, the white woman at the desk raised her eyebrows, and asked if I knew him. What kind of a question was that? I said yes. She responded: you know he got shot in the head, right? Yes. She asked who I was, and without thinking I said what I say when I go to visit Chuck in jail: that we're cousins.

A white male doctor in his early thirties walked past the desk at that point and asked if I needed directions, offering to walk with me to the NICU. It was now after 3:00 a.m. We walked together through closed and empty wings, and I realized that I wasn't scared of white men if they were wearing a lab coat. I explained to him that my cousin had been shot in the head. We moved through a bunch of security doors and into the NICU, and then right to the door of Chuck's room.

Chuck lay in the raised bed, his upper body covered in casts, a brace closed around his neck. His face was propped up high, elongating his neck, and thick white bandages covered his head. His face was bloated and his expression unfamiliar, like it belonged to someone else. The small TV on the wall played commercials and he was propped up to face the screen, as if he were watching them. The doctor gave me his card, saying that if I needed anything I should ask for him.

As soon as the doctor left, the nurse told me I couldn't be in the room; Chuck's condition was very critical. She explained that the family spokespeople were his uncle and grandfather, that she could release information only to them. I said okay. But nobody told me to leave, so I stayed an hour, then another, there in the hallway outside Chuck's room. Like I was standing watch.

At around 6:00 a.m., a flood of people rushed in with machines and tense expressions, and someone asked where the number to the family was. I yelled that I had it, and then a nurse picked up a speaker and yelled, "Code Blue." A man came in and said he was from the organ-donor program. He told me that Chuck was brain-dead, his brain not functioning, the bullet had gone in and split into a dozen pieces, too much blood. Chuck had no heartbeat and they were trying to get it back, but only for harvesting the organs because his brain was dead. I wondered: Like a coma? Can't they keep him alive with that? I called Miss Linda, Chuck's mother; I didn't know whether Chuck was dead, and if he was I didn't want to be the one to tell her. So I handed the phone to the organ guy. He told her that he was very sorry, but Chuck's brain was dead, too many pieces of bullet. He asked her if she'd like the organs to go to people who needed them, and she said, as I told him she would, that no part of his body would be going to anybody else.

I was asking to see him and they were telling me no, and I was crying, squatting on the floor among the medical staff, and then a guy told me that Chuck's heart had stopped. I was texting Mike that he was gone and that no, they weren't going to revive him; his brain was dead, it was just the organs they were hoping to save. Mike said, "Don't move. I'm on my way."

At this point it occurred to me that I'd snuck through a great deal of hospital that night, and had absolutely no business being there. I asked Mike via text if Miss Linda was mad that I'd stuck around. Mike said no, and left it at that.

One of the nurses said I could go into Chuck's room, so I crouched on the floor beside his bed. He'd been cleaned up again, the casts removed, the blood no longer oozing from his head. I put my arm over the rail and held his hand. I cried to him and told him that I loved him. I told him I was sorry. A kind male nurse came in and gave me a chair, offered apple juice. I sat with Chuck for an hour, maybe more. I noticed his watch lying on a white paper towel on the bedside table, and I remembered the day he got it, and how much he liked it, even though it was very plain, and I took it and put it in my purse, in the little pocket, and didn't tell anyone.

I was still there like that when Alex and Chuck's on-again, off-again girlfriend, Tanesha, entered the room. I immediately gave up my spot next to Chuck, in the chair the nice nurse had brought in. Tanesha was talking to him, and telling Alex and me what she saw: how he moved his arm because he was fighting, he always was a fighter; how she had followed the ambulance here. How could he leave her and leave his girls? She noticed that his body was beginning to grow stiff. Her legs were shaking and she was crying softly, saying she couldn't go to work today. Said, "You are my baby, why did you leave me?" She said she should have stayed last night. She told about how she had found Chuck on the ground with Tim on top of him, how Tim had phoned her and said come here, so she pulled back around and saw Chuck on the ground. Tim still at the station, held for questioning. And his brother dead.

Later, the detectives came in: three white guys in plain clothes. Hearing that I hadn't been at the scene when Chuck was shot, they rolled right past me, taking Tanesha and Alex outside the room for questioning. Alex, who didn't even live on 6th Street anymore, who now had a regular job and hadn't been anywhere nearby when Chuck was shot.

By this time I didn't know exactly who'd killed Chuck, but I had a pretty good idea. We'd spent much of every day together in the months before he'd been shot, and I'd also been around for the previous war. I was thinking I certainly could've helped narrow it down for the police, if they'd bothered to ask me. But they didn't, and so I was alone again in the room with Chuck. I held his hand. I talked to him. Mike texted me that the detectives grabbed him as he walked into the hospital, before he could even get up to the room.

Then Tanesha walked back into the room with the detectives, and said if she heard anything she would tell them. They gave her their card. They asked her if she thought that Mike knew the shooter's identity, to go with her gut. She said she didn't know. They left.

Mike got released from questioning and came up to the room and stood by Chuck's bed. He looked at Chuck and gave a firm nod of his head and said, "It's cool, it's cool," meaning: this will be handled; your death will be avenged. Then while looking down at Chuck, Mike cried a heaving, breathy cry. The sound of a person without much practice in crying, I thought.

Sitting in the room around Chuck's bed, we talked about bringing Reggie home from county jail on a funeral furlough. I said that if Reggie came home, all he was gonna do was go shoot someone, and Alex said, "Please—somebody gon' die regardless," and Mike nodded his head in agreement, and Tanesha, too. Alex counted one, two, three, four with his fingers. The number of people who would die. Then we talked about where the hell Chuck's baby-mom Brianna was. We thought she might have been on a trip out of town, because Chuck's mom had the girls at her house for the week. Had anyone gotten in touch with Brianna? Did she know?

More of Chuck's friends and neighbors have come in the room at this point. We didn't think Chuck's mother would come to the hospital— Miss Linda didn't like to leave the house except for her son's court dates, and in her state of shock and grief, she likely wouldn't make it over. After a couple of hours, some medical person came in and told us they'd have to take the body away. I walked outside with this guy and explained that we were waiting on Chuck's mother, and that they couldn't move the body until she arrived. He agreed to keep Chuck in the room for a couple more hours.

In the end, Miss Linda did come, accompanied by four young men from the block. She walked into the room and said quietly, "Let me see my son." I was in the waiting room across the hall with Alex, who by that time was snoring loudly. He'd been up since six o'clock the morning before.

Then Reggie called my phone from jail.

"Reggie, do you know?"

"Yeah, I know. I got to come home to see my brother go in the dirt."

I went into Chuck's room, now crowded with people. Miss Linda was sitting on the bed holding her son's hand, whimpering softly and rocking back and forth. She got on my phone with Reggie and said, "Uh huh, uh huh, uh huh, no, it was one bullet," then the phone died, and she passed it back to me. I pictured Reggie sitting in his cell grieving for his brother. I was squatting on the floor next to Chuck's neighbor, who was sitting on the chair. I'd asked the kind nurse to bring in apple juice and more chairs. Tanesha was on the other side of the bed, another neighbor sat on the floor, and two other guys perched on the windowsill.

Miss Linda lay on top of her son and moaned, "Oh baby, oh my baby." She held his hand and repeated, "Squeeze my hand, baby. Chuck, squeeze my hand." She rubbed his arms rapidly and forcefully, as if to warm his body. This made me cry and Tanesha cry. Then abruptly Miss Linda got up and walked out. I followed her and held out my arms, and she wept loudly into me. Tanesha came out and got on the other side of her, and the two of us held her up. Miss Linda said she wanted to go. Tanesha offered to drive her, and asked me if I would walk them down to the car. We were still holding Miss Linda up on either side. Miss Linda then asked if I would come immediately to the house. I said yes.

I'd meant to follow Tanesha in my own car, but somehow I couldn't seem to leave Chuck. After putting quarters in the meter, I came back to his room in time to see them putting him into the body bag, folding him to one side then the other, a tag on his big toe. I waited for an hour down at the ER to try to get his stuff back, but they told me that his belongings had been brought to the police station, held for evidence. Because of the nature of his death, they would be taking Chuck's body to the city morgue.

I charged my phone in the car, and as soon as it turned on, Miss Linda called and asked if I was on my way. I said yes. She said that if I couldn't be there, I should give the money I'd promised her for Pampers to Tanesha, who was looking after Chuck's daughters until their mother came back. She was worried about Chuck's daughters. She was without any of her sons. Reggie at CFCF on $10,000 bail. Chuck dead. And Tim, fifteen, who had seen him die, still held at the police station. Did he even know yet that Chuck hadn't made it?

In the car I fought my own anxiety, the anxiety that always came with large social gatherings on 6th Street. I remembered Mike telling me that I couldn't stand with the guys on the corner outside the hospital, and going into the ER to work out some alternate role, to be helpful in my difference. I remembered Chuck's girlfriend throwing daggers at me with her eyes, clearly suspicious about our relationship but unwilling to come right out and ask me about it. What right had I to be at the hospital, the only person permitted to remain through the night? And also the only one to escape police questioning? Chuck's thirty friends and relatives had been sent away, and his fifteen-year-old brother, who had seen him fall, and who loved him like a son loves a father, held for hours and hours at the police station. Had watched him fall, had crouched over him screaming before running away, Tanesha said. But I couldn't leave Chuck alone at the hospital. I wanted to be there if he made it through the night, and I wanted to be there if he died.

Late that afternoon, the police released Tim. He told us he hadn't eaten or slept in the full fourteen hours they'd held him. For the rest of the day, he barely spoke, his eyes far away. In the evening we gathered on Miss Linda's porch steps, and Tim sat down and looked out at nothing, tears slowly pooling and rolling down his cheeks. He brushed them away the same way he brushed away flies. Later, Tanesha and Mike and I took him to a diner for pancakes and cheese grits and turkey bacon. As we were leaving, I passed him the watch, its face now quite scratched, and he nodded a silent thank-you and put it on his wrist.

* * *

In the days leading up to the funeral, Miss Linda phoned me to come sit with her at the house and sometimes to stay the night. But she kept having to defend the presence of a white girl to the larger family and to people from out of town, and for this I felt ashamed and sorry. Chuck's father's family demanded that Miss Linda get the house fumigated before the funeral so the guests wouldn't be subjected to the cockroaches and flies lining the walls while they ate and mourned. When the fumigator guy arrived with his tank of insecticide, he demanded to know outright what a white woman like me was doing in the house, prompting Miss Linda to yell what had become her usual answer: "That's my fucking white girl. Is it a problem?" Chuck's smallest daughter, only six months old, was happy to get passed from woman to woman, but instantly began crying when I held her, prompting massive embarrassment on my part and a mixture of sympathy and curiosity from others.

Didn't I know how to take care of a baby? Or was she scared to be in a white woman's arms? Another child—the daughter of a cousin whom I'd never met before—spotted me and immediately leaped onto my lap, then clung to my leg for the rest of the evening. Her mother tried to pull her off, which made her start to cry, prompting her mother to sheepishly acknowledge: she likes white people.

Compounding the disturbance of my sheer presence were the mistakes I made in the weeks following Chuck's death. The first error was hugging Chuck's father when I saw him at the house. He'd left his wife and kids to grieve with Miss Linda, an act she regarded as a strong sign of his continued attachment to her, as well as of his love for his firstborn son. She'd banished her longtime boyfriend during his stay, though he did attend the funeral.

On the first night of mourning, we were sitting around the table outdoors, and Miss Linda was handing out the Rest in Peace T-shirts she had purchased from a kiosk at the Gallery, a downtown mall that caters to less affluent Black and white residents of the city. The T-shirts showed Chuck's smiling prom picture from the job training program on the front, with dates of his birth and death below it, along with the words "Gone but Never Forgotten."

I saw Chuck's father walk through the door. We both began to cry, and as he approached I got up and hugged him. Not a long embrace, a quick hug of sympathy.

Tanesha promptly informed Miss Linda that I had just hugged Chuck's father, and Miss Linda came over to yell at me and at him. He tried to laugh it off and calm her down, but she didn't calm down, not for fifteen minutes. "You know I don't play that!" she yelled.

How could I have forgotten that it's simply not appropriate for a young woman like me to embrace an older man who's not a family member? And no less the father of Miss Linda's firstborn? To think that I had compounded Miss Linda's grief with jealousy and conflict—I left that evening and planned to stay away until the day of the funeral. But Miss Linda phoned me at five in the morning to say that she couldn't sleep, and asked me to come back and sit with her.

The family didn't have enough money for the funeral home expenses, so we called the morgue and asked them to keep the body for a little longer. Days passed, and Reggie didn't get the furlough—the cops said it was too risky, given the circumstances of his brother's death.

* * *

After most of the extra cops had left the neighborhood, the hunt was on to find the man who had killed Chuck. Since Tim had seen the shooter from only a few feet away, many knew the man's name and the guys he hung out with. But the man had gone deep underground—nobody could figure out where he was hiding. As Reggie berated his boys each day from jail—what they weren't doing, how slow they were to avenge his brother's murder, what he would do if he were home—the 6th Street Boys acquired more and more guns, gearing up for what they assumed would be coming: part three of the 4th Street War.

Many nights, Mike and Steve drove around looking for the shooter, the guys who were part of his crew, or women connected to them who might be able to provide a good lead. On a few of these nights, Mike had nobody to ride along with him, so I volunteered. We started out around 3:00 a.m., with Mike in the passenger seat, his hand on his Glock as he directed me around the area. We peered into dark houses and looked at license plates and car models as Mike spoke on the phone with others who had information about the 4th Street Boys' whereabouts.

One night Mike thought he saw a 4th Street guy walk into a Chinese restaurant. He tucked his gun in his jeans, got out of the car, and hid in the adjacent alleyway. I waited in the car with the engine running, ready to speed off as soon as Mike ran back and got inside. But when the man came out with his food, Mike seemed to think this wasn't the man he'd thought it was. He walked back to the car and we drove on.

* * *

During the period surrounding Chuck's death, I started studying shoot-outs in earnest: how and when they happened and what the ongoing conflicts looked like over time. But I don't believe that I got into the car with Mike because I wanted to learn firsthand about violence, or even because I wanted to prove myself loyal or brave. I got into the car because, like Mike and Reggie, I wanted Chuck's killer to die.

Perhaps Chuck's death had broken something inside me. I stopped seeing the man who shot him as a man who, like the men I knew, was jobless and trying to make it at the bottom rung of a shrinking drug trade while dodging the police. I didn't care whether this man had believed his life was threatened when he came upon Chuck outside the Chinese takeout store, or felt that he couldn't afford to back down. I simply wanted him to pay for what he'd done, for what he'd taken away from us.

Looking back, I'm glad that I learned what it feels like to want a man to die—not simply to understand the desire for vengeance in others, but to feel it in my bones, at an emotional level eclipsing my own reason or sense of right and wrong. But to go out looking for this man, in a car with someone holding a gun? At the time and certainly in retrospect, my desire for vengeance scared me, more than the shootings I'd witnessed, more even than my ongoing fears for Mike's and Tim's safety, and certainly more than any fears for my own.

NOTES

PREFACE

1. US Department of Justice, "Prisoners 1925–81" (Washington, DC: Government Printing Office, 1982), 3.

2. Christopher Uggen, Jeff Manza, and Melissa Thompson, "Democracy and the Civil Reintegration of Criminal Offenders," *Annals of the American Academy of Political and Social Science* 605 (2006): 285, 287–88.

3. US Department of Justice, "Correctional Populations in the United States, 2011" (Washington, DC: Government Printing Office, 2012), 1.

4. Roy Walmsley, "World Prison Population List," 9th ed. (London: International Centre for Prison Studies, 2011), 3, 5.

5. US Department of Justice, "Correctional Populations in the United States, 2011" (Washington, DC: Government Printing Office, 2012), 3.

6. Alexandr Solzhenitsyn, *The Gulag Archipelago* (New York: Harper and Row, 1973).

7. On the first page of his landmark study of social conditions in Philadelphia's 7th Ward, W. E. B. Du Bois included the footnote, "I shall throughout this study use the term 'Negro,' to designate all persons of Negro descent, although the appellation is to some extent illogical. I shall, moreover, capitalize the word, because I believe that eight million Americans are entitled to a capital letter." I have capitalized the word Black in this work for the same reasons, and to follow him. W. E. B. Du Bois, *The Philadelphia Negro* (Philadelphia: University of Pennsylvania Press, 1899), 1.

8. The Pew Center on the States, "One in 100: Behind Bars in America 2008" (Washington, DC: Pew Charitable Trusts), 6.

9. Becky Pettit and Bruce Western, "Mass Imprisonment and the Life-Course: Race and Class Inequality in U.S. Incarceration," *American Sociological Review* 69 (2004): 151, 164.

INTRODUCTION

1. Katherine Beckett, *Making Crime Pay* (New York: Oxford University Press, 1997), 73; Jonathan Simon, *Governing through Crime* (New York: Oxford University Press, 2007), 241.

2. Katherine Beckett and Theodore Sasson, *The Politics of Injustice: Crime and Punishment in America* (Thousand Oaks, CA: Pine Forge Press, 2000), 5.

3. On the increasing economic hardship and spatial isolation faced by residents of segregated Black neighborhoods in US cities after 1970, see Loïc Wacquant and William Julius Wilson, "The Cost of Racial and Class Exclusion in the Inner City," *Annals of the American Academy of Political and Social Science* 501 (1989): 8–25.

4. Urban ethnographies have documented laissez-faire and corrupt policing in segregated Black neighborhoods from the late 1800s up until the 1980s. On the police turning a blind eye to gambling and prostitution in the Black community in the 1930s and 1940s, see St. Clair Drake and Horace R. Cayton, *Black Metropolis: A Study of Negro Life in a Northern City* (Chicago: University of Chicago Press, [1945] 1993), 524. On widespread corruption among city police during the 1960s, see Jonathan Rubinstein, *City Police* (New York: Farrar, Straus & Giroux, 1973). On the failure of the police to intervene when disputes arose among Black young men in the 1970s, see Elijah Anderson, *A Place on the Corner* (Chicago: University of Chicago Press, 1978), 2. On police allowing open-air drug markets to flourish in Black neighborhoods in the 1980s, see Terry Williams, *Crackhouse* (Reading, MA: Addison Wesley, 1992), 84. On the de facto system of justice that housing project leaders, drug dealers, and a few corrupt police officers enforced in the Chicago projects in the 1980s and 1990s, see Sudhir Venkatesh, *Off the Books: The Underground Economy of the Urban Poor* (Cambridge, MA: Harvard University Press, 2006).

5. Albert J. Reiss Jr., "Police Organization in the 20th Century," *Crime and Justice* 15 (1992): 56.

6. Data on the number of police officers in Philadelphia are taken from the Federal Bureau of Investigation, Uniform Crime Reports (1960 through 2000). Population estimates of Philadelphia are taken from the US Bureau of the Census.

7. For a detailed investigation of the creation and spread of tough crime policy and its connection to welfare retrenchment and market deregulation in the United States, see Loïc Wacquant, *Prisons of Poverty* (Minneapolis: Minnesota University Press, 2009).

8. Christopher Wildeman, "Parental Imprisonment, the Prison Boom, and the Concentration of Childhood Disadvantage," *Demography* 46 (2009): 270.

9. David Garland, "Introduction: The Meaning of Mass Imprisonment," in *Mass Imprisonment: Social Causes and Consequences*, ed. David Garland (London: Sage, 2001), 1–2.

10. On hyperincarceration specifically, see Loïc Wacquant, "Race, Class, and Hyperincarceration in Revanchist America," *Daedalus* 139, no. 3 (2010): 74–90. Wacquant's theoretical and empirical work on the expanding US penal system and its significance for American politics and race relations was a significant inspiration for this volume, and can be sampled in "The New Peculiar Institution: On the Prison as Surrogate Ghetto," *Theoretical Criminology* 4, no. 3 (2000): 377–88; "Deadly Symbiosis: When Ghetto and Prison Meet and Mesh," *Punishment & Society* 3, no. 1 (2001): 95–133; *Urban Outcasts: A Comparative Sociology of Advanced Marginality* (Cambridge: Polity Press, 2008); and *Punishing the Poor: The Neoliberal Government of Social Insecurity* (Durham, NC: Duke University Press, 2009).

11. Devah Pager, *Marked: Race, Crime, and Finding Work in an Era of Mass Incarceration* (Chicago: University of Chicago Press, 2007), 4–5.

12. Bruce Western, *Punishment and Inequality in America* (New York: Russell Sage Foundation, 2006), especially 191.

13. Of the 217 households surveyed by Chuck and me in 2007.

14. In these eighteen months of daily fieldwork, there were only five days in which I observed no police activity.

15. W. E. B. Du Bois, *The Philadelphia Negro* (Philadelphia: University of Pennsylvania Press [1899] 1996).

16. This key social divide in the Black community can be seen in Anderson's earliest book, *A Place on the Corner*. A further and more formal development can be found in "Decent and Street Families," chapter 1 in *Code of the Street* (New York: W. W. Norton, 1999), 35–65.

17. Even middle-class, respectable, and well-connected Black people in Philadelphia are aware of these distinctions to some extent. In 2007, I was asked to be in a working group writing a policy brief for congressional representative Chaka Fattah, who was running for mayor. The group was composed of me and six distinguished Black Philadelphians, including three attorneys, two long-established community organizers, and one writer for the *Philadelphia Daily News*. The first meeting was held in a high-rise building in Center City. When it wrapped, the elevator wasn't working, so we took the stairs. Nearing the second floor, we heard banging noises, and after a bit of discussion and more listening, we concluded that someone must be stuck inside the elevator. One of the lawyers suggested we call the fire department. At this suggestion to alert the authorities, the journalist quipped, "Hope nobody has any warrants!" There were chuckles all around.

CHAPTER ONE

1. An expression of affirmation, meaning roughly "Did I ever."

2. The terms *young boy* and *old head* have been used in the African Ameri-

can community at least since the 1970s. The words denote a mentoring relationship between an older and a younger man or boy, and imply some level of commitment to the welfare of the young boy from the old head and some level of deference and duty on the part of the young boy. Elijah Anderson first mentions the term *old head* in a footnote in *A Place on the Corner* (Chicago: University of Chicago Press, 1978), 225, then elaborates on the relationship between old heads and young boys in *Streetwise*: "The old head/young boy relationship was essentially one of mentor/protégé. The old head might be only two years older than the young boy or as much as thirty of forty years older; the boy was usually at least ten. The young boy readily deferred to the old head's chronological age and worldly experience" (Elijah Anderson, *Streetwise: Race, Class, and Change in an Urban Community* [Chicago: University of Chicago Press, 1990], 69). Anderson goes on to explain that traditional old heads who preached respectability are struggling to maintain their role with a new generation of young men facing a labor market with few decent jobs available to them. New old heads who grew up in street life are replacing the traditional male role models of previous decades (see also Elijah Anderson, *Code of the Street* [New York: W. W. Norton, 1999], 145–46). In keeping with Anderson's discussion, the old heads around 6th Street mentored young boys not on how to make it in respectable jobs but on the strategies for survival in a physically dangerous and heavily policed drug trade.

3. Mike and Chuck sometimes debated whether or not their group of friends could call themselves a gang or even a collective group at all. Philadelphia does not have neighborhood or citywide gangs like the Crips or Bloods, but instead has smaller street-based groups. Mike, Chuck, and their friends were bound to each other by their identification with 6th Street: they either grew up on the blocks crossing 6th Street or spent time there because a close relative had moved to the neighborhood. Five of them had "6th Street" tattooed on their arms, and when they and others wrote me letters from jail, they would end them with their nicknames, followed by "6th Street" or "4-ever-6." They sometimes called themselves the 6th Street Boys, the team, the squad, the clique, or the block. At other times, they forcefully denied they were a collective or group at all, although the fact that they bothered to discuss this might support their group identity rather than call it into question. In Scott Brooks's ethnography of Philadelphia basketball players in middle and high school, Jermaine explains the city's gang system succinctly: "It go by street, really. You got D Street, they represent they block; H street represent they block; K Street, J Street, like P Street. We ain't really got like Bloods and Crips. It just go by your street" (Scott N. Brooks, *Black Men Can't Shoot* [Chicago: University of Chicago Press, 2009], 149).

4. Writing about Philadelphia in the 1960s, Jonathan Rubinstein (*City Police*

[New York: Farrar, Straus & Giroux, 1973]) discusses the need for police officers to show "activity": the work the officers do that can be statistically counted and used informally to judge performance and merit.

CHAPTER TWO

1. It is noteworthy that in pursuits involving men and women, the women were, at least in all instances I observed, the hunters. That is, they took on the role of the police. The houses they were attempting to get the man back to were referred to by both parties as jail or prison, and when the men did get taken home, they and others referred to their girlfriends' having them on lockdown. That is, women were both the police and the wardens. This game version of the women getting the men home strongly parallels the serious role women play, both voluntarily and involuntarily, in the capture and imprisonment of the men in their lives, discussed in the next chapter.

2. The 111 occasions are not counted separately per man; some escapes from the police involved two or more people running away.

3. These numbers and descriptions of young men running from the police come from cases that I observed with my own eyes. I heard recounted far more chases than I observed, but I did not use these narratives as data. Comparing my observations with people's descriptions of the same incidents retold after the fact, I concluded that there is a bias toward reporting chases and getaways that involve known people, that involve elaborate attempts to get away, and that end in the police catching the person. From my observations, in most cases when men see the police and take flight, the police do not chase them at all. Those times the police do give chase, the man typically gets away rather than gets caught, and his successful getaway usually does not involve any creative or herculean efforts. Rather, he typically gets away in a quite mundane way, because the officer in pursuit runs slower or gives up faster. Accounts of chases are interesting in their own right, but are not good data for learning how men actually go about running from the police and the resulting success rates.

4. In Philadelphia, the courts can issue an arrest warrant if a person fails to pay fines for traffic violations or misses a court date in regard to these violations. A person can also be imprisoned for failing to pay these moving violations (Philadelphia County, 33 Pa.B. Doc. No. 2745 and Pa.B. Doc. No. 03–1110).

5. There are many reasons why people do not turn to the law when some crime has been perpetrated against them; having a precarious legal status is simply one of them. For a discussion of legal cynicism, see David S. Kirk and Andrew V. Papachristos, "Cultural Mechanisms and the Persistence

of Neighborhood Violence," *American Journal of Sociology* 116, no. 4 (2011): 1197–1205.

6. When a wanted man fearful of calling the police instead settles disputes with his own hands, this violence is *secondary deviance*—the additional crime a person commits because he has been labeled a criminal. Here the warrant serves as the label, creating more reason to commit crime and get into trouble than the reasons a man already had. For a discussion of secondary deviance in the labeling literature, see Howard Becker, *Outsiders: Studies in the Sociology of Deviance* (New York: Free Press of Glencoe, 1963), chap. 1, and Edwin M. Lemert, *Social Pathology: A Systematic Approach to the Theory of Sociopathic Behavior* (New York: McGraw-Hill, 1951), 75.

7. Ronny's cousin died during the summer, when I was out of town. Reggie called me a few times on the day of the funeral and gave me these updates.

8. Viviana A. Zelizer, *The Purchase of Intimacy* (Princeton, NJ: Princeton University Press, 2007).

9. Prisons and jails offer food, toiletries, clothing, phone cards, books, and other items through commissary accounts. The families and friends of inmates may send money to their loved one's account via the US mail or via online money transfer companies, such as jpay.com, that charge a fee for the service. The cash a man has in his pockets when taken into custody may also be moved into this account. Because the inmate is not permitted to possess or exchange currency, he or she never sees this money, and can use it only for items offered for sale by the prison. Typically, inmates are permitted to make purchases from their commissary account once a week. Child support and other court fines and fees are deducted automatically. In some jurisdictions, prisons require inmates to purchase their bus ticket home from this account, so the inmate may scramble to raise these funds from friends and family before he or she is granted release. This account is referred to as the books, as in "Can you please put some money on my books?"

10. Robberies during or after dice games were quite common around 6th Street at the time I was there. This makes sense, because men would be carrying large amounts of cash and were typically the sort who would not be able to go to the police. Chuck once described a two-man team who robbed dice games as their primary form of income and had been doing so for years, but I never met them personally.

11. Though wet was popular in many parts of Philadelphia, Steve was the only member of the 6th Street Boys who took it regularly. Around 6th Street, wet came in the form of dark crystallized leaves with a little shine sold in small glass vials and smoked in a cigarette or cigar wrapper (called a blunt). Its chemical composition is not at all clear to me, but I believe it involved tea or marijuana leaves soaked in embalming fluid and mixed with PCP.

12. Paying for a witness's hotel stay on the night before court is a typical way

to get a person not to show up. It serves as a way to compensate him or her, but more important, it ensures that the person won't be home if the police should try to drag him or her in to testify.

CHAPTER THREE

1. While conducting fieldwork, I became attentive to the particular moment that women discover a partner or son is wanted by the police by reading studies of people receiving life-altering news in hospitals and doctors' offices. There, family members learn that a loved one has a disease, not a warrant for arrest, but the shock and confusion are common to both, and the news may have a similarly transformative effect on relationships. For two excellent studies of hospital patients and their families receiving life-altering news, see David Sudnow, *Passing On: The Social Organization of Dying* (Englewood Cliffs, NJ: Prentice-Hall, 1967), chap. 5; and Doug Maynard, *Bad News, Good News: Conversational Order in Everyday Talk and Clinical Settings* (Chicago: University of Chicago Press, 2003), 9.

2. This conversation was recorded with permission on my iPhone. Some off-topic pieces of the discussion were omitted.

3. The way others tell it, Mike's mother didn't exactly tell his father to stop coming around—he did that all on his own.

4. The term *rider* has been discussed by Jeff Duncan-Andrade, who uses the spelling *rida*. He defines it as a "popular cultural term that refers to people who can be counted on in extreme duress." Jeff Duncan-Andrade, "Gangstas, Wankstas, and Ridas: Defining, Developing, and Supporting Effective Teachers in Urban Schools," *International Journal of Qualitative Studies in Education* 20, no. 6 (2007): 623.

5. There are few systematic studies of the legal and financial obligations incurred by people moving through the courts. In a unique study, Harris, Evans, and Beckett quantify the financial burden for a sample of people in Washington State. They find that those who have been convicted of misdemeanor or felony charges will owe on average more than $11,000 to the courts over their life span, and likely will pay significantly more than that because of the interest accruing on their legal debts. See Alexes Harris, Heather Evans, and Katherine Beckett, "Drawing Blood from Stones: Monetary Sanctions, Punishment and Inequality in the Contemporary United States," *American Journal of Sociology* 115 (2010): 1753–99.

6. Gresham Sykes, *Society of Captives* (Princeton, NJ: Princeton University Press, [1958] 2007), 63–83.

7. From a taped interview with two former members of the Philadelphia Warrant Unit, 2010.

8. These techniques as I describe them represent the women's perspective on

the police's efforts to secure their cooperation. For a contemporary treatment of police work from the officers' perspective, see Peter Moskos, *Cop in the Hood: My Year Policing Baltimore's Eastern District* (Princeton, NJ: Princeton University Press, 2008).

9. In Philadelphia, a man cannot visit a jail where he has been an inmate for six months after his release. In practice, this paperwork takes quite a while to go through, so that men who have ever been an inmate at a county jail are often denied visitation rights to any of the local jails. Prisons also run the names of visitors, making it dangerous for men with warrants or other legal entanglements to go there for visits. A third barrier to visitation is the canine unit, which is occasionally stationed in the prison or jail parking lot. Though visitors can refuse to allow the dogs to search their vehicles, they will be denied entrance to the facility.

10. For a detailed account of evictions among poor families in the United States, see Matthew Desmond, "Disposable Ties and the Urban Poor," *American Journal of Sociology* 117 (2012): 1295–1335; and Matthew Desmond, "Eviction and the Reproduction of Urban Poverty," *American Journal of Sociology* 118 (2012): 88–133.

11. Research suggests these are quite realistic fears. Incarceration increases the likelihood of infectious disease and stress-related illnesses, according to Michael Massoglia, "Incarceration as Exposure: The Prison, Infectious Disease, and Other Stress-Related Illnesses," *Journal of Health and Social Behavior* 49 (2008): 56–71. The same researcher has shown that incarceration causes long-term negative health effects. See Michael Massoglia, "Incarceration, Health, and Racial Disparities in Health," *Law and Society Review* 42 (2008): 275–306.

12. Of course, that Miss Linda was good at protecting Chuck, Reggie, and Tim from the police may also have contributed to the frequency of police raids, as her firm protectionist stance likely encouraged her sons' continued residency in the house. Other neighbors explained her ability to ride by the fact that in comparison with other women, Miss Linda had little to lose. Since her father owned the house, it wasn't as easy to evict her. Since the house was already in quite poor condition, she didn't fear the destruction caused by the raid as much as other women did. And since she held no job, the police couldn't threaten to notify her employer.

13. Michelle never admitted to this; Mike's lawyer showed his mother and me the statement at the arraignment.

14. For a nuanced account of the many excitements and pleasures to be found in breaking the law, see Jack Katz, *Seductions of Crime: Moral and Sensual Attractions in Doing Evil* (New York: Basic Books, 1990).

15. For an illuminating account of the complex ways in which women view the confinement of a loved one, including some surprising upsides to romantic involvement with a man sitting in prison, see Megan Comfort, *Doing Time*

Together: Love and Family in the Shadow of the Prison (Chicago: University of Chicago Press, 2007), chap. 5, especially 126–27, 174.

CHAPTER FOUR

1. Victor Rios, writing about Oakland, California, documents young people's efforts to push back against an expansive and putative criminal justice system, and describes young men's resistance to their criminalization. See Victor M. Rios, *Punished: Policing the Lives of Black and Latino Boys* (New York: New York University Press, 2011). Here young people are not resisting so much as making use of the police, the courts, and the prisons for their own purposes: they appropriate and manipulate criminal justice personnel and process for their own ends. This is perhaps more akin to the subtle transgressions and sub rosa dissent long documented in repressive regimes, from slaves on plantations—see John Blassingame, *The Slave Community: Plantation Life in the Antebellum South* (New York: Oxford University Press, [1972] 1979)—to peasants in authoritarian states—see James C. Scott, *Weapons of the Weak: Everyday Forms of Peasant Resistance* (New Haven, CT: Yale University Press, 1987).

2. Georg Rusche and Otto Kirchheimer discuss the pressing problem that early politicians and prison designers faced of making prisons sufficiently unpleasant as to deter even the lowest strata of society from crime. *Punishment and Social Structure* (New York, 1939), 105–6. For a thorough treatment of their work, see David Garland, *Punishment and Modern Society: A Study in Social Theory* (University of Chicago Press, 1990), 94.

3. Jack Katz discusses how would-be robbers risk that a victim may fight back. Randall Collins refers to this as the robber's failure to establish situational dominance. See Jack Katz, *Seductions of Crime: Moral and Sensual Attractions in Doing Evil* (New York: Basic Books, 1990); Randall Collins, *Violence: A Micro-Sociological Theory* (Princeton, NJ: Princeton University Press, 2008), 185.

4. See W. E. B. Du Bois, *The Philadelphia Negro* (Philadelphia: University of Pennsylvania Press [1899] 1996); St. Clair Drake and Horace R. Cayton, *Black Metropolis: A Study of Negro Life in a Northern City* (Chicago: University of Chicago Press, [1945] 1993); Elliot Liebow, *Tally's Corner* (Boston, MA: Little, Brown, 1967); Carol Stack, *All Our Kin: Strategies for Survival in a Black Community* (New York: Harper & Row, 1974); Kathryn Edin and Laura Lein, *Making Ends Meet* (New York: Russell Sage Foundation, 1997); Katherine Newman, *No Shame in My Game* (New York: Vintage and Russell Sage Foundation, 1999); Mitchell Duneier, *Sidewalk* (New York: Farrar, Straus and Giroux, 1999); and Elijah Anderson, *Code of the Street* (New York: W. W. Norton, 1999).

5. Liebow, *Tally's Corner*, 116–19.

6. In Pennsylvania, obtaining a driver's license requires a birth certificate or

passport, a social security card, and two proofs of residence (e.g. a lease or a bill with the person's name and address). Obtaining these items in turn requires identification and processing fees. The applicant must undergo a physical exam by a doctor, pay for and pass a written permit test, and either locate an insured and registered car with which to take the driving test or pay to rent one at the test site. Because men drove without proper documentation, they got tickets, which had to be paid before they could begin the license application process.

7. On this point see Liebow, *Tally's Corner*, 113.

8. Those on probation or parole from county jail typically are not given a curfew. Those on parole from a state-imposed sentence (which is a minimum of one year) often have more stringent requirements, which may include obeying a curfew, finding a job, finishing high school, calling the parole officer in the evening from the appointed house, staying away from others who have committed crimes, and so forth.

9. A person who is on parole in Pennsylvania must be paroled to a particular house, which must be inspected in advance and pass a number of requirements. A person cannot in most cases be paroled to his own independent residence. Those released on parole who do not have a house to which they might be paroled are sent to halfway houses.

10. A response to a verbal insult, meaning roughly "You think I'm a bitch now? You haven't seen anything yet."

11. A former Philadelphia probation officer told me that on an average day he received "countless calls" from, as he put it, "the baby-moms." He said that they would phone and try to get their boyfriends put in jail, and then when these men were in jail, they would phone him to try to get their boyfriends out again.

12. This is a fairly common thing to do. In fact, some people get others arrested simply to extort money from them, which they request in exchange for not showing up as a witness during the trial.

13. Since time for phone calls is quite limited, and inmates in county jail are permitted to make only local calls, a substantial need for three-way calling arises. Those in prison have an even greater need, since they typically can call only the numbers on their prearranged list. In the mid-2000s, the regulation against three-way calling was thought to be surmountable by blowing into the phone so that whoever was monitoring the call could not pick up the noise of the numbers being pressed during the three-way dialing.

CHAPTER FIVE

1. Kathleen Nolan provides a nuanced account of a heavily policed public school serving poor Black students in New York. There, the students' be-

havioral problems, such as wearing a hat or talking back to a teacher or po-lice officer, became criminal charges for which they stood trial and in some cases were sentenced to detention centers or jails. Kathleen Nolan, *Police in the Hallways: Discipline in an Urban High School* (Minneapolis: University of Minnesota Press, 2011), 53–64.

2. For a detailed account of the work women do to build and maintain re-lationships with partners who are sitting in prison, see Megan Comfort, *Doing Time Together: Love and Family in the Shadow of the Prison* (Chicago: University of Chicago Press, 2007).

3. As a young man sits in prison, the number of visitors tends to dwindle. Thus, at the beginning of Mike's sentences, his mother struggled to ac-commodate the friends and girlfriends eager to see him; in contrast, nearer to the end of a term she would implore them to make the drive, the goal then being to ensure that he'd receive a visit at least every two to three months.

4. In the Philadelphia criminal court, a case must move forward on the third preliminary hearing or get dismissed. On this date, no further postpone-ments or continuances are possible: the DA must present whatever evi-dence and witnesses he or she has been able to procure at that point. This date is commonly known as a Must Be Tried.

5. These notes were taken as Marie and Mike spoke, with a pen borrowed from the guard and written on the back of the visitor's sheet.

6. Though Mike and Chuck maintained this principle in the abstract, I no-ticed that when they were sent to jail, they did ask close relatives and girl-friends to bring in drugs or money. From my experience in visiting rooms, it is typically the main girlfriend or baby-mom who places marijuana or pills in her clothing and passes off to her boyfriend.

7. On the centrality of gift exchanges of food, clothing, child care, and other basic necessities in poor Black communities, see Carol Stack, *All Our Kin: Strategies for Survival in a Black Community* (New York: Harper & Row, 1974).

CHAPTER SIX

1. Shonda is referring to drug-screening machines that test for traces of illicit substances on the hands. The corrections officer wipes visitors' hands with a swab and puts it under a machine that generates a report of substances discovered.

2. This was not such a strange thing to say. A number of young people in the neighborhood were attempting to sell memoirs about their lives on the streets and in prison.

3. This conversation was taped with permission on my iPhone. Some irrel-evant pieces of the discussion were omitted.

4. The term *secondary legal jeopardy* echoes Megan Comfort's "secondary prisonization," a term she uses to describe how women come under the prisons' authority through their relationships with incarcerated partners. Megan Comfort, *Doing Time Together: Love and Family in the Shadow of the Prison* (Chicago: University of Chicago Press, 2007).

CHAPTER SEVEN

1. Becky Pettit and Bruce Western, "Mass Imprisonment and the Life-Course: Race and Class Inequality in U.S. Incarceration," *American Sociological Review* 69 (2004): 151, 164.
2. On the myriad restrictions and hardships that prompted Black sharecroppers to migrate to the North during this era, see Nicholas Lemann, *The Promised Land: The Great Black Migration and How It Changed America* (New York: Knopf Doubleday Publishing Group, 1992), chap. 1.
3. These suspicions have been echoed by scholars who have drawn strong connections between whites' growing unease in the Civil Rights and post–Civil Rights eras and the rise of tough-on-crime rhetoric, particularly the racially coded rhetoric of conservative politicians. See Katherine Beckett and Theodore Sasson, *The Politics of Injustice: Crime and Punishment in America* (Thousand Oaks, CA: Pine Forge Press, 2000), 53–54.
4. I wrote this conversation down as a text message to myself while it was going on and just after. As with other quotations, it should be taken as a close approximation of the wording and sequence, not a recording.
5. Noted while he spoke and directly afterward on a cell phone. Here I have omitted my small interjections, such as "yep," "uh huh," and "sure is" as well as other unrelated comments, such as those directed at the cat that had jumped up on the table.
6. See the appendix for a detailed account of Chuck's death.
7. I typed this conversation into my phone while it was happening—the quotes should be taken only as a close approximation.

CONCLUSION

1. Michelle Alexander, *The New Jim Crow: Mass Incarceration in the Age of Colorblindness* (New York: New Press, 2010); Loïc Wacquant, "Deadly Symbiosis: When Ghetto and Prison Meet and Mesh," *Punishment & Society* 3, no. 1 (2001): 95–133.
2. Leon F. Litwack, *Been in the Storm So Long: The Aftermath of Slavery* (New York: Knopf, 1979).
3. Vagrancy laws have resurfaced recently in the form of "quality of life" po-

licing. These laws lead to arrests for minor crimes such as panhandling, jumping turnstiles, sleeping in public places, and loitering. For these laws in New York City, see Mitchell Duneier, *Sidewalk* (New York: Farrar, Straus and Giroux, 1999). In Seattle see Katherine Beckett and Steve Herbert, *Banished: The New Social Control in Urban America* (New York: Oxford University Press, 2011).

APPENDIX

1. At first I thought that no whites lived in the neighborhood. Those we saw wore police uniforms or worked for the welfare office. Later I learned that a few whites did in fact live in the neighborhood—some had been there since the '50s, before it became a Black neighborhood; others had married in. Others were the white-looking children of a white and a Black parent. The very few whites working and living in the neighborhood would often nod to me when we passed each other on the street, in the special way that minorities do when they chance upon another of their kind.

2. See William Labov, *Language in the Inner City: Studies in the Black English Vernacular* (Philadelphia: University of Pennsylvania Press, 1972).

3. The difficulty I had renting in a Black section of the city should in no way be taken as comparable to the difficulty very likely to be experienced by a Black person moving to a white section of the city. Though real-estate agents were unwilling to rent to me, I don't believe they assumed I was dangerous or would become a blight on the neighborhood. They didn't turn me down because my stigmatized status would depreciate their property values. Rather, they often indicated that they thought I was too good for the apartments, so that in being turned down I didn't have to simultaneously suffer any insult to my person; I didn't experience what Elijah Anderson refers to as the acute disrespect that Black people encounter in dealing with whites. See Elijah Anderson, *The Cosmopolitan Canopy: Race and Civility in Everyday Life* (New York: Norton, 2011), 253.

4. On the difficulties faced by young men recovering from nonfatal gunshot wounds, see Jooyoung Lee, "Wounded: Life after the Shooting," *Annals of the American Academy of Political and Social Science* 642 (2012): 244–57.

5. Carol Stack, *All Our Kin: Strategies for Survival in a Black Community* (New York: Harper & Row, 1974).

6. Kathryn Edin and Laura Lein, *Making Ends Meet* (New York: Russell Sage Foundation, 1997).

7. Katherine Newman, *No Shame in My Game* (New York: Vintage and Russell Sage Foundation, 1999).

8. Ironically, for young men around 6th Street the term *buddy* means a woman whom one does sleep with, though not under the guise of any official ro-

mantic relationship. The term *friend* also has sexual connotations, and is rarely used to describe male friendship. Men call each other homies, partners, boys, or my man so-and-so.

9. Randall Collins, *Violence: A Micro-Sociological Theory* (Princeton, NJ: Princeton University Press, 2008), 186.

10. Erving Goffman describes participant observation as the "willingness to be a horse's ass." Erving Goffman, "On Fieldwork," *Journal of Contemporary Ethnography* 18, no. 2 (1989): 128.

11. A critique of this kind of identity story, as well as a critique of the ethnographer-centered narrative more broadly, can be found in Dave Grazian's unpublished paper, "The Riches of Embarrassment: The Presentation of Missteps, Mistakes and Pratfalls in Ethnography."

12. Mitchell Duneier, *Sidewalk* (New York: Farrar, Straus and Giroux, 1999), 11–12, 20–21, 334–39; see discussion in Robert M. Emerson, *Contemporary Field Research: Perspectives and Formulations* (Prospect Heights, IL: Waveland Press, 2001), 118–19.

13. Howard Becker, personal communication, September 11, 2013.

14. Anderson, *Cosmopolitan Canopy*, xiv–xv.

15. Ibid., 189, 191, 293.

16. For a nice contemporary treatment of the performance of race, see Shatima Jones, "Shaping Community" (unpublished manuscript).

17. My sense is that gender as well as race played a role in the lack of interest the police held for me. Philippe Bourgois has reported from his fieldwork in a Puerto Rican neighborhood in North Philadelphia that the police do stop people more frequently when he is around, as they assume that any white man in the neighborhood must be buying drugs. Personal personal communication after the panel "Criminalizing the City: 10th Annual Series of Public Conversations on Major Civic Issues Facing Philadelphia," Urban Studies Program, University of Pennsylvania, March 2012.

18. The frustration and shame with which poor young men of color view their reliance on the drug trade and their inability to obtain a "real job" have been a recurrent finding in the urban ethnographic literature over the past three decades. Anderson summed up this tension in a statement by a respondent: "Why is it so hard for me to get a job, and so easy for me to sell drugs?" (Elijah Anderson, presentation, Community Justice Symposium, Baltimore, Maryland, March 8–10, 2007). For particularly strong accounts of young men's struggles to leave the readily available but dangerous and morally tainted drug trade for low-wage work in the legal economy or for small-business ownership, see, for New York, Philippe Bourgois, *In Search of Respect* (New York: Cambridge University Press, 1995), and, for Springfield, Massachusetts, Timothy Black, *When a Heart Turns Rock Solid: The Lives of Three Puerto Rican Brothers On and Off the Streets* (New York: Pantheon Books, 2010).

19. Goffman, "On Fieldwork," 125–26.
20. Jennifer Hunt discusses how she worked out a nonsexual role in a group of male police officers in "An Ethnographer's Journey," *Chronicle of Higher Education*, September 2010; and "The Development of Rapport through the Negotiation of Gender in Field Work Among Police," *Human Organization* 43 (1984): 283–96. Also see the discussion in Emerson, *Contemporary Field Research*.
21. On this point see Emerson, *Contemporary Field Research*.
22. Anderson, *Cosmopolitan Canopy*, 40–42.
23. Collins (*Violence*, 185) points out that most would-be violence does not happen, but ends in bluster and empty threats. This certainly appeared to be the case for young men around 6th Street.